A LEAKY TENT IS A PIECE OF PARADISE

A LEAKY TENT IS A PIECE OF PARADISE

20 Young Writers on Finding a Place in the Natural World

Edited by Bonnie Tsui

SIERRA CLUB BOOKS
SAN FRANCISCO

The Sierra Club, founded in 1892 by John Muir, has devoted itself to the study and protection of the earth's scenic and ecological resources—mountains, wetlands, woodlands, wild shores and rivers, deserts and plains. The publishing program of the Sierra Club offers books to the public as a nonprofit educational service in the hope that they may enlarge the public's understanding of the Club's basic concerns. The point of view expressed in each book, however, does not necessarily represent that of the Club. The Sierra Club has some sixty chapters throughout the United States. For information about how you may participate in its programs to preserve wilderness and the quality of life, please address inquiries to Sierra Club, 85 Second Street, San Francisco, California 94105, or visit our website at www.sierraclub.org.

Published by Sierra Club Books
85 Second Street, San Francisco, CA 94105
www.sierraclub.org/books

Produced and distributed by
University of California Press
Berkeley and Los Angeles, California
University of California Press, Ltd.
London, England
www.ucpress.edu

Sierra Club, Sierra Club Books, and the Sierra Club design logos are registered trademarks of the Sierra Club.

Library of Congress Cataloging-in-Publication Data

A leaky tent is a piece of paradise: 20 young writers on finding a place in the natural world / edited by Bonnie Tsui. — 1st ed.
        p. cm.
    ISBN 1-57805-127-4 (alk. paper)
    1. Natural history—Authorship. 2. Natural history literature. I. Tsui, Bonnie.

QH81.T13 2007
508—dc22   2006042176

Book and cover design by Blue Design (www.bluedes.com)

Printed in the United States of America on New Leaf Ecobook 50 acid-free paper, which contains a minimum of 50 percent post-consumer waste, processed chlorine free. Of the balance, 25 percent is Forest Stewardship Council certified to contain no old-growth trees and to be pulped totally chlorine free.

First Edition
11 10 09 08 07
10 9 8 7 6 5 4 3 2 1

For Andy

Contents

Acknowledgments

I would like to thank all the writers who contributed their fine work to this volume. I am so pleased to have had the opportunity to work with such a diverse and talented group. Special thanks to Linda Gunnarson at Sierra Club Books for her thoughtful input, Lynsay Skiba for her feedback along the way, and Eva Dienel for helping me to realize the book in the first place. As always, my deepest gratitude to Matt for his love and support.

A LEAKY TENT IS A PIECE OF PARADISE

Introduction:
The Planting of Place

BONNIE TSUI

Be rather the Mungo Park, the Lewis and Clark and Frobisher, of your own streams and oceans; explore your own higher latitudes.

Henry David Thoreau, Walden, *1854*

Every schoolchild in America is taught to identify with those enterprising men who, for better or often for worse, plunged their various flags into this land so many centuries ago…. And even though we've heard phrases like "last frontier" and "final frontier" and "last best place" for ages, we all still carry some frontier within us. That's the reason that no matter what direction I, and the people like me, are traveling in our city-hopping lives, we're always headed West.

Sarah Vowell, "Uneasy Rider," Salon, *June 15, 1998*

despite the legacy of natural exploration that was left to me as a child of America, I didn't pee in the woods until I was in college. By this I mean that as a girl, I was not a big hiker, or camper, or backpacker, or any variation of land-based young outdoorswoman. I grew up in New York and thought I would, always and forever, live in New York. And though I did like to swim, I spent the bulk of my training time in chlorinated swimming pools around the greater metropolitan area, the ocean being available only in limited summertime engagements.

But somehow, during the period of protracted youth before age thirty, I eventually found a place out there that felt right to me. In our time, the years running up to age thirty are those in which most of us establish ourselves as "real people." We throw open the window and hope to find meaning in the world—and then promptly freak out. We obsess over the possibility and the geography of our life ambitions. Who are we? What do we want to do? How do we want to live? Sometimes, in the transition of growing older and finding our place, an aspect of natural connection we've always had—or find only then—comes to be useful in that search. A childhood tree house turns into a symbol of safety, reminding us to be brave enough to explore the big bad world beyond the clearing. Or an urban garden doubles as a lifeline to the rhythm of the seasons, situated as we might be amid the flashing lights and artificial constructions of a big city.

Nature has a knack for surpassing human impact. Big physical topographies and small details of landscape have always had a way of encouraging us to frame and view our lives in more realistic perspectives. It was on a semester abroad, halfway around the globe in the underwater canyons of Australia, that I found a place for myself outside my built environment. Here was an alternate natural world thriving thirty feet under the surface of the sea: bright cities of coral populated by fish and turtles that commuted between tall reef towers and around islands of sprouting anemone.

Schools of tangs zipped by, as yellow and speedy as taxicabs. It was thrilling to discover life in a medium at once so familiar and so foreign. Far away from poison ivy and mosquitoes (I had not yet encountered jellyfish), this suspension in water became my ideal way of surveying the frontier.

And when I came home after those months abroad, I talked about the experience to anyone who would listen, with the enthusiasm of a maverick explorer who has been the first to discover something new. On the me-specific scale, it was first and only and best—the first place where I'd really felt comfortable in nature, the only marine park I'd ever seen, the best means for me as a water lover to learn how to appreciate the planet's beauty and the efforts to preserve it. I suppose I started then to become the explorer I always wanted to be.

In the wide-open window of our twenties, when we're still figuring out the people we want to be, finding a place that makes us feel this way is transformative. This astonishing feeling of clarity—of being "all alive," as Thoreau termed it—somehow lends meaning to the rest of our days. Of course, in an ever-encroaching modern world, we've had to get more inventive with the specific ways we place ourselves in nature to seek out that sensation: by camping in leaky backyard tents; by chasing the annual crane migration; by jumping in a cargo plane bound for the Antarctic. We do it all in spite of allergies, physical limits, urban boundaries. Sometimes, we do it all without knowing why until we get there.

Three years ago, in an effort to pin this feeling down, I began to ask twenty writers aged thirty and under to tell me about the surprising ways and whereabouts in which they find connection to the natural world. There have been many observers of nature since Thoreau, but assembling an anthology of smart, refreshingly offbeat voices introduces a new interpretation of what nature writing can be at this age, and at this pivotal time of our lives.

These young writers' generosity and insight are evident in the gems they offer. Some essays, like Sam Moulton's hundred-day canoe diary about the Arctic, are engaging in their form. His journal observations bring a sharp immediacy to the journey he takes with three longtime friends, ranging from accounts of the frigidity of the water to the self-described idiocy of their pursuit. In Cecily Parks's literary parsing of her keraunophobia, she underscores the complexity of her feelings about the outdoors, and the ongoing battle between her bookish self and her bolder self.

Other stories are unusual in subject, like Christine DeLucia's meditation on life cycles in Massachusetts's Mount Auburn Cemetery, and Adam Baer's argument that the outdoor tennis court—carefully constructed as it is in a natural surround—is the built environment in which he is allowed to be primeval and, at last, to grow into a man.

Many writers found their way with humor, and I in turn found myself laughing out loud as I followed along. Cases in point: Hugh Ryan's discovery that a drag queen in four-inch heels could teach him all he needed to know about putting up a tent, and Nicole Davis's dogged, quixotic pursuit of historic road-trippers—whose tire treads led her memorably, and miserably, to a place called Mosquito Lake.

In their search for meaningful places, some contributors moved me with their depth of feeling. Alex P. Kellogg sees the physical environment as a serious player in his investigation of race and identity in Africa, and Andrea Walker, in her remembrance of hunting with her father, struggles with issues of morality and environmental stewardship. Liesl Schwabe's essay is lyrical and beautiful in its depiction of food as a meaningful connection to the seasons in her thoroughly urban life as a single mother in Brooklyn.

All twenty essays are original and thought-provoking, and when taken together, they are more enlightening for their quality and range of experience. There is familiarity, joy, and comfort in small places—Lilith Wood finds Alaska's mountainous beauty most poignant through narrow cracks in the built structure of the salmon cannery in which she works. And there is similar fulfillment to be found in the most unbound places of our planet, as allergy-ridden Gregory Mone discovers in the vast, pollen-free open water that is his Mother Nature. No matter where these writers find their homes—and it's often by getting lost that they find the places where they want to be—their distinctive stories illuminate questions and answers alike about self and place, belonging and rootlessness, preservation and destruction, the meeting of created and natural landscapes, the frontier without and within.

The places where we end up can be surprising. Sometimes we plant ourselves in them and thrive. Sometimes these places plant themselves in us. When I left Australia, the serene weightlessness of that undersea universe stayed with me. It has led me to pursue watery journeys among marine life all over the world, from New Zealand to Mexico to, recently, the depths of a Hawaiian aquarium pulsing with sharks. It stays with me still.

Once Upon a Time in a Tent

TIM NEVILLE

The first day of my senior year in high school started with a moment so traumatic that I eventually gave up on life and moved out of my parents' house and into a tent in the backyard: my girlfriend dumped me. I didn't move out right away. For weeks after being dumped, I wallowed in a funk but stayed indoors at home, hardly eating and never sleeping. Finally, no longer able to endure the pain that continually oozed through my watery eyes, I realized the road to salvation started with making my heartbreak manifest. So I moved outside. Living in a pod of angst pitched among the hissing wilds of a suburban sprinkler system could serve as a glaring reminder to everyone that, no matter how crappy your yard, life is still crappier.

The night I moved out, a Wednesday in November, started as every night had since the first day of school that year. There I lay again, twisting in bed like a half-killed snake on the highway. She wasn't coming back, yet I could not let her go. I was seventeen, had a letter in tennis, and took French. I was reaching the acme of youth and now I'd been dumped. Dumped hard. One day we were running naked through the woods. The next it was over. No fight. No other guy. Just run right over. There could only be one reason.

My room was ugly, too. Brown carpet, orange trim, a black poster with Chinese writing: I hated it all. I'd spent three-quarters of my life in that room already, and now it closed in around me like the darkness that was my future. I needed change. I'd proven to be a miserable failure in civilization; maybe I could do better in the wild. In English class I'd heard of a writer in New England who had lived alone on a lake. I needed a place like that, an outpost beyond society's cruel reach that wasn't too far away. I had school the next day.

The Saturday before, my brother, my best friend, and I had camped out in the backyard. We'd built a fire and roasted marshmallows and pretended summer had never gone. My parents had given us the tent the previous June. It was our first, a Coleman that came with a dozen poles virtually impossible to string together. You needed four people to rig it with any efficiency, and when you were done the tent still sagged and flapped and threatened to topple in a breeze.

But the tent's shortcomings were overshadowed by the novelty of being able to sleep outside. Before that June, I'd camped four times, always in a tiny pup tent that belonged to a Boy Scout who lived nearby. Our Coleman was palatial. It weighed close to twenty-five pounds and slept five people comfortably. I could even stand up inside. I'd left it up in the yard after the campout instead of taking it down. As I walked outside that first night, I was careful not to let the screen door slam.

The ground was heavy with a fresh rain, and leaves stuck to the bottoms of my shoes as I padded across the yard. With one arm I carried two sleeping bags, and with the other a pillow and a flashlight. The tent sighed a damp, musky odor when I unzipped the door and let the beam fall across the floor. Mostly dry. I unfurled my sleeping bags and lay in the center, away from the walls.

Take a look at me now, I thought.

We lived off Highway 50 on Maryland's rural Eastern Shore in a leafy, middle-class neighborhood called Kilbirnie. Getting to us required a drive down Bonhill Drive past vinyl-sided colonial homes to reach number eighty-eight, a blue rancher on the right. Nearly all our neighbors had spongy lawns mowed in three directions and well-manicured flowerbeds that bristled with azaleas and lilacs. Our yard had dandelions and prickly crabgrass with a yawning dirt patch in the middle. Each time Dad ran the mower, we'd run for cover as the blade raised a choking dust storm and threatened to whack gravel into our shins. Out back, we had no grass at all but scraggly trunks of holly, oak, and elm that separated our dirt from the neighbors' dogwoods. Dad ran the mower back there just to prove to Mom he did do yard work.

But ours was a woodsy haven, free to grow as subdivided nature mostly intended. Although it embarrassed my mother, our abomination was the best yard in Kilbirnie. While "Mr. Velvet" wouldn't let his kids even stand in his immaculate yard, we once built a small BMX track around ours, complete with jumps and a mandatory skid. Our yard was also the closest thing in Kilbirnie to a real camping spot. If you positioned the tent just right, you could open the door and see nothing but dark forest.

I settled in for the night. How could the world have curdled from sweet vibrancy to smelly surround in five words, "I want to be friends"? I denied the dump at first. Then I grieved. Eventually, I accepted my life as one of assigned loneliness.

I lived in the Coleman for nearly five months, though I was hardly down on myself that whole time. In January, I turned eighteen in the tent. Shortly after, something happened that sent my life on a rollicking course of global exploration and adventurous pursuits all designed just so I could play outside. I've filled two passports following that course so far, and in some way, each trip stems from the months I spent living fifty paces from the porch in a crappy tent.

Of course, I didn't know that then. But my miraculous awakening was well under way by the time March rolled around, when I was even ready to come back inside. The problem was, I couldn't. My parents had rented out my room.

At twenty-seven years old, Henry David Thoreau had a good ten years on me when, in 1845, he deliberately went to live in a cabin on Walden Pond. Boston practically sits on the pond's shore now, and whatever wilderness Thoreau took solace in is now a state park that welcomes as many as a thousand people a day. A friend went to Walden a few years ago to paddle an inflatable dragon across the murky waters. Such antics are not allowed today. In the twenty-first century, pool toys detract from everyone's communion with nature.

Even in Thoreau's day, Walden wasn't as remote as romantics like to think. The teacher himself admitted he was "naturally no hermit." His cabin and woodstove, placed upon a plot owned by Ralph Waldo Emerson, was only a mile, if that, from the nearest house. Guests came by—sometimes thirty at a time—with tobacco and wine.

There was nothing deliberate about my move into the tent, where I clawed for a life the gods had denied me. This was exile, a forced and deliciously melodramatic act of civil disobedience.

Yet the parallels between Thoreau and me were uncanny, even though I'd never actually read *Walden* back then. I too was alone but close to civilization—my mother could yell from the porch when dinner was ready. I too was naturally no hermit—the whole crux of my sadness being that solitude was something unpleasant. So I'd come inside to shower, do homework, and catch *The Wonder Years,* which always made me a little sadder. And, after word got out that I was living in a tent, at least two friends came to visit.

Of course, Thoreau had no idea his thoughts at the pond would prove to be the landscape behind his biggest literary splash, one that came only after he died. For my part, I had no intention of thinking about anything other than how I'd been dumped. I was already dead, and if my hermit-hood were to lead to anything good, I could certainly make room for her in the tent.

Holly was the most beautiful girl I'd ever seen. She was tall, with blue gems for eyes, jet black hair, and olive skin. She stuttered, especially when nervous, but when the words finally came, the tip of her nose bobbed as her lips struggled to keep up. Holly had been a freshman at Wicomico Senior High School, and I a sophomore, the first time I saw her. She was sitting in math class when I walked by, and she looked up. For weeks afterward, I would go out of my way to walk by, hoping she'd look up. Even if I were late to class, I'd still run through the halls to her classroom. There, I'd slow just before the door and casually toss in a glance as I meandered by. Sometimes she'd look. Other times she'd be talking to some other boy and I'd have to drop a book to get her attention. Satisfied, I'd finish my sprint to the other side of the school. Two months later, I asked her to slow-dance at a fund-raiser in the school cafeteria. She said yes, and we swayed to a gooey Phil Collins tune.

That night I fell in love with her, the principal's daughter.

A farmer's daughter would have been more welcome news, and more likely too. We lived in a town surrounded by soybean fields and chicken farms. At least I was an honor student, and I was certain the principal would approve. And I'm sure he did, at least until he caught my honor trying to get into his daughter's pants one day after school.

Not that I cared now that I was in the tent. Now it was over. It had been over before, but now it was over over, two years after I'd first seen her. Unlike the first time, this time she'd broken up with me—a soppy affair on a sunny September 4, when I cried heavily while parked at the docks. Now it was nearly winter and she'd already been seeing someone else long enough that people talked about them as if it had always been "them."

Before I moved into the tent, I tried to fill the void with things I knew, like work and school. I rekindled my interest in French, since I liked the idea of being able to describe my pain two ways (though *merde* pretty much summed it up). But everywhere I looked were reminders of my loss—namely, Holly herself.

Salisbury was a boring town of twenty thousand people; its only redeeming quality for a restless teen was the beach thirty miles away. But in winter, when the waves were too cold to surf and the boardwalk shops were boarded up, Salisbury fueled nothing other than a fervent desire to find another town. For work, I tore tickets at the movie theater in the new mall, a good place since friends came by when nothing was going on at Burger King, the high school hangout. Holly too had a job there, but after she dumped me she apparently was too good for the movie theater, so she dumped that too.

I met Holly's new boyfriend after I'd been living in the tent for about three weeks. I barely slept at all that night. I simply could not compete. He was older, maybe even twenty, with the long wavy black hair of his Mediterranean ancestors. He was despicably handsome for a hippie. I was growing my hair long, too, but he could already pull his into a ponytail. She started bringing him to the movie theater, but by that point I had moved from tickets to popcorn. Once I gave them a large but charged for a small. My options for winning her back were dwindling. *Deep, dark Greek man or generous boy with the popcorn buckets?* Holly would undoubtedly come running back.

She didn't. But "revolutions are never sudden," Thoreau wrote (I've since scanned his works), and neither was my decision to live in the tent. That first night I slept as soundly as I'd ever slept since the breakup—a deep rest against the lull of a limp drizzle. When morning came, I lay for an hour swaddled in my sleeping bag, watching the blue light of dawn filter through the tent. So I went out to sleep in the tent for a second night. Then a week. Then two.

At first, Mom, a schoolteacher with the hillbilly twang associated with her Appalachian roots, thought I was nuts for sleeping outside in November. Years later, she confessed that she worried about my being crushed by icicles and snow avalanching off the trees above. The Gulf Stream, however, keeps winters on the Eastern Shore so mild I don't think it snowed even once that year.

"How long do you plan to stay out there?" she asked me one morning. I'd been out there a week.

I hadn't thought about it. How long *could* I stay out there? A month? Two months? I decided to keep it simple: I would stay out there until I decided to come back in. I would know when that was.

"Forever," I said. She looked at me as if I were serious.

Connie and Charlotte came by a few weeks later. They were sisters several years older than me who lived at the other end of Bonhill Drive, at least until their father had an affair. Once the secret was out, he simply moved in with his mistress, who lived next door to him. Watching her husband work another lady's lawn had been too much for the mother. When adults had love troubles they didn't move into tents. They moved to Virginia. She eventually bought a new car there, with vanity plates that read NOTMRS.

Connie and Charlotte had been our babysitters for as long as I could remember, and were dear friends of the family. We once took Charlotte, then Connie, on vacations with us to Florida because my brother and I fought less when they were around. The sisters both had boyfriends and jobs, but little money and no desire yet to leave Salisbury. "Why don't you take Tim's room?" Mom suggested one night. "He's not using it."

They moved in a week later. The two of them shared my double bed and what closet space remained. In return, I got sisters.

My life still felt rudderless compared to the lives lived by my peers, who talked about college ad nauseam, but Connie and Charlotte added a vibe to 88 Bonhill that captured my attention more than the question of which schools had what SAT requirements. My parents went out more, leaving us younger ones to make dinner together on yo-yo nights, as in "Yo' on yo' own." Charlotte and I talked about her boyfriend. Connie let me borrow her car. They didn't see the pain splattered on the ever-moldier walls of the tent. They thought I was just a cool kid trying something different.

Even in suburbia, the forest began to come alive in ways once foreign to me when the rhythm of life in a tent took form. After planes stopped passing overhead, I could hear owls, and squirrels and birds at dawn. A raccoon once got into the neighbor's garbage and knocked over a can with such a racket that, for a moment, I sat terrified thinking we might have grizzlies in Maryland after all. One morning in December, I got up early and walked across Bonhill to a field nearby, hoping to catch the sunrise. I had no idea that dawn lasted so long in winter.

But more surprisingly, once I could hold my despair and run a hand along its saggy, tired edges, the woe didn't seem so boundless. The tent gradually became not a symbol of doom, but a very real refuge, my own pod of stability and control in a world that felt beyond control. Wind and rain could lash the tent and I would be warm and cozy—as long as I held the walls up and stayed in the middle and had a towel to mop up the mess. So many years later, things really haven't changed.

For Christmas that year, Mom gave me a zero-degree sleeping bag. By the time my birthday came, in January (fleece pajamas), the days had taken on an element of unpredictability that spiced everything else. Whereas a friend once rhapsodized about applying to Allegheny, I once raced through my yard in my underwear after the tent collapsed. I fell on the floor inside, hysterical with laughter, just as Dad was getting ready to do his morning sit-ups. Suddenly our ugly backyard seemed infinite in new adventures. How could I have missed this? And if simply seeing my backyard in a new light could be so interesting, what was life like in a place where everything was different from daybreak on, like in Montana or New Mexico or Egypt?

With a tent, I realized I could go anywhere and the thrill of adventure wouldn't end when the zipper came up. Love troubles seemed so ordinary—everyone had them. But here was a ticket to a whole new way of living. I was convinced I would never have another cookie-cutter day if I could shake up life from time to time. The way to a happy existence was so simple: All I had to do was step outside and never love again. I could handle that. If things ever got bad, I could always run home in my skivvies.

I tried at first to keep my new life a secret, at least from Holly, though I ached for her to know. *I'm living in a tent!* I'd whisper as she passed in the halls, though by the end of January I didn't care if she came running back. In fact, I wasn't sure I'd have room for her if she did. The tent was my very own first house, and I'd already started to fill it with clutter. I upgraded to an air mattress and redid the roof by hanging a tarp from a couple of pines. The plastic sheet flapped too much in the wind so I took it down. I had a small table, one chair, and a few books, including *The Catcher in the Rye,* which I actually did read. I started to entertain guests, namely, my brother, Jonathan, and my best friend, Pete. I even had a lamp powered by an extension cord from the back of the house, until Dad pointed out that I could get shocked.

Despite my accoutrements, living in a tent grew less peaceful. The floor was always clammy, and sometimes the smell of chicken shit from a nearby farm was so pungent I swore my innards were poisoned. But other nights—when a full moon lit up the forest or a soft rain feathered the tent—you couldn't have dragged me inside.

Sometime in February, the tent finally gave up and could take no more. The roof inside now dribbled from an accumulation of water as slight as melting frost. When it rained, water pooled on the floor and soaked my cotton sleeping bag. Worse, the mold now crept a good foot up the walls.

For the second time in four months, I decided to move. I took out my sleeping bags, the air mattress, the candles that had replaced the lamp, and transplanted the whole outfit from the backyard to the back porch. There, I re-rigged the tent. I was now under a roof and could bang my elbow on the house from inside the tent, but I was still outside. When Dad grew tired of the tent mashed against the backdoor, I took it down and slept inside on the couch. Feeling like a cheater, I sometimes slept on the porch but without the tent, which seemed like a great compromise for staying outside but not in the rain. By the middle of March, I came back inside to sleep on the living room floor. Soon I found a new, bigger adventure.

Instead of going to college, I'd spend a year in Switzerland as an exchange student. The idea thrilled me. I'd never seen mountains bigger than the Poconos and now I'd be living in the Alps. I could finally learn to snowboard. I'd drink *petits cafés* and *vin* and become fluent in another language. The world seemed so big from my backyard. Here was a chance to find its edges, and I wouldn't even need a tent. Like Thoreau, I was ready to "extract honey from the flowers of the world."

But two months before I left, as the trees over Bonhill Drive sprouted tender leaves of spring, a flower blossomed that I had vowed never to let take root again.

Her name was Nicole.

Nicole was the most beautiful girl I had ever seen. She was tall and far wittier than the other one. She had slender, milky white legs that poured from shorts too small to contain all that loveliness. Nicole had the best laugh, an infectious, goofy cackle that sometimes backed up in her nose as a snort. She loved speaking French *(quelle coincidence!)* and was at the top of her class. I once found a flower and a note from her inviting me to dinner tucked under the wiper on my car. It was a Thursday, so her mother, an art professor at the college, wouldn't be home until late.

We rolled around her living room floor between stacks of newspapers, first wrestling, then kissing for so long our mouths ached. The next week, I cut out letters from a magazine and pasted them into a ransom note I left on her car, signing it with the nickname she'd given me.

iF YoU EveR WAnT tO SeE TIm AgAIn, iNVitE Him tO DInNEr. FUnnY sTUfF eXPeCteD

mONsieUR ProF. d'aMOuR.

We swore we'd write each other every Sunday while I was in Switzerland. For the first six months we did. I'd sit in a café with a bandana around my neck to write her letters about learning to windsurf on Lake Geneva or to describe my favorite street in Coppet, a medieval town nearby. I saved her letters in a yellow box.

Gradually, I missed a week, then two, then a month, and soon her letters, too, stopped coming. Still, fifty weeks later she was waiting for me at the airport when I came home. Jonathan, Pete, and a dozen friends were there, along with my grandmother, who hugged me first.

Nicole and I went camping at the beach that summer, using the same Coleman I'd lived in the year before. Nothing was the same. The tent was rotten and filthy. Nicole was as beautiful as ever, but she was leaving in a month to go to France for a yearlong exchange. I was on my way to South Carolina for college, which I ended up hating. So I moved to Montana because I thought it might look like Switzerland. It didn't, but I stayed for six years. I eventually met Heidi there.

Heidi and I have just bought our first house, but we still go camping. I have a new tent, my fourth, and the adventures get bigger each year. I'm a journalist now and people pay me to go to places like Fiji and Egypt.

If Heidi can't come, she meets me at the airport when I return. She really is the most beautiful woman I've ever seen.

A few months ago, Heidi and I went back to Maryland for Pete's wedding and to see my parents, who have since moved into their dream house on the Wicomico River. Pete lives in Salisbury now and has a lovely wife and a beautiful baby girl with big brown eyes. He'd asked me to be his best man, and we surfed a warm swell on the day he got married. Sunburned, with salt in my hair, I gave a corny speech about the times we camped in the Coleman at the beach and spun an even cornier metaphor about a wave and a surfer coming together "in an ocean of infinite possibility" to create something unique and more powerful than either. One lady cried. Another said I should be a writer.

A few days before the ceremony, I drove through Kilbirnie. The neighborhood is practically old now—what, thirty years?—compared to the glistening crops of the latest housing boom in Bend, Oregon, where I now live. The trees standing over Bonhill are mature, the lawns as manicured as ever. Mr. Velvet's remains exceptional.

As I rounded the corner and 88 Bonhill came into view, I saw a lush carpet of Kentucky blue or some other serious grass out front. Out back, they'd thinned the trees and planted grass. The backyard looked like every other backyard. I couldn't be sure, but I thought they even had a sprinkler system.

Not that there's anything wrong with that. Mine goes off every day at five A.M. Even so, there's a brown patch by the tomato plant where the sprinklers don't reach. It's not a hideous dirt patch yet, but if it ever comes to that, Heidi and I can always cover it with a tent.

The End of Strawberries, the Beginning of Peaches

LIESL SCHWABE

ate on a Friday night we got the news: the strawberries that were meant to be delivered the next morning from upstate were in bad shape. The order had been a little risky to begin with, expecting so many strawberries to last into the double digits of July. The notion wasn't necessarily unheard of, but at the eleventh hour it wasn't panning out. Which is why on the subsequent Saturday morning, Ethan—the chef of the restaurant where I wait tables—and I were able to find such a good parking spot one block away from the Grand Army Plaza Green Market, the kind found there only at seven thirty in the morning. Ethan goes to the market every Saturday morning to stock up on produce for the week, though usually not quite so early. This Saturday morning, however, we were responding to the emergency occasioned by the end of the strawberries, and we needed to do so well before the doors of the restaurant opened for weekend brunch at eleven. The menu would be written after the fact. What would be served, at least when it came to the specifics of the pancakes and the waffles and the garnishes, would depend on what waited for us in crates and baskets and in the backs of trucks. We had come to load up on the next boon of summer, peaches.

I live in Brooklyn, New York, in a third-floor walk-up with no more outdoor space than a fire escape. My apartment is two blocks from the Brooklyn-Queens Expressway and three blocks from the Gowanus Canal, which, though cleaner in recent years, is still notorious for its toxic content and Day-Glo ripples. Despite annual resolutions, I do not belong to my community garden. My old and brakeless bike has been locked to the stoop for seven months and is rusting at an almost visible pace. My five-year-old native New Yorker son is afraid of bees, has never liked the feel of grass under his bare feet, and once asked, as we drove upstate for the weekend, when we would "get away from all these trees." From the looks of it, any stabs to prove my connection to the natural world, let alone its importance to me, might seem dubious.

Nevertheless, as seasons blossom into themselves, what has become more reliable to me than the return of warm weather is the return of green, not only to the trees in the park at the top of the hill but also to the plate. For the last four years, I have waited tables at a tiny restaurant just down the street from the Green Market. The menu is entirely seasonal, and the vast majority of both our produce and our meat is local, grown within a five-hundred-mile radius. Over time, I have acclimated to the rhythms of what's harvested when, not as a farmer or gardener or chef, but as a devoted observer, a student of sorts, wide eyed and curious, anxious to see what's arrived in the kitchen each week.

The changes in temperature and light are seasonal shifts I know by sight and feel. But how these transformations manifest in food—in spring-running shad, in midsummer stone fruit, in the root vegetables of late fall—is what has become instinctual to me. Unexpectedly, I have developed a sense of the terra firma while living and working in Brooklyn, as if my internal calendar is finally in step with the solar one. Knowing what's pushed itself up through the dirt and toward the sun, and what's grown plump and ripe, has changed not only how I eat but also how I live, as a reluctant grown-up, as a single mother, as an individual who, over a lifetime of constant moving and indecision, has struggled and struggled with how to feel as firmly planted as a beet and as clear as a farmer about what I'm supposed to do each morning when I wake.

When I started waiting tables at Rosewater, I was really—like most waitresses—just looking to make some cash. My son was almost two at the time, and I had been staying home with him since he was born. Working a few nights a week allowed me to continue to stay with him during the day while also earning some money and trying to remember what it was like to be an individual. I was twenty-five years old and had basically turned from beer-drinking college student to breast-feeding stay-at-home mother overnight. I had very little sense of myself, if any, especially in my new role as adult and parent. Local produce was the last thing on my mind. I needed money. A friend got me the job. What I lacked in knowledge about the grape varietals from the Finger Lakes, I made up for with overzealous excitement at being around adults and conversing in sentences that used all parts of speech. At that time, I didn't cook, hadn't eaten meat in over fifteen years, and was fuzzy on the difference between arugula and watercress.

While growing up in the Midwest as the only child of a single mother, I was acutely aware of what was at least cast as a very fine line between surviving and not. Grocery shopping with Mom was one of the first events in which I remember really trying not to exist, at least in the sense of having needs, like requiring food and clothing. While I realize now that the situation was rarely, if ever, as tight as it felt at the time, to my egocentric child's mind—according to which I was directly responsible for our financial state—our buying the expensive brand of yogurt (or, in later hippie high school years, the coveted organic brand) over the cheap one, or even considering the gourmet potato chips at all, would have pushed us over the edge. Food in abundance, pretty food, food that seemed permissible only on holidays—pecans, juice not from concentrate, whipping cream—I felt the luxury of such indulgences could never outweigh their cost, both literally and psychologically. My anxiety also hovered around the notion of quantity. Obviously I understood we had to *eat,* but did there really have to be so much in our cart? Did the two of us really require *that* many bags, that long a register tape, that much expense? Watching my mother roll her eyes and puff out an exasperated sigh as she wrote out the check each week made me wonder if there was a way to consume less, to need less, to simply get by on as little as possible.

In sketching an appropriate portrait of my childhood relationship with food, I must note that my divorced parents maintained essentially opposite approaches to just about everything, but particularly toward the necessity of sustenance. I spent every other weekend, one school night a week, and some vacations with my father. He lived in the belfry of a defunct church, made experimental films, and never cooked. My mother required (frozen) vegetables at every meal, served a breakfast you could set your watch to, and was adamant about proper etiquette, even when it was just the two of us. But in between their diverging tastes and tendencies, I found myself again and again with an underlying penchant for self-deprivation.

Trying to will the grocery bill down was not so different from trying to will my feet to stop growing or trying to will last year's winter coat to fit. In the simplest terms, I wanted to cost less. And while I knew well enough that one could not carry on through Midwestern winters without shoes and boots and coats that fit, food did seem to be the one arena of consumption that one could—or should—be able to skimp on. In the black-and-white logic of my child's mind, it really seemed that what could have been saved, had we not needed to eat so much, would have made a difference somewhere else.

◎   ◎   ◎

At the Green Market, Ethan spent over five hundred dollars on produce—namely, greens (purslane, wild amaranth, lamb's-quarters), fava beans (young enough not to have to be peeled twice), peaches, kohlrabi, and tomatoes. I love the Green Market no matter what. I love Grand Army Plaza, in the shadow of Brooklyn's own victorious Arc de Triomphe, across from the proud solidity of the public library and the entrance to Prospect Park. The landmarks around the market are massive and undeniable; the setting alone demands some reverence for boldly taking up space in the world. As we made our first stop, we chatted with Kira, the blond and freckled farmer from New Paltz. She'd been up since three fifteen that morning, about the same time I'd gone to sleep after waiting tables the night before. I stammered a bit, not only because I was wooed by the colors of the pattypan squash and the lavender but also because I still envy people who seem so sturdy, who seem sure of the need for themselves exactly where they are and have the dirt under their fingernails to prove it. I go to the market by myself all the time. But I like going to the market with Ethan because seeing that much money change hands for that much food—the two of us making two trips to the car with a pushcart and crates, carrying so many fava beans that our backs hurt—feels like tangible, visceral proof that I exist exactly where I need to, too.

Despite my worry, the cupboards of my childhood homes were always full. Signs of my Depression-raised grandparents were evident in my mother's own second-generation excess supply of untouched canned soups and condensed milk. The shelves were stocked, but in such a way that were I to peer into them, nothing would strike me as actually being edible. We kept ample amounts of flour and sugar and oatmeal and Cream of Wheat and more and more of said canned soup. We never ran low on instant corn muffin mix or Jell-O or baking soda. While I'm sure that we did actually consume some of these powders and cans and mixes, they felt so un-food-like in their unforgiving, unappetizingly geometric shapes piled high in the cabinets that I could never connect the sensation of hunger, or the cessation of hunger, with the appearance of a can of Libby precut green beans.

My father, meanwhile, rarely kept more than a can of smoked oysters and a six-pack of Black Label in his kitchen. My nights with him usually entailed going to the bar for burgers and fries. This, until vegetarianism seemed to me, at age ten, the more sophisticated option for what was otherwise determined to be my "picky" eating habits—at which point I began to order grilled cheese, Swiss on rye, at the bar. Nights spent at home with my dad often included ramen noodles or Uncle Ben's instant rice with canned salmon. We used chopsticks and sat on the stoop and felt, in our way, cosmopolitan, although I didn't like how the vertebrae of the salmon stuck like wet Kleenex in my teeth, or the way that some of the fish flesh was a darker color. My dad told me that if I were blind I wouldn't know the difference.

Not surprisingly, I came of age terrified to spend a cent, as it turned out, on the basics. Plane tickets were, to me, always justified, and luckily, I went to college at a time when thrift stores were still cheap and chic. Predictably, there's something about being young and striving toward a bohemian ideal that makes renting tiny rooms without windows for small amounts of money seem almost glamorous. But I held on tightest to my wallet when it came to food, which remained in my eyes the ultimate luxury, the most consumable, impermanent opulence. Occupied with the same childhood concept that deprivation would somehow get me somewhere, I decided that being profoundly cheap and needing next to nothing would mean something significant someday. As if some score-keeping God would eventually reward me for my selflessness.

In my late teens and early twenties, I moved back and forth around the globe several times and owned little more than a cast-iron skillet that I usually left in my mother's attic. At the grocery store every week wherever I was, but particularly at the Safeway on Market Street in San Francisco, where the mist releasers over the produce aisles also generated faux lightning and subtle thunder, I whimpered as I paid and continued to wish, at age twenty-two, that shopping for food didn't feel exactly like paying the electricity bill. The only times I felt more frustrated than when I paid for groceries was when I returned home, to makeshift kitchens with no spices. I wanted to use the food I had bought well, and I wanted to know how to cook vegetables I wanted to eat, but I simply didn't know what to do or where to begin.

During the same postcollege stint in San Francisco where the Safeway made me feel like the wrong combination of too old and too young all at once, another quiet moment burned itself into my mind, representing everything I wanted and everything I was too afraid to make happen. I walked into a friend's kitchen, a long, clean kitchen, to find his roommate sitting on newspaper on the floor and painting the wooden table yellow. The chairs were upturned and her hair was tied back under a bandana. I felt so lost and so envious all at once, as if this very moment were some sign of arrival at some place I could never get to, no matter how many stamps in my passport or how many times I skipped lunch while thinking the money saved could ever be worth it. Here was a girl my own age who owned furniture, and painted it yellow, and knew where she lived.

Presently, I have lived in my apartment for over six years, longer than I've ever lived anywhere my whole life. I don't love it. Some days I don't even like it. The block is stinky and industrial. The landlord refuses to fix the front door. The apartment itself is narrow and cramped. Yet it has provided the threshold over which I crossed as a woman in labor and back again as a mother, over which my son has walked countless times to school, and over which his father stepped when we separated. This apartment is also where I learned to cook and, more importantly, to eat. While it would be an oversimplification to say such hurdles and the stretches in between could be symbolized by the food I've prepared for myself and served to friends, it would be a mistake not to recognize the importance of these parallels.

During my years at the restaurant, I have learned which months correspond to which vegetables, watched the chefs test the temperature of the meat with their knuckles, and seen how each plate is balanced not only according to flavor and texture but also according to color and garnish.

This is reflected in the time spent in my own hallway of a kitchen. In fits and starts I have grown bolder and more tactile. As a relative newcomer to the enchantments of being a carnivore, the challenge of preparing meat continues to prove the most rewarding. I am still a little surprised at just how good a pork chop can taste, particularly when it comes out of my own oven.

Unlike vegetables, which can be eaten raw or kept at a knife's distance or pushed to the back of the fridge for a morning omelet or cooked well enough even if they're a day or two past their prime, there's no denying the need for human intervention when it comes to the meat on the chopping board, red or brown or pink and slick. Cooking meat demands some kind of authority, some kind of responsibility, and some kind of necessary grasp on what flesh feels like when it's raw. Squeamish at first, taking off my rings to knead spices into ground lamb and squish it into kabobs, I was shocked at how pleasing I found the sensation. I had been a staunch vegetarian for fifteen years. But I came ravenously back to meat, learning—as I did with produce—of the farms and farmers who raised the animals. And with this came the awareness of the diet of the animals that lay dead with their hooves intact in the walk-in cooler in the basement of the restaurant.

Inseparable from what I do as a waitress and what I serve in my home has been my membership at the local food cooperative, the largest of its kind in the country. The co-op has a funny reputation, not just around Brooklyn, but around the whole of New York City. When two squad leaders (that's really what we call them) were busted for sharing their work slot, instead of both working their own, proper, two-and-three-quarter-hour shifts, the indictment made the *New York Times*. Nonmembers giggle over rumors of the Stalinist vibe. Former members alternate between grimacing at the memory of copious makeup shifts and recalling, often wistfully, just how cheap the Belgian beer and the organic chicken and the hippie beauty products were and just how abundant the produce was.

Current members, of whom there are over twelve thousand, commiserate in every aisle about the love-hate relationship inspired by having to work at a grocery store in order to shop there.

For a while, my shift at the co-op had me in the basement, wearing a denim apron, cutting small portions of cheese from big wheels, and weighing them out to sell. This same shift entailed bagging dried fruit from big bulk boxes, tying up tiny bits of spices, and being able to tell at a glance the difference between Arbequina olives and Provençal. While this has been my favorite shift, I've also worked the checkout, where I chat with other members about what they do with celery root or yucca or eggplant. Working checkout also includes the delightful survey of who buys what. While I try not to let my judgment get the best of me, seeing who stocks up on three cases of frozen burritos and who insists that their sea salt be Celtic does provide some kind of window into human behavior that I find endlessly fascinating. Some husbands and wives know that if one unloads the cart, the other should pack up the groceries, while other couples seem only to squabble over why one or the other bought so many mushrooms, or bought mushrooms at all, really, since she or he should know by now how much she or he never really liked them. Meanwhile, the groceries pile up, and neither the husband nor the wife is bothering to bag anything up to take home.

The greens and the fruit at the Park Slope Food Co-op are not as pristine as at the Green Market, and I don't get to shake hands with the farmer when I buy something. But the requirement of making thousands of members work in order to shop—though hectic when it comes to managing squad leaders and shifts—almost completely precludes the need for full-time employees, which ultimately keeps the price of everything, from organic plums to vitamins to European chocolate, at just over wholesale cost. This has put me in the previously unthinkable position of simply having to buy baskets and cartfuls of food, usually organic and often even local, every week. Because it's too cheap not to, because having a child requires being at home, and because I am finally old enough to recognize that keeping myself present requires the physical routine of feeling where my body is in the world. Washing greens, marinating meat, chopping garlic—these are the routines that form the transition from day to night, from who I want to be in the world to who I want to be in my home. Cooking not only provides me with the nourishment to live and thrive but also brings with it the patterns and regularity to help me make sense of my days.

My son, though stubborn in his refusal to eat much that isn't beige, knows his way around the co-op. We buy him as much yogurt and baked tofu as he will eat. He has started to learn different varieties of apples, and knows that Winesaps, his favorite, grow only in winter. Even though he doesn't like avocados or apricots yet, I put him in charge of picking them out of the bins and feeling which ones are ready to be eaten. We talk about each type of vegetable that I put into our cart; even as he wrinkles up his nose, he is learning to identify different greens and nuts and cuts of meat. I am still unmethodical. I still have a hard time convincing myself that even if I don't feel like eating kale today, I might on Wednesday. I still get overwhelmed in the produce aisle when the mist comes down and makes the mustard greens and the parsnips wet, because everything just looks so alive and so exactly itself. I still see other vegetables in other people's carts and wonder if they feel more at home in their kitchens with their legumes than I ever will in mine. But, unlike at the San Francisco Safeway, I now know how to begin. I can chop and simmer and come back down to the place where I live and feel the heat of the burner from the other side of the oven mitt, even if I have been distracted again by my habits of daydreams and frustration.

At the Green Market, in the strong sun of morning, I like watching the people as much as I do the bushels of fruit and vegetables and the bartering to acquire them. The market draws an eclectic group of Brook-lynites armed with babies and dogs and wagons. They mill around, poking at what's ripe and smelling everything. Living in New York City, one is blessed with these moments, when everyone in sight is doing something somewhat intimate, like deciding on the food they will prepare in their kitchens and feed to their families. At the same time, the force and buzz of doing such tasks collectively, of coming out in such numbers as to buy up several truckloads' worth of zucchini and goat cheese, makes me real-ize how much I am a part of something larger, even when I'm back in my apartment, alone with my basil and my dandelion greens. I am seduced completely by the nostalgia too, by the awareness that real, individual people will trade money for food and shake hands to secure the deal. The farmers at the Green Market take food stamps, but can't give change, and throw in an extra tomato to make up the difference. Bartering over food seems as timeless as the need for food itself. Doing so in a group reminds me how central the business of the tradition is.

In the summer, buying peaches, a whole bag of peaches, maybe even eight or nine and maybe even all for myself, I almost laugh out loud at how this is the one place in my life where I indulge in the luxury of excess. At the market or at the co-op, I push myself to buy as much as I can carry, as much as I can hold. The process reaffirms, in some primordial way, that I am alive and joyfully so, that I will feel hunger and I will feel full. One summer night, now a few years past, when it was raining and still light out and we went outside to smell the rain, a friend said to me that eating a peach was what he thought he would miss most after dying.

In the winter, I repeat to myself what I've learned, that Brussels sprouts are never ready to eat before the first frost. I remember this when the days are too short and the wind too unforgiving. I remember the necessity of frost like I do the winter solstice, that the gifts that arrive from the darkest points of the year are what carry us. When the market is empty and even the crates of apples and gallon jugs of cider are gone for the season, and the only people around are scurrying to the library or breathing out visible breath with their dogs, I consider then, like a secret, what is growing underground. I know that fennel, green peas, artichokes, and morel mushrooms will come again, with no shortage of metaphor or beauty. While it's hard to shake completely the longing for a feeling of somehow belonging somewhere more than I do, I wait out the winters, knowing that spring will bring nourishment and familiarity not unlike belonging after all.

When We Were Kings

TIM HEFFERNAN

On my desk is an atlas open to a page illustrating the Nevada-California border. Against the blank white spaces that signify desert country, some names leap out: Death Valley, Ash Meadows, the Last Chance Range, Oasis, Goldfield, Gold Point. Had I opened the atlas to, say, Massachusetts, the names would have been very different. The colonists who arrived there in the 1600s longed to recreate their past lives and gave their new towns the names of the towns they had left behind: Boston, Cambridge, Holyoke, Gloucester. But the people who settled the American West were not colonists; they were pioneers. They named the mountains and valleys for the hardships they caused, and the towns for the hopes they placed in them.

It makes no difference to the cartographer that many of those hopes were dashed, that, today, Goldfield is a ghost town while Death Valley is considered a national treasure. Names are fixed at the moment they are given and do not change with the tides of taste and fortune. Even Las Vegas, a yellow stain on my map, had origins far lovelier than the images its name conjures today. Las Vegas, Nevada, "the Pastures in the Land of Snow": how beautiful it must have seemed to the early Spanish ranchers who watered their cattle in its many streams.

[42]

But there is one place on my map whose name, I think, still fits. North of Vegas, west of Goldfield, not very far from Death Valley, is a small black dot labeled Deep Springs. It is now a college, but it began its life as a ranch sometime in the 1870s, and the men who homesteaded it chose its name for a simple reason: the waters there never run dry.

I first saw Deep Springs College in the spring of 1995 as a high school senior, when I was an applicant. Just after sunrise on the day I arrived, I boarded a Greyhound bus at the Las Vegas depot and headed north on Nevada State Highway 95, aiming for its junction with Route 168, where a van from the college would pick me up.

Vegas is a strange place for many reasons, but what struck me that day—and what still strikes me every time I visit—was the fact that it has no suburbs in the traditional sense. It simply ends—*snick*—at the backside of its latest housing development, and there the desert takes over. One moment we were among houses; the next, we were alone in the sand and scrub. I imagined that morning that the first man on the moon might have felt the same shock the moment the airlock door slammed closed and he stepped out into the lunar dust. Behind us both: chambers filled with cool air, clean water, lights, companionship. Ahead: silent, beautiful, terrifying space.

The few human encampments we passed en route to the junction with 168 gave me a sense that the inhabitants consider the desert alien, a place to be avoided. First came the bored, boring town of Indian Wells—a handful of buildings and trailers huddled beside a creek, surrounded by mountains that block all sight of the desert beyond.

After that, Mercury. The site of aboveground nuclear bomb tests in the 1950s, it is marked now by signs warning travelers that to stop is to risk arrest. The craters are still there, alive with radiation, and the military maintains a small base, but the place is otherwise dead, and it's hard to imagine anyone wanting to stop anyway. (In Ike's time, on the other hand, the public was welcome, and patriotic vacationers would drive out from Vegas to watch the mushroom clouds bloom.)

And finally, at the junction itself, the Cottontail Ranch—a brothel, and the only human habitation for miles. On later trips, I would stop in to buy a cold Coke or one of the surprisingly classy souvenir T-shirts before heading back to Deep Springs, and I remember most distinctly how dark it was inside. The building has no windows.

I was raised in the East, in New England and then Miami, and spent many of my childhood summers in the Blue Ridge Mountains of West Virginia, where my grandparents owned a farm. These are regions of trees and twisting roads, of rain and tangled thickets, of ranch houses in neat rows separated by neatly fenced yards—regions, in short, destined by their history to be characterized by boundaries, subdivisions, and blocked views. And so I found it sad to see the residents of the West, the Big Sky Country, trying so hard to recreate those characteristics in the one place in America where they aren't inevitable. All that space, and yet everyone was living on half-acre plots. All those views, and yet their shades were drawn. The desert, unfenced, unowned, and seemingly un-limited, felt completely foreign to me as it swept past the windows of the bus, but it didn't feel threatening, and I think I began to fall in love with it that morning.

I fell completely in love with it that afternoon, when I first looked down from Gilbert Pass into the place that would become my home.

Deep Springs sits in a high valley of the same name at the very eastern edge of California. To be geologically precise, it sits in a depression—a bowl with no outlet—a fact in which we students took wry pleasure, es-pecially during the bleak days of winter. Regardless, to the fifty people who live in it—the twenty-six students and the faculty, staff, and their families—it is simply the Valley, and it is breathtaking. The campus lies at its higher, eastern end; the handful of buildings and eighty-five acres of alfalfa stand out against the brown earth like a fly on a wall and are similarly dwarfed by the immensity of the terrain. The Valley's western tip, twelve miles distant, is dominated by a seasonal salt lake, which goes dry and turns blindingly white during the summer. A single, two-lane highway passes through the Valley, straight as a string pulled taut, designed for speed. Otherwise, only the mountains that encircle the Valley—the Inyos to the south and the mighty Whites to the north—offer relief for the eye and for the gut. Without their protection, the college would be utterly isolated, a raft adrift on a sea of sand.

In truth, I knew all this before I arrived; for months, I'd read and reread the school brochure, memorizing its written promises and its photos—shabby dorm rooms littered with books and work boots, sunset over the Sierra Nevada, a black-and-white panorama of the Valley taken in the 1920s, identical to one taken sixty years later. It was a teenage kind of infatuation—emotionally fraught, dreamy as cinema—which is why, I guess, seeing Deep Springs for the first time was so thrilling. The only thing I can compare it to is that other teenage triumph, the return of a crush's affections. The Valley opened ever wider as we descended from the pass, and our future together seemed to unfold with it.

As it turned out, my application was rejected—and rightly so, although I was too hurt at the time to recognize it. But I reapplied the next year and got in. Iris, a staff member who sat on the applications committee, called me with the news. "Remember that Kafka story I told you about?" she asked. "Well, welcome to the penal colony."

Deep Springs does have something of a prison-camp quality. The student body of twenty-six, the smallest of any college in the world, is all male. The students work, among other places, in the fields of the college's cattle ranch, raising the alfalfa that feeds the herd of 450 during the winter, and in the school kitchen, cooking the community's meals and washing the dishes afterward. Adult supervision is minimal and is only a force to the extent that the students respect it.

And then there is the college's remoteness. The nearest bar, which students are forbidden to visit anyway, is twenty-two miles away and is called the Boonies. While classes are in session, in fact, students are forbidden to visit any outside civilization—defined, by student body consensus, as any place where people outnumber cows. So the neighboring towns remained a mystery to us, and us to them; for a long time, thanks to the tall tales of one of the school's former mechanics, many locals believed that Deep Springs was a reform school for child murderers and avoided it like the plague.

Journalists who write about Deep Springs—and they do so on a regular basis, like clockwork and migrating birds—tend to emphasize that remoteness, sensing a sort of transformative magic in the distances that separate the college from anything that might be called civilization. They invariably decide that the school is either a cult of freakish geniuses or an avatar of the Old West (self-made men struggling against nature: the graybeard of American mythology) and curse or exalt its isolation accordingly. And yet when I think of the Valley today, isolation is the last thing it calls to mind.

I remember instead the intensity of friendship and an intimacy with my surroundings that I have not experienced since I graduated and do not expect to experience again. A month after we had gone to our senior proms (or, just as likely, skipped them: nerds of a feather), we threw our duffel bags into our dusty Deep Springs dorm rooms, walked out onto the Main Porch, and beheld the community over which, by virtue of being admitted as students, we had been given control. It was our responsibility to hire and fire the faculty. We chose the incoming classes. We made the rules of behavior by which we agreed to live and had the power to punish transgressors. Admittedly, as kingdoms go, Deep Springs is tiny, insignificant, a speck on the map—if it even appears on the map, which it often doesn't. But to our young selves, it was the world in its entirety. It was where we would change from boys into men, and what we learned there we learned, to steal an insight from Edward Hoagland, "when we were nineteen, when it mattered."

But we didn't know any of this when we arrived. For all its uniqueness, life at Deep Springs simply felt like life as usual: a series of screwups and hard lessons learned.

And screw up we did, with unerring skill. Most of us were city boys; the simple physical running of farm and ranch equipment seemed, at first, extravagantly complex. During my first term, when I was the mechanic's assistant ("mech's ass," informally), I managed to bash a pickup truck into a wall, ram a piece of baling wire through two of my fingers, and drive a backhoe into a tree. Chuck, the mechanic, met these displays of ineptitude with teacherly patience. After making sure the backhoe—and the tree—were okay, he had only this to say: "This thing weighs eighteen thousand pounds. It don't brake like a car." That was enough. I drove on eggshells ever after.

Naturally, most of the screwups were easily repaired and took on a sort of slapstick quality in hindsight. Francis underestimating the strength of an orphaned calf, which escaped and ran loose among the dorm and school buildings until he tackled it into a snowbank. The farm team boys accidentally knocking sprinkler heads off the irrigation lines, creating instant Old Faithfuls that turned the alfalfa fields into short-lived swamps. Abe driving ten miles through the mountains, horse trailer in tow, with the big ranch truck's emergency brake locked in the on position—eventually one of us wondered aloud why the clouds we were kicking up were black instead of white like the dirt of the road.

But some of the mistakes were serious. Nick accidentally tore up the water main that supplied the kitchen and dorm; three days of bucket-brigade duty followed, while the depleted farm team had to work double shifts to bring the alfalfa crop in on time. Jeff drove a farm truck with an empty oil pan until one of the red-hot pistons smashed through a cylinder wall, permanently ruining the whole engine. That meant one less vehicle, one less efficient worker, and a week's labor lost while the new engine was installed and a couple grand disappeared from the school's meager coffers.

The list goes on: blown transmissions on the tractors because nobody checked the fluids; horses hurt during joyrides in the desert, temporarily worthless for the important job of herding the cows; sewers backed up because someone flushed what should have gone into the trash. We all bombed once in a while, and we were always soon forgiven. It was, after all, just dumb kids' stuff. But forgiveness notwithstanding, the sense of personal shame was powerful. Mess up and hurt yourself, that's fine. Mess up and hurt your entire community? Not so easy to swallow. Most of us came to Deep Springs precisely because we wanted to be part of something larger than ourselves. Few of us, I think, arrived prepared for the risks and defeats of civic engagement.

Nowhere was that more apparent than in "SB," the Friday night legislative session of the student body. There, the week's events would be discussed, with the student chairmen of the applications, curriculum, and review committees providing reports. There might be a round of the week's best anecdotes or a call for volunteers for a side project somebody had dreamed up. After that came the hard stuff: voting on whatever sense-of-the-body motions had been proposed by students during the preceding few days. Maybe someone felt we needed to ban smoking indoors. Maybe we had to think about putting down one of the SB pets—Bert, the ancient pit bull who pooped where he pleased, or Petri, the cranky, hoary three-legged tom whose granddad, it was rumored, was a genuine bobcat. Maybe we should throw away our one television—being so far from town, we got no broadcast TV, but we rented videos, and some students considered them an unwelcome outside influence.

The debates could be tortuous affairs, and not only because they often lasted until two or three o'clock in the morning. At stake in every effort to change the rules that bound us to certain responsibilities was the much larger question of where the boundary between the individual and the community lay. And in a democracy of twenty-six, "the community" and "my friends" were nearly the same thing. Which definition dominated depended on the day.

And when it came to deciding rules for the community, friendship often lost. At various points, I stopped speaking to one classmate or another. Or maybe they stopped speaking to me. One student stopped speaking to anyone. For a time, the SB broke in half, with the rebels forming their own governing body, the BS. The acrimony was genuine; even today referring to a bit of political nastiness on my part, one former classmate reminds me that he can forgive but not forget.

It is hard to imagine now what all the fuss was about, but then it's hard to imagine what it was like to be a teenager at all, with its extremes of love and hate. It is easy, however, to remember how these miniature crises felt insurmountable, and how, after being on the losing end of a vote, Deep Springs suddenly felt alien and cruel. Being voted down didn't make you think you were wrong; it made you feel like you didn't belong there at all.

There was one cure, and we all took it: escape to the desert and the mountains. They were literally outside the back door of the dorm building, and a ten-minute walk would take me out of sight of anything made by human hands. Then, and only then, was I ever alone at Deep Springs, and it was glorious. Many times I simply lay on a flat boulder for an hour or two, listening to the wind and chucking pebbles absentmindedly, and returned to the campus feeling completely refreshed. Nobody had missed me, and I hadn't missed anyone, and that, really, was what made these short escapes so enjoyable. Being irreplaceable—or at least believing that you are—is a wearisome burden at any age.

But we also took longer trips, deep into the hills, among the pines and sage. There were treasures to discover up there—old mine shafts, snowbanks in July, a lone apple tree planted by a nameless prospector years ago. Petroglyphs on lonely boulders, Paiute huts above tree line, an arrowhead once in a while. Hawks and eagles—red-tailed, golden—kept watch from the cliffs. Wild horses patrolled the flats. After a storm, columns of white smoke rose from the ridgelines, the work of lightning upon dry pines. They gave an electric edge to the land, an eerie sense of abandonment, as if an unseen army had fled our approach, leaving its campfires behind.

Sometimes we stayed out there for a night, or for a week if we had the time. The White Mountains, especially, welcomed those longer stays: they are enormous and almost completely empty of people. In places, the only signs of modern civilization were the contrails of jets passing noiselessly, high overhead, and the wind erased them quickly enough.

Those hikes were often more like tramps, just aimless wanderings with only vague destinations in mind, which made it all the more important to keep our eyes open. Not only so that we'd have something to do, although that was one motivation, but we also had to pay attention to where we were and what we had seen so that we could find our way back. That was the strange thing about those trips—we never took maps.

And why would we? Hiking in the intermountain West is a very different thing from hiking in the forested East and on the jungly Pacific coast, where most of us grew up. Sight lines are long, and trees are sparse. The tallest trees might reach fifteen feet, and knee-high scrub predominates. The dominant geological features are canyons and ridges, which alternately lead hikers to the peaks and funnel them to the valleys. It's simple and, except for dehydration, not really dangerous to go on a walkabout; the weather is predictable, the rattlesnakes are shy, and it is difficult to become too badly disoriented.

That said, there are also very few trails; the terrain invites through-travelers to improvise. This is a great courtesy. Instead of knowing what was out there, we got to experience the thrill of discovery.

Far up one canyon, I found a group of Joshua trees, the only ones for miles around. Nobody before me had ever reported them, and for all I know I am still the only person who has ever seen them. On another hike, my classmate John and I came across a small clan of endangered pineapple cactus clinging to a bare hillside. The young ones were sprouting from the roots of their dead elders, whose lacy skeletons, fine and white as fish bones, in turn covered their children in a protective embrace. Later that day—footsore and exhausted from traveling much farther than we had planned to—we stumbled down our millionth rocky slope and found ourselves, almost miraculously, standing in the shade of a cottonwood grove, with the rich smell of clay and moss filling our nostrils. We had only heard about Paradise Springs, and so it was especially sweet to have found it under such circumstances. And its cold waters tasted especially sweet, too, seeing as we'd drunk our bottles dry hours before.

We all had times like that, and they made us feel as though we belonged to the country, the way being told a secret makes you feel you belong among the secret-sharer's trusted friends. Those Joshua trees, those cacti, those springs, the old blown-glass medicine bottles we sometimes kicked up, the stone ax head a classmate found: these had been the land's secrets, and when we discovered them, they became ours, too. Even the simplest things, like learning which fork in the canyon would take you to the swimming hole, had an air of whispered confidence about them. It took hard work to coax knowledge out of the reluctant landscape, and close observation to learn the signs that would allow us to visit its hidden places again. To this day I know parts of the Valley and its mountains as well as I know my own apartment, know exactly what is out there right down to individual rocks and trees, precisely because I explored them blind. If I'd used maps, I never would have seen half of what I did. Maps, after all, have a tendency to tell you where *not* to go.

Or maybe it's just that they only show what has already been found, and we, as social creatures, tend to congregate in those familiar places. A name on a map says, "This place is known to us humans. It has been discovered. It is not savage. You are welcome here." To name something is to claim it, and this is the right of its first visitors. Conquering kings gave names to their lands. So did we.

Students who went to Deep Springs long before I did christened the Druid, a stone spire on a ridge behind the college that looks remarkably like the sculptures of Easter Island. They named the Elephant, an isolated hill on the Valley floor that does, in fact, look like a supine pachyderm with its trunk stretched along the ground. They named Chocolate Mountain for its cap of dark brown basalt. I thought I'd found something worthy of a title once, too: a high-walled, narrow slot between two house-size boulders that my classmate Nick and I accidentally stumbled into (and then carefully inched down) while returning from a hike. The Cut? The Alleyway? What would it be called? Back on campus, I told the farmer Andy, a former student himself, about our discovery. He recognized it immediately. "We used to call it Pinch Canyon," he said. Sometimes, kings simply inherit.

I graduated from Deep Springs seven years ago, and when I go back the school feels foreign. I am a grown-up, the students are teenagers, and in any case it is their institution now, to do with as they please. But the Valley still feels like home: it hasn't changed.

Since we left, a surprising number of my classmates (seven, including me) have become writers of one sort or another—essayists, journalists, authors of fiction. Several others have gone into law, focusing on endlessly debatable, intrinsically abstract subjects: the First Amendment, Native American rights. One is a fisherman, captaining a boat he owns. One will soon become an Episcopalian minister.

It would not be too great a stretch, I think, to find in these diverse careers a common thread of venture-into-the-unknown. The writers dig into other people's consciences; the lawyers and the minister dig into their own; the fisherman pursues prey he cannot see, in an environment he cannot control.

Did the Valley and the mountains teach us to be this way? I don't think so. In reading essays about wilderness, I often come across some variation on the phrase "I went there to find myself," and I always suspect that the opposite was the case. Wilderness shows us by its very essence precisely what we are not. And we go into it to escape precisely what we are: social creatures bound to grand systems that we must engage with or be ruined by.

Put another way, the human aspect of exploration consists in the act, not the stage. A certain kind of person is attracted to places like Deep Springs, where community and democracy are necessary, beneficial aspects of our lives. A certain kind of person is attracted to the opposite—to the middles of nowhere that still survive, where conquest, even illusory, is crucial to the sense of self. What's curious is only this: how often those people are one and the same. I suspect it's a case of one trait demanding an equal and opposite reaction, as when the messy plurality of community life is counterbalanced by the clarity of solitude.

Or maybe the reaction is only opposite, not equal. I find it meaningful that the greatest thrill I've experienced since leaving Deep Springs came on a hike in the Sierra Nevada, and it's telling that, as in the old days, I didn't take a map. Instead, my friend Dan and I bushwhacked and scrambled our way up the southern—and steepest, it turns out—face of Mount Tom. We didn't bring enough water, we didn't bring climbing gear, and nobody knew where we were going. We did the opposite of everything the books told us to do. I suppose that's why, when I finally stood on the summit, I didn't feel like I was on top of Mount Tom. It was my mountain, Mount Tim, Mount Me. I felt I'd earned the right to call it mine. And I suspect that anyone who has made his own way through a wilderness knows exactly what I am talking about.

Four Points

ANDREA WALKER

I hunt with a Remington 760 pump, .243 caliber with 100-grain bullets. It's a good gun for a girl because it's lightweight and doesn't have
a lot of recoil. Still, the day after I learn to shoot it, a black-and-blue
mark the size of my fist will appear in the notch between my right shoulder and collarbone, where I cradle the butt of the rifle. I am twelve years
old, and it is late November, a few days before Pennsylvania's antlered
deer season begins.

The shooting range my father takes me to is in an old cow pasture
beyond the fields where the county fair is held each August. I begin
by trying to pop tin cans off hay bales, the bullets making a satisfying
ping when they connect with the cheap metal, sending the Campbell's
soup and StarKist tuna containers sputtering backward and sideways.
Eventually my father ties paper targets onto the bales, and over the
course of an hour the punctures I make in them inch closer to the
center. The exercise of firing the gun becomes mindless and abstract; a
different kind of perception takes over. I smell the smoke from a distant
burn pile and the acrid tang of the spent shells. I hear dry cornhusks rattling in the wind. The front pocket of my coat is full of bullets, and they
have a pleasing heft, pressing against my right thigh.

One week earlier, my father and I had attended a two-day hunting safety school in a cinderblock recreation hall attached to the local Elks Lodge. Men in camouflage suits and work boots sat on rows of picnic table benches with their sons. I was not the only female—two or three other women in their twenties or thirties sat attentively beside their husbands—but I was the only girl. Along with the teenagers, I took a test to make sure I knew how far I was supposed to stay from other buildings and hunters (200 yards), and how much fluorescent orange I was required to wear on my back, head, and chest (250 inches).

As we are riding home from the shooting range, my father reminds me what I will need to pack for our trip: several pairs of long underwear and thick socks, insulated boots, a warm hat, flannel shirts, and turtlenecks. Because the heater has not warmed up, the vents blast cold air into the cabin of the truck, making me shiver inside my new Gore-Tex jacket. A squirrel stops in the road up ahead, fixing its gaze on us and flicking its tail rapidly several times in succession. My father does not slow down to accommodate it, and just as I am about to cry out, the animal darts away. I realize that the palms of my hands are sweating, and I wipe them on my jeans, wondering how I will have the courage to kill an animal bigger than I am. I weigh ninety pounds and wear braces and have dirty-blonde hair cut by my mother with a pair of kitchen scissors to save money. I have not thought about my reasons for going hunting any more than I would have thought about why we eat beef four times a week, why we go to church on Sundays, why we vacation every other year in the same gray clapboard house at the Jersey shore. As far as I can tell, hunting is like most activities in this rural, south-central part of the state—something people do because their fathers have done it before them.

We hunt on my uncle's land in the Pocono Mountains. It's a three-hour drive north on Interstate 81, past Amish farms and destitute mining towns, to a twelve-mile-long lake set deep in the woods. The twenty-six hundred acres are held collectively by the ten families who own cabins like my uncle's. Most are standard A-frames, some covered with unpainted shingles. Inside, they have stone fireplaces and furniture deemed too worn or ramshackle to stay in someone's primary residence, meaning kitchen tables that wobble and armchairs with stuffing popping out of their upholstery. Most of the cabins have wooden decks and picture windows looking out onto the water. My uncle's has a bearskin rug with the head and claws attached, a kitchen with 1950s appliances, two bedrooms with sagging mattresses and piles of thin blankets, and closets that smell of mothballs and must.

For me as a child, the cabin was a place of ease and contentment where we came for summer vacations when we did not go the beach. More than anything else, I loved crawling into one of the beds as soon as the sky or wind suggested that a thunderstorm was approaching, opening the window ever so slightly so that I could listen to the sound of water falling on the full green leaves. I caught toads and salamanders in the damp corners under the deck, holding them overnight in my aunt's Tupperware so I could play with them the next day, and invariably waking to find them limp and sour smelling. I learned to swim and to row, to fish and to walk in the woods without getting lost. I learned to tell a pike from a bass from a trout, and the call of a screech owl from that of a horned and a barred. I learned to tell the difference between maple and hickory leaves, the tail of a muskrat from that of an otter.

But this visit is different, and I can sense it from the businesslike way my father orders me to bring the bags in from the car, telling me where to lay my rifle.

That evening, we meet the other men for dinner in the lodge, a long wooden building set under towering white pine trees at the northern point of the lake. When it was built in the late 1800s by the Philadelphia industrialist who bought this land for his hunting parties, the lodge was painted light blue; it had a green shingle roof and a tongue-and-groove porch that circled it. The wide screened windows were opened up in the summer, and a cook came up from the city every season, sleeping on a cot beside the coal stove at night. In the winter, men went out on the lake with a sled to cut blocks of ice, which they kept in a shed and covered with sawdust. They ran water in from the spring, and in the warm weather they had dances on the wide plank floors. Now the paint has peeled and weathered to a dingy gray and the roof has been patched with black shingles rather than green, giving it the appearance of a crazy quilt. A group of us mill about in front of the fireplaces—so big I could lie down inside them—eating sandwiches made from cold cuts someone has spread out on the antique pool table, its velvet worn down to the wood in several places.

I am the first female in the history of the camp to go hunting, and the men don't know what to make of me. They still tell jokes, but leave out the obscene parts, or they talk in clusters on the other side of the room so that my father and I can't hear. Some shake my hand and wish me luck; a few offer small, faintly derisive smiles, asking whether I really plan on shooting something. There is still no indoor plumbing in the lodge, and it is too cold to contemplate putting my bare skin against the seat in the outhouse, so I cross my legs as I stand by the door and stare out into the darkness. I think of the first women who came here, accompanying their men to the hunt, staying in the one-room cabins containing only beds and fireplaces, a table, and a bowl for water. I try to picture them sitting in the wicker rocking chairs at the lodge, gossiping and warming their hands by the fire as shots rang out across the lake and the men called out to each other in sharp, quick barks of victory or defeat.

My father stands behind me and puts his hand on my shoulder, indicating it is time for us to leave. "We'll get up at four A.M. tomorrow," he tells me as we walk back to our cabin. When we cross over the bridge, I pause to listen to the water rushing over the dam and kick a few loose stones over the edge, trying to keep my feet warm. "It's a cloudy night tonight," my father observes. "The deer will be on the move in the morning."

We hunt in two groups: the standers and the drivers. The standers form a straight line going up the side of the mountain, about two hundred feet apart from each other. They position themselves behind trees, or clumps of rock if they can find them, so that they won't be seen by the deer running straight at them. The drivers form a similar line, a mile or so down from the standers, and walk toward them in unison, gradually pushing the deer forward. It's an efficient system, like a vise being turned tighter and tighter. In the first hour, a group of deer weave in and out of the trees ahead of us as my father and I are driving. My father holds his hand out for me to stop and looks at them through the scope of his rifle. The sun is just coming up over the mountain above us, filtering pinkish light through the bare branches. An icy wind, one of the first of the season, cuts across the ridge of my nose as my father lowers the gun. "Too far away," he says.

A good shot is important to my father. I am told to aim for the shoulder of the deer, because that is where the heart and lungs are located, and a shot to that area will kill the animal quickly, with the least amount of pain. If I hit the deer and he isn't killed immediately I will have to track him by following the blood trail; a deer can run for a long time if its adrenaline starts pumping. Better to stay still and wait for five or ten minutes, my father instructs me, because often the deer will lie down and bleed out.

As we walk in the woods, my father speaks to me in a low, even voice, sometimes gesturing toward the ground, or up above us, where he wants me to observe something closely. We keep an eye out for scrapes and rubs, indicating that a deer has been through the area recently. Rubs are made by male deer chafing their antlers against young tree trunks, trying to remove the soft covering that grows on their horns in the spring, a velvety skin that helps to nourish the bone. The rubs look like short knife strokes in the saplings, spots where the bark is chipped away. Scrapes are places where the bucks have pawed at the ground and urinated, stirring up the leaves and dirt to mark their territory and attract a mate. Scrapes are often found where there are low branches hanging overheard, since the does have glands in their eyes and noses that secrete oils onto them, another way of leaving a sign for the next visitor. The buck will come to check on his scrapes each day, and when he finds that a female has been there he will pick up her scent, tracking her like a bloodhound.

I learn that good places to hunt, if you are by yourself, are downwind of a scrape, near the place deer enter and exit a field, or above a ridge where they travel. Deer eat acorns, corn, young grass, and soybeans. They like white oak acorns better than those from red oaks because the white have less acid. Their eyesight is not good, but they have a keen sense of hearing and smell. Deer are nocturnal animals, bedding down during the day and moving about at night to feed. The best hours to hunt are during sunrise and right at dusk, since those are the times when the deer will travel between their feeding and bedding places. Deer move about when it's windy because the wind makes it harder for them to hear predators approaching, and they get nervous. A similar thing happens after a storm, when water is dripping from the trees. On clear nights, when deer can see better, they are more content to stay in one place and eat, while on cloudy nights they remain in motion. The day after a clear night, deer will be more apt to stay bedded down, since their bellies are full, but after a cloudy night they will have to find food.

Every few minutes of walking, we stop, pause to look around, and listen. Sometimes my father will reach in his pocket to put a clump of chewing tobacco in the side of his mouth, but mostly we are just waiting, observing the world around us, trying to fine-tune our senses to pick up the slightest hint of movement, the sound of a single twig snapping. Ninety-eight percent of hunting is just this, I realize. Shooting the deer takes a minute or less. Most of the time you just watch and wait.

Before the Pennsylvania Game Commission was created in 1895, there were no official limits on the number of deer you could shoot (historians believe laws were sometimes passed but not enforced). Most regions were not heavily populated, and people who hunted did so for the meat, which they stored and ate over the course of the winter. Deer were abundant but not innumerable, as many believe, because their numbers were held in check by natural predators such as wolves and mountain lions, by Native American harvests, and by the extent of mature forestland. Deer have an easier time finding food in fields and farmland, and a tougher time in heavily wooded areas. The deer population declined dramatically in the late 1800s as hunters began to kill for sport rather than subsistence, and the Game Commission came into existence for the purpose of protecting and conserving the herd. New harvest laws were passed in the early 1900s reducing the seasonal limit from two to one deer and protecting antlerless deer from being shot. Because the laws were enforced for the first time, the deer population began to grow dramatically, and by the 1920s the population was so large that the commission began issuing statewide licenses for does.

Today the Game Commission has twenty-two separate license allocations throughout the state, and the number issued each year varies by region, with the commission engaging in a complex series of calculations in an attempt to reach what they call the "optimum deer density" and "biological carrying capacity." This is more loosely defined as the number of deer that can be supported by a given region without endangering the diversity of other plant and animal life within it. Factors considered each year (outlined in a forty-six-page document entitled *Population Management Plan for White-Tailed Deer in Pennsylvania*) include previous population trends, winter mortality rates, yearly reproductive success, and the overall health of the herd. Game Commissioners walk creek beds in the winter to count the number of deer who have died from cold or starvation, and stalk fields of young grass in the spring to try to count the number of fawns. Deer are tagged for the purpose of various studies, and hunters are required to turn in the details of their kills on a "harvest report." Game Commissioners examine the deer taken to meat processors and collect data about sex, age, health, and antler characteristics. A computer algorithm processes this data to determine whether the harvests are on target for that year and what numbers they should aim for in the upcoming season. Ultimately, the commission's best research leads them to conclude that "there are approximately twice the number of deer in Pennsylvania than can be supported during the winter without overbrowsing forested habitats."

All this is a fancier version of the hypothetical my father poses when I ask him how he responds to people who say hunting is cruel. "Imagine," he said, "if just for one season we didn't hunt. Since we long ago killed off the mountain lions and wolves that ate our sheep and cattle, there are no predators for the deer except humans. If we didn't shoot them, their numbers would rise to the point where the current habitat couldn't support them. They would kill off additional plant species and disrupt the behavior of the animals that depend on those plants. They would come down in our yards and gardens looking for food. They would destroy farmland and the young trees planted to replace those cut for timber. They would be hit by cars or starve to death, slowly and painfully, in the winter."

As the overall number of hunters in the state diminishes, and suburban sprawl results in fewer places to hunt each year, the conditions are in place for many of my father's predictions to become realities. Since 1968, the Game Commission reports, sales of junior hunting licenses have slipped 40 percent, a decline that in recent years seems to have stabilized but not shown signs of reversing. Although actual (and up-to-date) figures are hard to come by, a 2001 survey conducted by the U.S. Department of the Interior's Fish and Wildlife Service showed that more than 50 percent of those who hunted in the state were between the ages of thirty-five and fifty-four, with less than 6 percent of hunters aged sixteen and under. The survey says that the number of female hunters sixteen and under is too small to be statistically significant.

It is late in the afternoon on our first day of hunting when I see the buck. My father and I are standing close to the water, up near the straggly stream that feeds the lake. The ground is covered with dead leaves, and the deer, when I first spot them, are similarly colored, like spots of a dull beige fabric being wound through a series of bobbins. I struggle to focus the scope on my rifle, seeing the trees in the distance become fuzzy, then distinct. My father points toward my pocket, where I finger four bullets and slip them into the chamber.

"There's a six-point in there," he says softly. "A nice one, too."

I get a glimpse of the buck, in with the other deer, but their continuous movement confuses me, and the area displayed in the scope is so small I have a hard time keeping him in its range.

"When they smell us, they're going to stop, and that's when you shoot."

And just as my father says this, the doe at the head of the group goes completely immobile, and then the deer behind her freeze, as if an electric current has just passed through them. When I turn up the scope, it brings the buck's face into such detail that I can watch his nostrils flaring. I lower the crosshairs, down to the patch of white between his front legs, and then I stop. The deer beside him moves in front, blocking my line of fire. I can't be sure of my shot. I hesitate.

Sound explodes from farther up the mountain, a cracking that reverberates off the lake and lingers in the air for a moment. In the time it takes me to lower the gun, the deer have wheeled about and fled. Their upturned tails bob for a minute in the distance, quick brushstrokes of white in a landscape saturated with every conceivable shade of brown: fawn, ochre, mushroom, and taupe. My father has an amused expression on his face as he lifts his baseball cap to scratch his head, spitting tobacco juice to one side.

"You'll get him next time," he says with a smile.

Three men kill deer on the first day of our hunt, and my father insists that I help gut the last one. We walk up to the carcass, and the man who shot it looks into its eyes before nudging it with his foot. "There'll be a film over the eyes if they're dead," my father explains to me, "but you have to be careful because sometimes the shot'll just shock them, and they may be lying down startled but get up and run off the second you walk over." I help hold the buck's hind legs apart as the shooter gets his knife under the skin at the back of the belly, cutting slowly toward the chest, taking care not to puncture the membrane the surrounds the internal organs like a pouch. "If you do it right," my father says, "you can just roll that whole sac out, without having to cut into it, which can taint the meat." We remove the diaphragm, and then the lungs and heart, which one of the men wraps in paper with the liver to put in a cooler. The organs are warm and smaller than I expected. I find it hard to tell them apart. I wipe my hands in some leaves as steam rolls up from the innards, which my father says foxes and coyotes will come to eat. Nothing is wasted, I learn. If a buck dies in the woods, even the antlers will be something for mice to chew on, a source of calcium.

That evening, we have dinner in the lodge again, and I drink my first beer, staring up at the stuffed pheasants and grouse mounted on shelves above the fireplaces. I step out on the porch to see a moon bright as a strobe light illuminating small ripples on the lake, a few flakes of snow in the air above them. The deer killed earlier in the day are hanging from one of the thick pine boughs near the dock, a limb that has been used for so many years the ropes have worn troughs in it. The wind makes a soughing noise in the long-needled branches and the bodies sway a bit, the heels and antlers occasionally clicking against each other. As I watch them move, I am seized by the irrational urge to crawl up inside one of the carcasses and wear it like a coat around me, the skin a barrier against the coming winter's chill, the antlers an elaborate headdress that would beautify and protect.

As I reach the end of my twenties, I begin to wonder what I am missing by living so far from my father. Though we are only six hours' distance by car (I now live in a small town in Connecticut), we might as well be on opposite sides of the world. He wakes up early to go hunting and fishing, to plant trees and tend his twenty acres of grass and gardens, while I negotiate a series of trains and elevators to sit in a cubicle, to interact with the world through a series of keystrokes. Some days I am so busy that the thought of moving back to Pennsylvania never crosses my mind, and then sometimes I will be waiting for a streetlight to change, or getting into a taxi, when the need will assert itself like a sharp pain in my chest, a sudden shock of estrangement.

When my longing is most intense, I try to remind myself of how much I misremember about my past. I tell myself that I construct my memories of hunting as enchanted times, rather than ones filled with anxiety and doubt. I make my father kindly rather than gruff, the woods poetic rather than desolate and austere. But I also remember the weight of the deer's organs in my hand, the vinegary, rotten odor of its still-warm insides, and the knowledge that a certain kind of killing can be a form of respect, a communion with the environment that is essential to the protection and preservation of it. I know then that I miss hunting too much not to return to it, in whatever form and fashion the circumstances of my life now can accommodate.

I shoot my deer on the last day of the hunt, as my father and I are driving near one of the ridges. It's a rocky area, full of shale and slate boulders, remnants of long-ago volcanic eruptions and the shifting of the continental plates that formed this region. The mountains in Pennsylvania are old and worn down, whittled to a smoothness that is comforting, a size that seems manageable rather than dwarfing. In the valleys between them are small, rolling hills filled with some of the richest soil in the world, fields pocked with sandstone and feldspar, limestone made from the shells of crustaceans swimming in the oceans that once covered this ground. As we walk, my father tells me to go on ahead of him. He says he is going to sit and watch near a scrape he has found. I am hesitant to move forward alone, and he must sense this, because he tries to concoct a theory about the deer turning off on a trail beneath us, rather than coming this high up the mountain. In an instant I perceive that he is giving me an easy out; he thinks I don't really want to shoot something, but would rather walk back to the lodge while he waits to see if the drivers push any deer through. I want to stay and argue with him, but I also believe there will be other chances. I am twelve years old and think that things will go on this way indefinitely—that there will be time and opportunity to go hunting every season, every Monday after Thanksgiving.

After I've gone a few hundred yards ahead of my father, I hear the sound of something running in the distance. It is a loud, chaotic noise, the repeated sound of wood splintering and snapping, and I realize it must be a whole herd of deer, charging up toward the skyline. I crouch down behind a tree trunk, trying to steady my rifle in the crux of the Y shape formed by its branches.

I can't yet see myself riding home in our pickup with a dead deer in the back of it. I can't see myself chewing on the tough, gamey meat all winter or mounting the antlers on a plaque above my desk or bed. I think about being the first woman to shoot a deer at the lake and wonder whether the men will think of me differently. I think of my father and wonder whether he will see me as a different person, someone more like him than he realized. But when the four-point steps into my crosshairs, I am not thinking about anything. The buck slows to a walk and stops to lift his head, cocking his ear to catch the sound of my breathing. When he takes the next step, I open my eyes a little wider and breathe with him for a moment, before pressing back on the trigger.

Sissies in the Wood

HUGH RYAN

"**h**ey."

Joe frequently started conversations this way when he was unsure of how he would be received—a neutral gambit that announced his intention to say something unpleasant without actually doing so. I thought of it as his warning shot. I waited, head on his chest, wishing I was one of those people who fell asleep immediately after having sex.

"Want to go camping? In Tennessee?"

I rolled over and laughed, thankful that my worries of a moment ago were just the product of a hyperactive imagination. Joe didn't join my laughter. After a minute of silence, I rolled back. "You *are* joking, right?" I saw the corner of his mouth quirk up and an eager gleam flare in his eyes. He was quivering with poorly contained excitement, like a puppy trying not to wet the floor. I decided to cut him off before it was too late. I moved to face the wall. "No."

Even turned away from Joe, I could feel the intensity of his desire to spend time in Tennessee—a place where, if we were lucky, it was the wildlife that would kill us. I had seen *Deliverance;* I knew what happened to city folk in the woods. A full five minutes passed as I attempted to will myself into unconsciousness. I knew from experience that Joe would still be staring at my back, his smile, if anything, larger than before. He was capable of prolonged fits of enthusiasm at levels that would have killed an ordinary man. Eventually, I rolled back to face him.

"Do you really want to do this? Couldn't you just call me a homo and steal my lunch money? Can't we relive my painful childhood memories that way? Or better yet, we could play a game of dodgeball, and you can peg me in the face. Doesn't that seem like a fun idea?"

I sounded whiny, petulant, and sissified. In other words, I sounded exactly like myself, and I was quite happy that way. I had spent years perfecting my sissy-hood. In high school, when most other sissies either had been beaten into submission or had hidden themselves under nerdy, bookish personas, I flitted through the halls wearing a necklace of faerie dust, sprinkling it on anyone who got in my face. I wasn't incapable of manly behavior—I outright rejected it.

The only time I ever went camping, it was an utter disaster. My memories of the trip are spotty, a montage of scenes out of a wilderness safety video—the "what not to do" sequences only. Reel 1: Hours spent running around the campground crying, after my older brother accidentally left me in the woods alone. Reel 2: Teenagers in a car calling me a fag as they drove by. Reel 3: Finding my family just before a skunk came along and sprayed our dog. Reel 4: Picking a flower that left painful sores all over my hands.

As far as I was concerned, camping was the stuff of which nightmares were made.

I resisted the idea that night, but over the course of the next few days Joe's enthusiasm broke me down. I agreed to go. He tried to get me excited about the place itself, some commune run by a queer artist group called the Radical Faeries, but once I had given in, my only line of defense was to pretend that it wasn't happening. He could make me go, but he couldn't make me enjoy myself.

❋　　❋　　❋

"Miss Thing, take your tent out of my yard or I will cut you. Don't make me take my pumps off and come over there. You heard me. Get!"

I was hallucinating. That was the only explanation for what was happening here. This being my second camping trip ever, I wasn't sure what to expect. However, had someone asked me to list situations I was reasonably certain would not occur in the woods, this would have been way up there. It had to be some sort of fever dream. I was not standing in the forest being harangued by a drag queen in four-inch heels. I waited for her to disappear, at which point I could collapse on the ground and sleep until the end of this vacation from hell.

Another voice floated out from behind her. I could just see someone moving inside a tent I had not noticed before, ten feet farther back in the woods.

"Don't mind her. Queen woke up on the wrong side of the sleeping bag today. What she meant to say was, 'You're quite welcome t—'"

"Bitch, I said what I meant to say, and if you think I am having my view ruined by a bunch of dirty homosexuals, well you have got another thing coming." With that, she rounded on me, six feet two inches of raging drag queen fury. She was in her forties, dressed in a tight pair of leopard print stretch-velour bell bottoms and a torn Mickey Mouse T-shirt. She was beautiful, with a face like Angela Bassett and biceps to match, and she was about to kill me. I was ready to drop my tent and run when she burst into laughter and crumpled to the ground.

"Hoo boy! Get a look at him. Like as to wet his pants in another second. 'Oh Lordy! Somebody help me! There's a big black drag queen a-comin' for me.' Hah!"

She was now rolling on the ground, tears running down her face, taking huge gasping breaths in between gales of laughter. I was frozen above her, and I could just make out her voice saying, "Run, Forrest, run!" over and over again. Where was Joe when I needed him? After all, this had been his idea in the first place. He had sent me to choose a camping spot while he got a cart to bring down the rest of our stuff. As though choosing a camping spot was something I had any clue how to do. He might as well have asked me to build him a log cabin.

"Sorry about her." The voice from inside the tent had emerged and shown itself to belong to a white guy in his late thirties. He was wearing baggy pants with flames stitched along the seams, a matching shirt, and fiery face paint to top it all off. He was easily twice my size, as tall as the giggling queen at my feet, except he wasn't wearing heels. His hair contained equal, and equally unnatural, patches of red and black. "I'm Burn, and you've already had the dubious pleasure of meeting Delicious—call her Deli. Don't worry, she's harmless."

I took a deep breath. I might not know a single thing about the woods, but I knew a whole lot when it came to catty queens. "Oh, I wasn't afraid of her. I was just worried her pants might give me a rash if they touched me—some of us can't wear cheap synthetic fabrics, you know. They're hell on good skin."

There was a moment of complete silence. I heard birds chirping, the gentle breeze blowing through the leaves around us, and somewhere far off the sound of wood being chopped. Maybe this was the famed tranquility so many bad nature writers yapped on about. Or maybe it was the last sound I was ever going to hear. Then Deli's laughter pealed again, with Burn's sounding a low bass note to match it.

Once she had managed to regain some of her composure, Deli purred, "Mmmmmm.... Burn, baby, I think we'll keep this one." Then she reached one long elegant arm toward me, every inch of her regal again. "Be a dear, and give me a hand up," she said. I let go of the things I was holding and reached out to her. She grasped my hand and levered her way back to standing, nearly pulling me down in the process. She was as strong as she was tall. I went to pick a stray leaf from her hair, and she waved me away.

"Don't worry about that, sugar. By next year, every woman on a runway in Paris will have maple leaves in her hair. You know they're always stealing their best ideas from us." Deli paused to size me up. "So we're going to be neighbors, eh? Well, I guess it could be worse. You've never been here before, have you? You by yourself? Welcome home. How'd you find your way here? Let's get that tent set up. You got a tarp?"

I attempted to answer her first round of questions. "Yes. No. No. My boyfriend, he told me about it. He's getting the rest of our stuff. It's his tent, and I have no idea how to put it up. Maybe there's a tarp in there? I don't know. . . . I'll just wait for him."

When I was through, Deli snorted and held out her hand. I stared at it, unsure what she wanted. Were we going to dance? At this point, I wouldn't be surprised. In an exasperated voice, she said, "Your tent. Give it here. If you wait for a man once, you'll be waiting around for him for the rest of your life. Now watch."

Unceremoniously, she took the bag from my hands, upended it, and shook the contents out on the ground. Quickly, she used the tip of her spike-heeled shoes to push the various bits into separate piles. "Okay, listen up, because I'm only going through this once. These are your spikes. You use these to secure the tent to the ground. Don't look at me like you don't know how to do it, baby. Just slip it into the hole and pound away. This is your fly. Think of it like a condom. . . . "

She was the first person on this trip who reminded me of . . . well, me. The guys who had met us at the airport were all like Joe, competent and scruffy and sort of manly. I had managed to avoid knowing much about the Radical Faeries, but I had assumed they were all like that. Deli, with her outfit and her attitude, seemed as if she should feel as out of place here as I did. As she explained each piece of equipment on the ground in front me, it became clear that my expectations of her, and of this place, were very wrong.

I tried to listen to what she was saying, but my brain just kept repeating, "How the hell does she know all this stuff?" I didn't know how to set up a tent. I didn't think guys like us ever knew how to do stuff like that. I mean, we were sissies. This was the whole reason I didn't want to go camping in the first place. I was a city fag. Taking me camping was like releasing a litter of kittens into rush-hour traffic: vaguely amusing, but destined to end with blood and cuteness smeared across the pavement. Yet here was someone who made me look butch, and she was setting up the tent in what must have been record time.

When Joe arrived with the rest of our stuff, the tent was done. First, Deli had shown me what was wrong with the place I had originally chosen. Aside from being in front of her tent, the ground there was sloped ("I know you'd look good wet, baby, but there, even in a light rain, you'd end up soaked"), and home to a number of large roots ("Two words: beauty sleep. Every queen needs hers, and you'd never get any on top of those"). While we prospected for a good site nearby, Burn gathered up great armfuls of dry leaves, which eventually we spread in the place Deli choose. It turned out that I did have a tarp, so we put it over the leaves ("It's like a stone-age featherbed"). She showed me how to lace the poles through the pockets of the tent itself (here she said nothing, but she gave me a look that made me feel incredibly dirty), and with that, it was up.

For a second, I reveled in the incredulous look on Joe's face when he saw the tent. I wanted to jump up and down and squeal, "Look what I can do!" Then I got pissed. The time it takes me to go from zero to bitch needs to be measured with the same type of instruments that calculate the fractional existence of radioactive elements. Why did he assume I couldn't do it? Okay, I had thought the same thing, and without Deli I wouldn't have been able to. But this was different. It wasn't okay for him to think it, too.

I decided to play it cool. "Tent's up," I said, in my best approximation of Joe's own nonchalant voice. I'd let him say something before I savaged him for his disparaging thoughts. I wanted to wait until I could throw his own words back at him.

"Cool," Joe responded. He dumped our stuff out of the cart, introduced himself to Burn and Deli, and then said, "I'm hungry. You guys want to go get lunch?"

This was not going as I intended it. Surely he would say something. Even if it wasn't something I could use against him, the least he could do was praise me for what I had accomplished. This was impressive! Didn't he understand that? Maybe I just needed to make it clearer that I had set up the tent.

Before anyone had a chance to answer Joe's question, I burst out: "It wasn't as hard as I thought it would be. Putting up the tent. It was pretty easy really. And there it is. All set up and waiting. Pretty cool, huh? I mean, it's not like it's the first time I've set one up or anything. But it's still pretty cool. Right?"

I stopped. I was babbling in a way that made everyone else wince with awkwardness. My laid-back cool of a moment ago was gone. Why did I need him to say something? Was I really just trying to get him to be condescending? That would be pretty sick. Clever, but sick. No one knew how to respond to my little outburst, so I decided to act as though it hadn't happened.

"Yeah, uh, lunch sounds good. Let's go get lunch. Deli, Burn, want to come?"

It was going to be a long week.

As we trudged back up the hill toward the main area of the grounds, I began wondering about what we were going to eat. Words like *Spam* and *freeze-dried* kept popping into my head. Wasn't that supposed to be part of camping, eating horrible food? I had some snacks hidden among my bags, but I suddenly began worrying whether they would be enough to see me through the week. If I had paid a little more attention to my surroundings, and a little less to my internal monologue, my fears might have been allayed.

On our walk, we passed by abundant gardens, a herd of goats, and more chickens than I would ever care to count. In my life, these things had little actual relation to food, so I paid them no mind. Even some of the flowers we walked by were edible, though I wouldn't know that until lunch was served. What looked to be a loose assemblage of rotting logs was actually a shiitake mushroom growing area. There was more organic food in that short walk than in all the aisles of my local Whole Foods Market combined—I just couldn't see it. For most of my life, I had avoided making any connection between the food that appeared on my plate and the rest of the world. At eighteen, I'd had a vague realization that yummy, tasty "meat" came from fuzzy, cuddly "animals" and, thus, had stopped eating it. Beyond that, I just knew that food was more expensive in Manhattan, cheaper in Brooklyn, and tended to have its origins in Red States or South America.

Even without noticing the food we were passing, I had a lot to take in. Interspersed with the growing areas were small houses where the permanent residents lived. Each was unique, designed by the person, or people, who lived inside. We passed log cabins, small shacks, yurts, tents, and stone dwellings in a variety of shapes and sizes. Some were painted, others covered in mosaic made from broken dishware. Deli pointed out houses where her friends lived, rattling off a list of names that sounded a bit like the cast of a *My Little Pony* episode. Sparkle, Wing Song, Gizmo, and other such names were interspersed with more common ones like Eric and Amanda. I definitely wasn't in Kansas anymore.

Amid the rural setting, I was amazed to see solar panels attached to a number of houses, along with other more arcane pieces of technology that I couldn't identify. Outside one building, I stopped, confused.

"Ummm . . . what is that?"

"Sauna," Joe said. "There's a shower and a tub in there too. The system on top collects and heats the rain water."

A sauna. In the middle of the woods. It was the gayest thing I'd ever heard of. I loved it. Maybe I should have listened more carefully when Joe was describing this place.

"Wow . . . damn." Deli and Burn laughed at the reverence in my voice. If I could choose, I might live in a sauna. In New York, my favorite was a Russian bathhouse in the East Village, where old Eastern European women flagellated themselves with oak leaves and poured buckets of freezing water on their heads. I had a suspicion that this sauna might actually be rather similar, right down to the hairy, muscular arms encased in 1940s-style women's bathing suits.

"Aren't you glad I made you come?" said Joe, jokingly. Before my brain had a chance to consult on the matter, my mouth was off and running.

"You didn't make me. I wanted to come." A blatant lie, as he'd all but dragged me kicking and screaming. I'd refused even to learn the name of the place, referring to it only as "Camp Deliverance." What was I doing? Joe just turned away from me. After a second, we all continued walking.

By the time we reached the main house, I had forgotten lunch entirely. I was too busy fuming. This trip was turning out to be as much a failure as my last camping escapade. Maybe I had been right: I wasn't cut out for this "woods" thing. Glumly, I followed Joe, Deli, and Burn up the rickety wooden steps of the house and into a scene that nothing could have prepared me for.

There was food everywhere. The kitchen itself was bigger than my apartment, with ceilings that were easily fifteen feet high. One whole wall was covered in shelves housing carefully labeled glass jars. Teas, spices, grains, dried fruit, some that I recognized and some completely new to me. I saw apricots and hibiscus flowers, granola, lentils, pasta . . . but what were those brown podlike things? The little kid in me wanted to run over and start opening jars, to sniff the spices and run my hands through the dry goods, but there were other things to look at first.

On the wall opposite the shelves were two large industrial sinks, a six-burner gas stove, and what looked to be a working woodstove. In between were two islands, one laid out with lunch and one with a cluster of faeries hard at work preparing dinner. Most were chopping vegetables under the direction of a squat, muscular young woman with a Mohawk and a rattail. The rest were singing along to "Papa Was a Rolling Stone." Above their heads hung a bewildering array of pots, woks, skillets, and colanders ranging in size from a one-cup saucepan to a cast-iron skillet three feet in diameter. The room was rough, homemade, and painted in a dozen different colors. In total, it looked like Williams-Sonoma redesigned by the Unabomber and then overrun by the last vestiges of Haight-Ashbury.

Dominating the lunch table was a massive bowl of fruit salad: strawberries, honeydew melon, and peach slices accented here and there with a scattering of blackberries, mint leaves, and bright orange flowers. Beside that was a pot of rice at least two and a half feet tall, clearly meant to go with the still-sizzling vegetables sitting next to it. Beyond that were a few loaves of bread, a large bowl of sauce, a teapot with some mysterious steam rising up from it, a bowl of punch, and other dishes that were still covered.

Mute with awe, I followed Burn over to one of the sinks. A sign hung above it: "We know where your hands have been and we liked it. Now we'd like you to wash them." Burn handed me the soap, and I ran my hands under the water while trying to formulate the questions I dearly wanted to ask. Finally, I just sputtered, "Where did this all come from?"

Burn smiled. "The food? Lunch? The house?" His eyes were twinkling, and I could tell he was enjoying my astonishment, the way a native New Yorker takes pride in watching a first-time visitor gape at the Chrysler Building. I hate feeling like a tourist, but I had no choice but to go with it. This place was astounding.

"Yes," I responded. "All of it." Burn chuckled, and we relinquished the sink to Joe and Deli.

While I heaped my plate full of food, Burn ran through a quick history of our lunch. "Some of it's grown here," he said, "and mostly the residents—we call them stewards—save that stuff to eat year-round. This place is a nonprofit, and everyone who comes down is encouraged to donate as much as they can. A lot of that money goes to support these gatherings. The stewards try to buy local food, or get organic and fair trade stuff. I like the local stuff best—it tastes better. No chemicals pissing the flavor away. Anyone who's got time can just go into the kitchen and help cook it all up." By now, our plates were in danger of toppling over from the food heaped on them. I scooped up some silverware and began tasting.

"This is delicious." I heard a throat-clearing noise behind me. "Uh . . . sorry, Deli. No pun intended." I began to laugh, but nearly choked on the strawberry I had popped into my mouth. I made a mental note to swallow the food before I tried to compliment it again and followed Burn out onto the deck. Here were more than a dozen long tables, each seating eight to ten people. Nearest us was a woman dressed all in black, braiding the unbelievably thick mane of scarlet hair that went all the way down to her waist. Next to her, two men in psychedelic paisley body suits juggled small metal balls back and forth. A man in tattered cutoff jean shorts and no shirt lay snoozing on a long bench, his handlebar mustache at first masking the incredibly intricate tattoos that crawled around his mouth. And it went on from there. It was too much for me to take in. It looked like a biker convention hosted by Rainbow Brite.

"You know," I remarked to Burn, "either I need to get over being surprised by everything, or I need to get used to having my jaw hanging open."

"Well, keep your mouth open wide like that, and I bet you'll make a whole lot of friends fast," Burn said, laughing. Then he grew serious for a moment. "Nurture that feeling of surprise. It's beautiful. There's a lot of surprising stuff out here, if you leave yourself open to it. Hell, you could surprise yourself." Then he was all smiles again.

"Let's sit over there," Joe said, coming up behind us. I hadn't noticed him until his arm moved past to point out a table with four empty seats. I settled into the crook of his elbow, happy to feel its strength and the way it fit familiarly around my hips. Then I pulled away and started toward the table he had suggested.

I spent most of lunch in a reverie, listening with half a mind to the conversation going on around me. I chimed in occasionally, usually to answer a direct question, but for the most part I stayed in my head. The food was amazing; both the flavor and the texture were worlds better than the produce I was accustomed to getting in the city. I was pushing the last few bits of stir-fry in circles around my plate when a man in a long dress emerged from the kitchen and yelled over the din of the crowd. "We desperately need folks to help out with dinner. If you've got the time, we've got some vegetables that need some faerie love. Blessed be." Burn's words flashed through my mind. Surprise myself, eh?

"I'll help!" I didn't know what the hell I was doing. I couldn't cook for this many people. This was a complete mistake. And it felt good.

"You sure about this?" Joe asked.

I shot him a frosty glance over my shoulder as I got up. "Of course I'm sure." Then I was on my way to the kitchen.

❀   ❀   ❀

Three days later I was still in the kitchen. At least, it felt as if I hadn't left. I'd somehow volunteered for every meal, though unintentionally. After helping with that first dinner, I was exhausted, and I crashed long before Joe made it to the tent. I wanted to calm down and sleep late. Shortly after dawn, however, I found myself urgently needing to pee. I started to get up, looked down toward my feet, and froze.

"Joe," I hissed. "Get up. There's a scorpion in the tent."

"I know. I was watching it," he replied. "And it can't hear you."

"You know?!" I yelled back, choosing for the moment to ignore his sarcasm. "Then. Why. Isn't. It. Dead?"

"We probably put our tent on its home. I doubt it's even that poisonous. I'll catch it and let it go outside."

"Yeah, right. It'll sting you. Or no, you'll release it, and it'll sting me when I get out to pee. This is wonderful." I was working myself up to constrained hysteria, trying to channel all my fury into my eyes and voice, while avoiding any movement lest the scorpion decide I needed to be taken out.

Joe, meanwhile, had gotten to his knees and grabbed the wide-mouthed Nalgene water bottle that he usually kept attached to his bag. Slowly, he opened the tent flap, poured out the dregs of water, and then trapped the scorpion under the empty bottle. Next, he put his hand inside the sleeping bag under the scorpion, flipped everything over, and held up the now trapped arachnid.

"See?" he said, and smiled. "No need to kill him."

I could have shoved the damn scorpion down his throat.

"Oh, I see how it is. You'll eat animals, but you won't squish one when it's trying to kill me!" This wasn't exactly fair. Yes, I was a vegetarian and Joe was not, but I had long ago given up any claims to moral superiority on this point and considered it a decision people had to make for themselves. Joe just looked so smug, I couldn't help but throw it in his face, knowing he felt bad about it.

Silently, Joe turned and left the tent. I followed him outside, pulling on pants as he looked for a suitable location to release our unwelcome visitor. "I'm going to . . . to . . . to go help with breakfast!" I announced, and stalked off.

Thus, I found myself back in the kitchen. Over a pot of strong coffee—the good stuff, which was in short supply—I woke up enough to think about what had happened. The scorpion could have hurt one of us, but it was also clear that Joe could take care of it. He was right, too, that we had probably disturbed its home. It wasn't something to which I had given much thought. Insects and animals were just there, or they weren't. They didn't live anywhere, unless they were pets. Before I could get lost in the ramifications of this thought, the faerie who had volunteered to supervise breakfast cleared his throat. Sleepily, he began, "So . . . we're, uh . . ., going to make some wild-blueberry and spelt pancakes. I picked the berries yesterday, so we should be good. But, uh . . ., before we start, anyone want to do some yoga?"

I had done yoga a few times before, but had found that rooms full of stressed-out businesspeople were both less relaxing and less stimulating than I had been promised. But here, it was a different story. First thing in the morning, outside, with the sun shining on me, surrounded by a loose conglomeration of people spread out across a hillside, I found it possible to really breathe.

Fifteen minutes into the meditation, I found myself at peace, and into that moment of peace swept a number of realizations, not the least of them being that I was behaving like a two-year-old. I was so intent on punishing Joe for bringing me to a place I had decided not to like that I had refused to consider the possibility that I might enjoy parts of it. While I had no doubt that this was, to some degree, a successful strategy—since I seemed to be preventing Joe from enjoying himself, too—I had to wonder if I was winning a battle to lose the war. The opposite approach, pretending to enjoy myself simply for Joe's sake, was impossible. I had a feeling that if I did this to make Joe happy, I would be as miserable as I was while doing it to spite him. What I needed was to do this for myself—and then to decide how I felt about it.

After thirty minutes of practice poses, when the slowly waking campers began grumbling for breakfast, we knew we had to return to the kitchen. To my surprise, I no longer wanted to feed Joe the scorpion for breakfast. I felt calm. I took that sense of tranquility back to the kitchen with me and quickly found that chopping vegetables could be just as meditative as yoga. It was a place where I could feel comfortable *and* useful and also get to meet a few new people. And if I hid there, I wouldn't have to face Joe and admit how childishly I had been behaving. So I stayed in the kitchen. For three days.

The number and kind of faeries that I cooked with ebbed and flowed with the meal in question. Some nights it would be a huge party, with dozens of people dancing, chopping, and helping to decorate the kitchen for some esoteric theme (the "Jewish Love Boat" was my favorite, though the "New Orleans Bordello" was a great excuse to wear a skimpy nonoutfit). Other times it was a smaller group, and I did get to know people. Some, like me, were there for the first time; others had been coming for decades. I met a two-year-old clinging to her father's skirts, and an eighty-year-old man who had been a faerie since the group started.

A few were the brawny mountain-folk whom I had imagined living in the woods, and a large number were men and women who, like Joe, exuded a competent manliness. Most, however, were people whom I would not have imagined surviving, let alone thriving, in the woods. Urban queens, young lipstick lesbians, people with AIDS, older people with chronic disabilities—the sheer variety of bodies and attitudes that found or made a place for themselves here amazed me. It was far from a perfect rainbow, the percentage of white, upper-middle class men being much higher than I was accustomed too. Yet still, it began to shake something loose in my mind.

Somehow, despite my near-perfect feminist-queer credentials—the degree in women's studies, the job as a social worker with queer youth—I had been harboring a pernicious and unexamined belief. I loved sissies. I loved being a sissy. Subconsciously, though, I believed there were things that sissies did not, and could not, do. Somewhere along the line, manliness had become a code word for competence, and I had abandoned whole ranges of activities to the provenance of people who were "not like me." Watching the queerest of the queer chop wood, clean an outhouse, and help build a new barn, I realized again just how strong one had to be to stand outside traditional gender roles.

Had others said to me that there were things I categorically could not do, I would have screamed at them. Not being able to scream at myself, I had chosen Joe as my stand-in. Not, I was to quick to remind myself, that he didn't deserve it. He thought the same way I did. There was the slight chance, however, that I had been a bit harsh. Given the number of people at the gathering, and my artful hiding in the kitchen, I had barely seen Joe after the first day. I tried to turn in for the night at times when I knew he wouldn't be in the tent yet, or long after he himself had fallen asleep. On my fourth night in the kitchen, somewhere between chopping vegetables, singing every song from *The Little Mermaid*—in chorus—and serving a vegan tomato-and-basil risotto, I decided that I had an apology to make.

❂　　❂　　❂

It was dark by the time I finally got back to the tent, and I could hear Joe breathing low and rhythmically from inside the sleeping bag. I can just apologize in the morning, I thought. I undressed quietly and got in next to him, knowing as I did it that it would be tough to avoid waking him up. There was no warning shot this time.

"Are you mad at me?"

A difficult question. Normally, I would have given some answer that was nominally correct and then just gone with it, arguing my point of view until at least I was convinced. I opened my mouth, and then shut it again. The whole point of this week, I had decided, was to do new things. He deserved the truth. The confused, nonsensical, and incoherent truth.

"Yes. No. I don't know. No. I'm not."

"Then...?"

"Look, I'm just... I'm mad at myself, I guess. I've been having a great time here, and I'm mad that I didn't come here earlier. Or really, mad that I haven't wanted to come. Or didn't think..." I paused here, struggling to compress realizations about the way I had lived the last twenty-three years of my life into a few sentences.

"I'm used to being a big sissy. I guess I assumed this meant there were certain things I just wouldn't be interested in, and I'm really pissed with myself for thinking that way. So every time you said what I was thinking, I bit your head off. And I'm not saying you don't deserve it somewhat too. Just that I should be yelling at myself more than I should be yelling at you."

"Huh." Joe shifted his body against mine, his arm finding purchase around my shoulders.

I waited. Slowly, his breathing turned to a gentle snoring, and I knew the conversation was at an end. I had no idea what Joe was thinking, but I had said my piece, and he had heard it, and that was enough for now.

Freed from the obligation I had felt toward Joe, I thought about the rest of the time I had down here. Five more days—what did I want from those days? I had no idea. I had stepped so far beyond my world that I was still getting my bearings. I just knew I wanted more—more woods, more faeries, more drag queens in camping gear, and leather bears cooking vegan breakfasts. Were there places like this in New York? Or if not like this, at least places where I could get outside again and feel comfortable? How would I go about finding them? And what should I wear while I was doing it? Eventually, as I lay in my sleeping bag, I went from thinking to dreaming, crossing a thin line that seemed, on that mountainside, much thinner than usual. There was a lot to do in the morning. And in this case, my wildest dreams were more likely to help me navigate than any anxious thoughts.

Little Stick Land

SAM MOULTON

Day 1 | May 29 | 0 miles

So much depends on the weather, and this morning we awake to both sunny skies and a hefty tailwind. This is a good sign. We lash the red boat to the yellow boat with our freshly cut bow and stern lines and fashion a makeshift sail out of our dark green tarp, some spare guy lines, and two of our paddles. A few bowlines and slipknots later, we have a crude, two-canoe catamaran. It's an old trick, and it works. We sail twenty miles north under an open blue sky.

Day 7 | June 4 | 124 miles

Fending off swarms of blackflies, dragging our gear-laden canoe upstream, exhausted and dehydrated and up to my crotch in ice-cold spring runoff, I now think our endeavor just seems impossible and dumb.

To make matters worse, we have only a rough idea of where we are on the Blondeau River. Unlike most of the waters in northern Saskatchewan—which is rocky and rugged and beautiful and chock-full of clear lakes and unbridled rivers—the Blondeau is a small, stinky stream of a river. It lacks direction, looping back on itself constantly like a Lab chasing its tail, and we'll be glad to be done with it. What we do know: at some point near its marshy headwaters, we have to find an old trapper's route, leave the river, and lake-hop northwest into a different watershed.

We're looking for waters that will carry us north and west and, appropriately enough, closer to the border with the Northwest Territories. There, we will once again shoulder all our gear, this time heading for a river system destined for Hudson Bay. But we don't want to go to the bay. No, no. If everything goes as planned, we'll head farther north still, schlepping our canoes and all our gear and food over one more height of land, and, on the other side, launch our boats on a river that will lead us to the top of the continent.

The plan was born a year and a half ago when three friends of mine— Brook, Mike, and Luke, but Luke mostly—latched onto the idea of canoeing to the Arctic Ocean. We determined that, if we were to time it right, and start as far north as we could—where the dirt roads end at the open-pit uranium mines, and hardscrabble First Nation settlements dot the northern third of the province—and start late in the spring just after the ice broke up, it would be possible to reach salt water by the end of the summer, before all the tundra's rivers and lakes froze up again. The ice-free window varies quite a bit from year to year. Some years, the biggest lakes never thaw out completely, but in an average year there are a hundred days of open water to work with.

"Ice to ice," Luke said to me on the phone when he asked me to join the expedition. I liked the sound of it. Serious and significant, in a continental and cyclical sort of way. (Later, when trying to impress a girl or, more likely, a potential sponsor, I will wield the phrase for dramatic effect.) I signed on, and we pieced together a route we thought we could complete in about ninety days.

We'd have to get resupplied once by floatplane and, when we reached the ocean, hitch a ride to Uqsuqtuq, an Inuit hamlet of about a thousand hardy souls on King William Island, just off the mainland. Uqsuqtuq means "lots of blubber" in Inuktitut, the Inuit native language. You'll find it labeled on most maps with its English name, Ghoa Haven.

The Blondeau, however, was never really part of the plan. In fact, the only reason we're going up it right now is because we jumped the gun. Wollaston, the lake we wanted to start on, was still not quite thawed out when we arrived. So instead of sitting around, watching ice chunks blow about and waiting for breakup, we opted for plan B, starting 150 miles farther south, going up the Blondeau.

Which brings me back to my crotch. I'm trying to stay positive, reminding myself of the incredible disappearing act we've masterminded. After a year and a half of late-night scheming and nonstop planning—researching, training, obsessing, sewing, dreaming, debating, practicing, dehydrating food, and reinforcing gear—we've finally managed to leave our usual lives behind for three months.

But I've been doing the math—I'm pretty sure we all have—and it's simply not adding up. We knew we'd be slow at the start, heading up a swollen river, heavily provisioned—eleven packs, some eight hundred pounds of food and gear, all told. I feel like a pack animal. Each portage requires all four of us to make three separate trips. There, back. There, back. There.

Several of our food packs weigh over a hundred pounds each and require two people to load on one person's back. I'm almost embarrassed to reveal their contents. We packed more like dewy-eyed sailors on one of those ridiculous British navy sailing explorations—the kind in which those aboard had no idea what they were in for, the kind that rarely made it back home—than weight-conscious modern adventurers. We've got fifty pounds of cheese, fifty pounds of summer sausage. Our spice kit alone weighs twenty pounds, the fishing tackle thirty. Luke even brought a freaking fish scale. We've got a dozen or so books, a cast-iron frying pan, and a comically heavy wooden box we built ourselves for carrying tools and pots and pans, called a wanigan, a traditional wooden kitchen-box used for canoe tripping. They come in all shapes and sizes, but since only a few boutique woodworkers still make them, we decided to build our own. Imagine ripping an oak cabinet out of your kitchen, fastening leather straps on the back, riveting a cutting board to the top, and you have a fair idea of the overbuilt and uncomfortable box we intend to lug across the tundra.

If we want to make the Arctic Ocean by the end of August, we figure, we'll need to average about seventeen miles a day. Since we waved good-bye to our dads—who had been kind enough to drive us three thousand miles to our dropoff, as well as pay for gas—we've been busting ass. Even so, these last few days we've been averaging only around ten. Clearly this is not the result of one or two poor decisions but rather the product of a series of delusional and overly ambitious calculations. I was yearning for a real adventure, to be sure, but this is beginning to seem downright Sisyphean.

Day 13 | June 10 | 224 miles

We catch up to the ice this morning—and finally reach the lake where we had hoped to start. Today, however, our timing is perfect. Temperatures in the high sixties, mostly clear skies, and strong northeasterly winds have pushed the remaining pack ice into Wollaston's southwestern bays, and we're able to skirt the lingering frozen and shifting slabs to the east.

Many days it's been too windy or wavy to carry on sustained conversations with my paddling partner or the other boat. But not today. Today it's eerily calm. A forest fire rages to the northeast, sending mushrooms of smoke straight up into the sky and dusting everything with a light film of ash. The lake is heaving ever so slightly. It feels like paddling across the belly of a sleeping giant.

Voices carry on days like today. Conversations have no beginnings or ends and span entire mornings. Mike tells me about growing up in Bozeman. How he used to dress up like Huck Finn, play the trumpet, and listen to jazz with his dad. Occasionally he and his brother and his dad—who is a blacksmith and farrier, among other things—stacked two anvils on top of each other, put some gunpowder in between them and, much to his mom's dismay, blew them up. He tells me about water rights in Montana. He tells me he'll never—ever—own a cell phone.

Luke tells me about some of the first snowboard descents he notched in the Grand Tetons. He tells me about schmoozing with wealthy land-owners in Jackson and teaches me the ins and outs of easements and other fundamentals of land conservation. He sums up Jared Diamond's arguments in *Guns, Germs, and Steel*. He tells me about scrambling with friends over a mountain pass in Wyoming to attend a bluegrass festival in Idaho.

Brook tells me about drinking malts and eating popcorn and watching ABC's family movie on Sunday nights with his family. He tells me about his dreams—he has remarkably vivid dreams and tremendous recall. He works with disabled and mentally ill children, and his stories about the kids' difficult and troubled lives are heartbreaking and disturbing. He also tells me that when he was little his dad, who owns a vending machine business (and gave us two hundred Snickers bars for the trip), put a soda machine in at his house for the kids who played soccer in the field across the street. Only twenty-five cents! But then the mailman started buying them, and the water softener guy, and soon deliverymen from all over his hometown of Janesville started swinging by on their routes. His dad had to get rid of it.

We talk and inch our way north, and each night we set up our tempo-rary home with amazing speed and efficiency. It takes just twenty minutes to unload and secure the boats, set up the tents, collect firewood, build a fire ring, start a fire, get water boiling, and rummage through all our food packs for dinner ingredients.

It's simple living, but rambling across such an unforgiving landscape isn't easy on the body. The sun bumps on my hands, which appeared on day two, are back in full force. My navy-blue-and-white-striped thrift store shirt has already turned sky blue and tan. I have a chapped lower lip split down the middle and intermittently bloody. (Unlike Brook, who puts lip salve on religiously and is kind enough to remind me periodically, I'm not so good about reapplying.)

I'm already deeply tanned. A thin layer of perma-dirt covers much of my body. The line between my palms and the tops of my hands is like night and day. My arms are bitten and scraped to hell. My beard seems to be growing faster than usual. My back is sore. And an old injury has come back to say hello. The tendons in my right shoulder are aflame, an unpleasant reality that asserts itself, with searing little stabs of acute pain, with the first few hundred paddle strokes every morning.

Day 18 | June 15 | 334 miles

Our first rest day of the trip. After several days of bouncing down the Fond du Lac River, we're at Manitou Falls, a spot so spectacular—and with such great walleye fishing—that we decide to take a voluntary breather. Repair some blown-out pack straps, inventory our food packs, check to see if any bags of milk powder or pancake mix have exploded.

We rolled into camp late the night before and baked a massive frying pan of lasagna with summer sausage, fresh garlic, and rehydrated broccoli in a large oven someone had constructed out of sandstone rocks and left behind. For the first time, I checked my watch, which was buried at the bottom of a drybag, below wadded bunches of wool shirts and fleece tights. I ate just-baked lasagna. At midnight, the sun finally slipped out of sight. We've made a conscious effort to travel without the handicap of time in our heads. I thought it would be a big deal to live completely off the clock. It isn't. Eating, sleeping, paddling—expedition canoeing isn't exactly rocket science.

By far the most difficult thing we do is negotiate whitewater, and we've already had a few close calls. Running technically challenging rapids in a loaded, seventeen-foot canoe isn't easy—it's sort of like trying to drive an eighteen-wheeler with ailing brakes down a steeply winding mountain road—and we can't afford to make any mistakes. A capsize could end the trip—or worse. So we play it safe. The previous day, we portaged part of Thompson's rapid, the first major set of the trip. We thought for a while about running it, and then we thought of the explorer David Thompson.

In 1796, David Thompson, the first European to explore the Fond du Lac, almost died lining up what has become his namesake rapid. He lost nearly everything, including his life, when his boat dumped—and he spent the next several weeks, starved and nearly naked, hunting and foraging for food with his two native guides. It was such an ordeal, and his account so harrowing, that no one mounted an official expedition of the Fond du Lac for an entire century.

Other than the addition of a few fire pits and a couple of overgrown portage trails, probably not much has changed since then. Only the tiniest trickle of folks paddle the Fond du Lac these days. Most of those who do, sign the registry—a dirty notebook shoved in a rusted-out tin can that lives inside a massive stone cairn on the left shore and dates back to the early 1980s. I pore over the entries. A group of goofy young Canadians—"four hosers with nothing profound to say." A solo paddler whose campsite just got raided by a black bear, a few terse words from some cold and wet Germans, and an open invitation to hot coffee and free lodging from the owner of a now-defunct fly-in fishing lodge downriver.

Finally, I come across my own entry, which, not surprisingly, is also the most recent one. The previous September, my friend John and I paddled the Fond du Lac on a shorter, late-season journey. I had a magazine assignment to investigate a geological anomaly—some massive sand dunes—on the south shore of a big lake at the river's end. We could have floatplaned in and out, but since John and I both happened to be between jobs, we decided it would be more fun, and more adventuresome, to take the long way there.

It's hard to believe I was in this same spot just eight months ago. If you add it up, and if we don't have any mishaps like Thompson's, I'll end up having spent four months in a canoe in the Canadian bush this year alone. A third of the entire year. You'd think I was on the lam.

My life in a canoe started when I was twelve. My parents sent me to a summer camp in northern Wisconsin that specializes in wilderness trips, and in canoeing in particular. Manito-wish. There are a handful of camps like it in Maine, Canada, Wisconsin, Minnesota—all over the North Woods. Keewaydin. Menoygn. Widgiwagan. Most have difficult-to-pronounce Native American names, and all of them are institutions steeped in rowdy traditions and history, with a dedicated cult of staff and alumni.

It was the best place I'd ever been. The counselors were the coolest guys I had ever met. I learned about girls. I learned how to steer a canoe (the J stroke), how to start a fire in the rain (birch bark), how to pop a canoe onto my shoulders with my knees (a widgi flip).

I was hooked. So were Brook and Luke, who were also campers there. We begged our parents to come back summer after summer so we could go on longer and longer trips. Fourteen days, twenty-one days, thirty-three days. Then, during college, we worked on staff. Brook recruited Mike Wolfe, his best friend from school, and we all began to lead lengthy backpacking, sea kayaking, and canoeing trips, working our way toward leading the Canuck.

The Canuck is Manito-wish's flagship trip, a thirty-day canoeing trip in northern Saskatchewan. There may be only one or two a summer, and if you're one of the lucky few who get to lead one, they name a canoe after you.

When we left, the Sam Moulton, the Luke Manger-Lynch, and the Brook Yeomans were all sitting next to Boulder Lake on canoe racks with the rest of the camp's massive flotilla. Luke's boat was already wa-terlogged and a bit bow-heavy, but otherwise they were in good shape. Soon, we thought, stick-legged eleven-year-olds would start paddling all of them around the North Woods, doing all the stuff they're taught not to do—dragging them up muddy creeks, ramming them into beaver dams, and dropping them on rocks.

Day 31 | June 28 | 445 miles

The wind plays games with your head. We've been pinned down for the last day and a half and, looking at another long night in the tents, starting to oscillate. For the past several minutes, Brook and I have been stand-ing on the shore, passing the binoculars back and forth, having a rather pointless and unproductive discussion.

He's convinced that there are fewer whitecaps on the lake, that it's finally letting up. He hands me the binocs to look for myself. I glass the water, trying to detect the same subtle signals that Brook has observed.

But it looks the same. The same as it did a half hour ago, when our roles were reversed and I was the one who was certain the wind was letting up a bit. The same, more or less, as it has looked for the past thirty-six hours.

We've had this same conversation dozens of times already in the past month, and it's becoming increasingly clear that we'll be having it often in the future too. We're just stubborn and anxious to keep moving. While we're not rushing, we're certainly not laid-back either. If it's not prohibitively windy out, we're out there moving north. We're learning to deal with the wind—it's the blackflies that really drive us insane.

We have defenses—bug shirts with full head-nets built in, a bug tent with four walls of mosquito netting to cook and hang out in—but the flies are truly evil little buggers. It would be one thing if, like mosquitoes, blackflies just bit and were done with it. Instead, they secrete an enzyme that liquefies the skin. They never run out of the stuff, and creep into every cranny and crevice. My hands, arms, and face are all puffy and pocked with red, and I have two collections of welts the size of softballs where they've nailed me through the mesh lining in my pants pockets.

If we were to stand completely still for several minutes, they would cover us from head to toe. We'd look like the stupid guys on TV shows who allow bees to swarm over them. Even going number two becomes an ordeal, and we've had to break out our secret weapon, a giant-size tube of heavy-duty mesh known as the "shit sock" or "poop tent."

Using it can be a bit tricky. Once you've found a good spot, collected some sufficiently smooth rocks of the right size for wiping, and dug a hole in the ground, you duck under the netting, stake it as best you can so that it hangs away from your body, pull down your pants, squat over the hole, and do your business. Efficiency is everything, because if you get hung up in one of the separate steps—usually getting the netting just right—you're forced to expose, for several more precious seconds, the oh-so-sensitive flesh on the backs of your legs and bare bottom. The Inuit had no such elaborate defenses. They just dealt. I can't even imagine.

Day 43 | July 10 | 725 miles

The trees are getting smaller, people sightings more infrequent. We've been clawing our way north for the past several weeks, navigating the most isolated and out-of-the-way waterways of the trip. We stumble across a wolf so fluffy and white and big that my first thought is that it's a polar bear, despite the fact that I know polar bears aren't that white and never wander this far inland.

We're not quite in full-blown tundra yet, but rather in what's referred to as the transitional zone—a unique and undulating ecosystem that exists between the boreal forest to the south and the treeless barrens above. It's the ancient homeland of the Déné people, or Caribou-Eaters. And before their world turned upside down, before the earth started to get inexplicably warm, before the animals they hunted changed their migration patterns, before the Déné began to starve, and before the Canadian government made the difficult decision to relocate them to a few centralized hamlets—they made this harsh environment their home. They call their world the land of little sticks.

It is a truly inhospitable land, interrupted only by the occasional winding esker, a lunarlike landscape that during this time of year is a rich tapestry of lime greens and oranges and yellows interrupted by braids and blobs of bright blue. It is so desolate and expansive that it is at once reassuring (no one can sneak up on you) and intimidating (what are we doing out here?).

Water is the only efficient mode of travel. Portaging even short distances is an exhausting and stumbly affair; walking great distances over the alternately lumpy, uneven, rocky, and marshy taiga would be absolute hell. Which is exactly what explorer Samuel Hearne, the first white man to travel overland from Hudson Bay to the Arctic Ocean, did in 1770, looking for copper with his Chipewayan guides.

Like our surroundings, we too have been transitioning. The muscles in my upper body and arms have grown immense. The sleeves of my T-shirt that used to drape loosely around my biceps are now almost taut. And though it may sound far-fetched, I feel as if all my senses have been heightened. Like I can see farther. Smell more acutely. My beard's getting quite bushy, and I had no idea I had so much neck hair. I feel—and am starting to look—like Jason Bateman's half-human, half-lupine character in *Teen Wolf.*

It has been harder for me to discern the changes in my trip mates. Luke's whiskers are still minimal, and both Brook and Mike began the trip with long, bushy beards. (When they stand together, they look like ZZ Top gone savage.) I'd been wondering just how much we'd degenerated over the past few weeks—and then Luke illustrated it today with the following.

Though it's the height of summer on most of the continent, the Canada geese, our most constant companions, are still molting, fueling an ongoing debate as to whether it would be possible to run one down on land. Though there are some ethical concerns about actually attempting to do such a thing, we all agree on this much: the place is lousy with them, and we long ago grew weary of our mostly reconstituted and mushy food. We all crave meat, dream of bacon.

The geese seem acutely aware of their vulnerability and therefore skittish. We tried chasing some the other day just for kicks. They honked noisily and, with heads down and long necks outstretched, were surprising agile and hysterically fast. But this afternoon, Luke gets a good jump on a small gaggle. The chase narrows to one bird, and with several judicious whacks with a paddle the debate is over. We roast the victim over an open fire and then gnaw on the bones until nightfall.

Day 45 | July 12 | 754 miles

Resupply! We find the two blue steel barrels and cardboard-and-duct-tape-reinforced box of fuel intact, sealed, and upright, exactly where the bush pilot had dropped them a few weeks earlier. Since we first started planning the trip, the issue of our resupply—whether it would be possible to find the provisions easily, whether we would reach them at the appropriate time, whether barren-land grizzlies would have gotten to them first—was never far from our thoughts.

Part of our anxiety resulted from the fact that the pilot gave us the barrel's precise UTM coordinates, which usually allow one to find a location in a flash with a GPS unit. The only problem: we didn't have a GPS, so we had to pinpoint the spot by hand, on our 1:250,000 (1 inch equals 250,000 inches) scale maps. But don't get the wrong idea. While we made a conscious effort to be as low-tech as possible, we did have a few battery-powered gadgets in our packs: a VHF line-of-sight radio, an Epirb (a more generic version of a personal locator device), and, after much pretrip debate, a satellite phone.

At first, I was the only person who wanted to take a satellite phone. We all knew it had the potential to alter our decision making in subtle ways—knowing in the backs of our minds that we could contact the rest of the world in an instant. It's a complex and thorny issue, and depending on how you look at it, the device either could be a lifesaver or actually could increase the chances that we'd find ourselves in a life-threatening situation.

But it became increasingly clear that the debate wasn't really about risk management. Among the four of us, we've logged hundreds and hundreds of days in the backcountry. We were okay with being on our own if things went wrong. No, the real matter at hand was more philosophical. It concerned style, notions of self-reliance, and, ultimately, what it really meant to let go.

In the end, whether or not to bring a phone became a moot discussion. Since we had no way of knowing exactly when, give or take a week or two, we would reach the Arctic Ocean, we needed a reliable way to contact our Inuit boat pickup. We could either rent an unwieldy twenty-pound Vietnam-era radiophone or bring a tiny one-pound satellite phone. And when a company agreed to lend us a sat phone for free, the debate was over.

Day 55 | July 22 | 1051 miles

It's a weird world we live in where you can paddle across some of the continent's wildest lakes and rivers for nearly two months, seeing no one—save for a few plump fisherman who pay thousands of dollars to be flown into rustic fish camps so they can catch, and release, fish of prehistoric proportions—and then, smack dab in the middle of the biggest and remotest section of wilderness on the planet, run into two dozen people.

We're on the Thelon River, several hundred miles west of Hudson Bay and almost directly in the center of Canada. The Thelon is the super-highway of the subarctic, draining the entire torso of Canada before depositing its precious freshwater into the bay. The entire length of the river is rollicking and beautiful, but the section we're on now, known as the Thelon Oasis, is the prettiest and mellowest. It has such high concentrations of musk ox, wolves, birds, and herds of caribou—thousands and thousands of them—that naturalists have described it as the Serengeti of North America.

For all these reasons, it's a popular destination for serious wilderness canoeists. Several outfitters fly paying customers to the choicest stretch of river, let them float leisurely downstream, and then pluck them out of the tundra a week or two later. And, as it's now mid-July, it's prime fly-in time: in the past three days alone, we've stopped and chatted with a group from Phoenix, a young couple from Thunder Bay, Ontario, another couple from Alaska, some Iowans, some Norwegians, and a group from Jackson Hole that included a couple in their late seventies. I'm happy enough to see everybody, but would just as soon not. I love that they love this place, too. I really do. It's just that they remind me of things I'm trying to forget—that even the most remote corners of the planet are less "wild" then I want them to be, that I was born several centuries too late, that I am not the brave, pioneering, and burly explorer I feel I could have, or should have, been.

But last night was truly surreal, as we had an impromptu dinner party with a group of four young Canadians with whom we'd been leapfrogging downriver for the past week. More than the other groups, they are like us. They are in their twenties and on an epic journey of their own, a trip that began in one of their backyards in Yellowknife (the capital of the Northwest Territories) and will end, sixty days later, on a western arm of Hudson Bay.

A friend of theirs is a floatplane pilot, and they just rendezvoused with him for what they called a "nonessential drop." Fresh apples and oranges, several bottles of Chardonnay, and finger puppets and other small trinkets from their families and lovers. We had a tremendous feast in their absurdly tall bug tent, and I woke up this morning with a fierce hangover.

Day 57 | July 24 | 1109 miles

At first, you can't make out individual caribou, just a mass of moving blotches of mottled grays and blacks and tans and browns. Then, as we paddle farther downriver, a sea of antlers becomes apparent. We secure our boats in an eddy, scramble up the ridge, and insinuate ourselves into the herd.

We approach in a low crouch, slowly, before dropping to our bellies. We literally crawl into the middle of the herd. There are thousands of caribou all around us.

They're confused, indecisive. Mike and Brook are taking what I imagine will be unbelievable photos—roll after roll of *National Geographic*-close photos. Then they're out of film. The herd begins to get organized, and when several animals get spooked, the entire throng finally starts running away from the river. And we run with them, and for a few brief moments it is a free-for-all, all of us, beast and man, thundering across the tundra together at full tilt.

Day 59 | July 26 | 1129 miles

The farther we get up the Tibielik River, the more obvious it becomes that this morass of water and quicksand is more akin to an effluvial plane than a bona fide river. We've spent the last day and a half poling, dragging, pushing, tracking, and pulling our canoes. At one point, the sand is so deep that it sucks us in up to our thighs. Every step is like postholing in deep snow, only worse, because the sand and water create powerful suction. Several times, we almost lose our boots in the muck (which would be very bad indeed). At one point, it takes Mike and me an exhausting half hour to slog one hundred yards.

Getting through this final watershed is the big unknown of the trip, our crux move, and we'd suspected there would be low water here late in the summer. To our knowledge, no one has ever paddled up or down any section of the Tibielik, but, after talking to others, we know that many of the smaller tributaries in this area are navigable only for a few weeks after breakup.

We pull out the maps and assess. We know we have to stop clawing upriver—it's a waste of time and energy, neither of which we really have to spare. We could portage, but even in the best-case scenario the section is at least ten miles, which of course means fifty miles of walking for us. Plus, we just added five hundred pounds of food to our canoes two weeks ago. The only other option is to turn around, backtrack a day and a half to the Thelon, roll the dice, and hope that a tributary farther downstream will have more water. We roll the dice.

Day 66 | August 2 | 1212 miles

This afternoon we realize that the food in one of our packs has somehow become infused with white gas vapors. We'd all been burping up gassy belches since lunch, but it was Brook who first noticed that his stomach was queasy, and that he was feeling a bit light-headed. Not our brightest move—putting gas and food in the same pack (though in different pack liners)—but still the infusion is rather strange, as none of the gas containers appear to be punctured and, at this point, all our food is double- and triple-bagged to prevent blowout.

It wouldn't be such a big deal if it hadn't happened to our tastiest and most calorically rich food: several bags of gorp, a dozen Snickers, twenty pounds of cheddar cheese. Some food appears to be tainted only slightly, while a few things would be all but inedible under any other circumstances.

We make a halfhearted attempt to air it all out on our tarp, and while we're doing so, two Inuit guys pull up in a motorboat to say hello. They've got a puppy and a four-month-old baby with them. They live in Baker

Lake, an Inuit hamlet about a hundred miles downriver, and they're out for a long weekend of hunting and fishing. It's a surreal encounter, us fly-fishing next to a colorful tapestry of M&Ms and raisins and nuts spread out across a tarp, them looking at us curiously. They give us some butter-scotch hard candies. One of the guys keeps insisting that the warehouse where he works in Baker Lake is the size of Boston Garden. And then they're gone.

Day 77 | August 13 | 1359 miles

The weather has been getting increasingly nasty these past several weeks—near-freezing temperatures, consistently high winds, and very little sun. But it's the piercing quality of the wind that I find most remark-able. Never have I felt such a bracing, bone-chilling wind before—not even in Wisconsin, in the dead of winter.

Everyone's flesh is feeling the bite, but nowhere is it more obvious than in my disfigured and swollen hands. (I can't stand paddling with neoprene gloves on and have, therefore, exposed my hands more than the others have their own.) The most affected area is the base of my fingers, between the back of my hand and first knuckle. Each digit is a blotchy mess of raw and open blisters that I've lamely tried to wrap with white athletic tape because nothing else will stay on.

Snow has started to fall, and the long, slow drumroll of winter has clearly begun. Already, the birds have set off on their annual migration south. On the coldest and wettest days, despite our layers of clothing and heat-trapping, snap-on spray decks, we can't even keep ourselves warm while paddling and are forced to pull over to warm up—to run around in circles, do jumping jacks, wave our arms like windmills.

But our spirits are high. The bitter winds have blown the bugs away, we have plenty of food, and abandoning the Tibielik proved to be the right call. Today we finally reached the Meadowbank River, which feeds the Back River, which will carry us all the way to the ocean.

The Arctic Circle, unbelievably, is now just a few days' paddle away.

The detritus of everyday life has finally been washed away. Synapses have been scrubbed clean. I'm certainly starved for new stimuli, but I've never felt more lucid. My thoughts drift south more and more frequently—I wonder what family and friends are doing, how they're doing. I wonder if they're thinking of us. Other times my ears burn, as they say. I hallucinate about fresh fruit, dalliances with ex-girlfriends, and how much money I'd pay to be able to listen to the Rolling Stones' *Exile on Main Street*—but mostly just about juicy peaches and laundry fresh from the dryer.

Day 85 | August 21 | 1579 miles

A light dusting of snow has fallen on the headlands to the east. My water bottle is partially frozen, and a thin layer of frost covers our tents and boats like a veil. There's a gentle breeze when we shove off this morning, but it lasts for only an hour before the clouds once again gather and darken. The wind veers around, intensifies, and begins to pound us with waves of sleet, rain, and snow.

Midmorning, we finally cross the Arctic Circle—sixty-six degrees north—and the weather only gets worse. Here in the Back River's yawning delta we've got nowhere to hide. Choppy waves batter us, and we're getting blown around like kites. We're soaking wet, mildly hypothermic, and making almost no forward progress. We take refuge on a debris-strewn island, the highest point of land we can find. We drag the boats out of the water, past the high-water mark, set up the tents quickly, inhale some hot food, and promptly fall asleep.

A few hours later—how many, I'm not sure—the storm has mellowed. Mike gets up to go to the bathroom and makes the sickening discovery that the tide has risen and carried the boats away. We fly out of the tents. Miraculously, we can still see them—both upright, and both beached on the opposite shore about a half mile away. We're stunned. How could we be so spectacularly stupid? We have tidal charts, for God's sake! We'd consulted them last night. We pulled the boats up . . . we always do . . . the tide is only supposed to be a few inches here this time of year.

Then the sinking realization of how absolutely and completely fucked we are sets in.

We're now stranded on a tiny speck of an island with virtually no supplies. Because we were so cold and harried, we unpacked only what we needed to warm up. The boats have everything we need to survive—or initiate a rescue: all our food, the satellite phone, our Epirb. All we have are a few Snickers and our line-of-sight radio. It's a sick joke. Though our boats are intact and within sight, we have no way to get to them.

Our world collapses. We have a day or two's worth of food, but that's it. Nobody knows where we are exactly. Both the Royal Canadian Mounted Police and our expedition coordinator back in Wisconsin have a rough idea of where we should be, but because of the uncertain nature and time line of our trip, neither one of them would necessarily grow concerned about our whereabouts for several weeks.

We must solve the problem. We quickly dismiss the most obvious and tempting solution—that someone simply swims for the boats. The air and water temperature are prohibitively cold, the time in the water too long. If the distance were shorter—a couple of hundred yards or less—maybe we would have gone for it. The grim reality is that debilitating hypothermia would set in well before someone could reach shore.

What we desperately need is another craft. We take quick inventory of the refuse strewn about the island—a half dozen empty fifty-gallon fuel barrels, a five-foot plank of wood. Using guy lines from our tent fly, we cobble together a raft with three barrels and the wood. Too tippy and unstable. We add two more barrels to the design and come up with a smarter and more secure system of knots. In a few minutes, we have a larger, more confidence-inspiring vessel. It's not ideal, but a quick dry run determines that our creation can float two people.

We outfit Brook and Luke and gently shove them off. The wind is with them . . . they float slowly and serenely to the shore . . . the raft stays together . . . it works! They paddle back, we quickly retrieve the second boat, and the crisis is over in less than thirty minutes.

Day 86 | August 22 | 1581 miles

The water I'm drinking has a faint but unquestionably salty aftertaste. Despite hiking quite a way inland, we haven't been able to find nonbrackish water today. The ocean overpowers everything up here. Though we hardly speak of them today, yesterday's events weigh heavily upon us. It all happened so fast, and was over so quickly, that it feels as if it didn't really happen—like we all had the same scary dream one night.

We attempt to paddle again this morning, but the wind and waves beat us down. Under these conditions, we simply cannot make any significant forward progress. With the weather showing no sign of letting up, and no more significant heights of land to hide behind, we decide to finally lay down our paddles. It's a difficult decision—we've been on the loose for so long. We feel like we could keep chugging along indefinitely. Like the four of us—communicating only with glances and gestures and grunts—have enough energy and chutzpah to start our own colony. Enough to conquer entire nations.

Had we technically reached the ocean? No. Were we just a few short miles from our goal? Yes. Did it make any sense whatsoever to head farther out in the delta, with nowhere to hide from the weather and no guarantee of potable water? No. Did any of this matter to anyone else in the world besides the four of us? No. Did we have anything left to prove to ourselves, to one another—or to the rest of the world? No.

We're a mess of mixed emotions. We break out the phone and call Jacob, our contact in Ghoa Haven. He tells us that his friend Saul will come and pick us up. Sit tight, he says. It's only about sixty miles of travel, but depending on the weather, it may take a few days.

Day 89 | August 25 | 1581 miles

Saul and his soft-spoken son Colin show up the day after our call. Then, for two days, we bounce across the Arctic Ocean in a twenty-two-foot-long open-hulled motorboat Saul named the *Snow Walker*. Towing our yellow canoe behind us, with the red one strapped lengthwise across the bow, all six of us crammed into the tiny cabin, we must be a comical sight to behold.

Out on the water, we fall in with three other motorboats holding three Inuit families who had been out for the final hunting and fishing trip of the season and who were heading back to Ghoa Haven. By chance, we'd all camped in the same general area and—chugging for King William Island at roughly the same speed—had formed an ad hoc flotilla en route.

We make good time for a while, and then sometime around midnight the wind kicks up, forcing us off the water once again. The swells get bigger and choppier, and we follow the others to a well-known local campsite—a small, protected cove somewhere along Adelaide Peninsula.

In the morning we wake up with the Inuit. It feels strange to wake up with company. Their traditional, gold-rush-era wood-and-canvas tents make our taut, brightly colored domes look silly and alien. We get our first good look at the Arctic Ocean, and it's nasty, all white-capped and churning from last night's high winds. We meet the Inuit families we saw only briefly in the flicker of headlamps last night. There are young children and deeply wrinkled and weathered grandparents and everyone in between.

They think we're crazy and more or less tell us as much. Why would we come all this way—*in canoes*—just to say hello, turn around, and fly home? We don't have a pat answer. What can we say? We don't know where to start. Each of us has talked to only three other people over the past three months!

So we pull out our maps and show them the last bit of our route, how we got from the Thelon to here. The Inuit all nod. One of the elders perks up when we point out the island we stayed on when we let our guard down, when we got lucky. His son translates for us, explaining to us that his dad says the island is "good medicine," that the government used to have a medical clinic there in the summers in the 1960s, and that Inuit tribes from all over the Far North used to make an annual pilgrimage there. This time we nod. We say nothing of our grave folly. We're embarrassed.

Instead we swap stories and sample each other's food, though all we have left are dehydrated vegetables and some fifteen pounds of instant mashed potatoes. We play with the kids and drink cup after cup of Red Rose brand tea, the Inuit's favorite. They're curious how our tiny stoves and multipurpose tools work, and what it's like where we've come from. We want to know how they track caribou and navigate the open ocean without maps, and what it's like to live here. We all look out at the ocean and, though no one says anything, we all wonder when it will calm down.

The next night, the winds will finally diminish, the swells will subside, and we'll all make a late-night run to King William Island. There, we'll be welcomed into a young couple's home, there'll be a drum circle at the community center in our honor, and, based on his first impressions, an Inuit elder will give us each a name—Luke will be Uyarak (Rock), Mike will be Kublu (Thumb), Brook will be Nagruck (Horn), and I will be Kukik (Nail). We'll barter our rescue ropes for musk ox hides, we'll befriend a young artist named Danny, we'll eat frozen caribou fat, we'll listen to AC/DC, and we'll arrange to have our canoes sent home on a barge down the coast and, finally, up the McKenzie River. We'll beg one of the few white guys on the island to fly us south for a bargain price.

But those are all stories from a different world, a world in which the wind doesn't reign supreme. For now, all we can do is watch it blow.

On Keraunophobia

CECILY PARKS

> The fear of lightning is one of the most distressing infirmities
> a human being can be afflicted with. It is mostly confined
> to women; but now and then you find it in a little dog, and
> sometimes in a man.
>
> *Mark Twain, "Mrs. McWilliams and the Lightning"*

Iate one March evening in northwestern Wyoming, my mother and I were driving home from a movie. The film was about the Rwandan genocide, and the contrast between the violence and chaos we saw onscreen and the windblown, drifted meadows we cut across on our way home was so stunning that it was difficult for either of us to speak. This was a landscape characterized primarily by silence: the moon reflecting off snow brought the mountains around us into high relief, but the highway remained flat and dark to the point of inscrutability, and when I tapped the brakes and the massive fifteen-year-old Chevy Suburban we were in began to fishtail, the silence gained weight. Black ice. I knew enough about black ice not to brake, and I did my best to steer into the skid. About a hundred yards ahead of us were three cars stopped at various angles both on and off the highway, and I could see the silhouettes of people moving in and out of the shafts of light cast by headlights. Our heavy vehicle swung like a pendulum from one lane to the other—slowly, deliberately—and somehow, at the last minute, I guided it into a snowbank at the side of the road, a stone's throw away from the mess of cars. With a soft crunch, we stopped. "If I'm ever on the *Titanic*," my mother said wearily, "I want you with me."

How dearly I wish I could tell a string of stories that unfold like this one: natural disaster strikes and I emerge as the capable yet down-to-earth heroine, shaking my head in an "It was nothing" way before I go off into the wild world to rescue someone else, even if my arsenal contains merely a steady hand on the wheel. Or maybe the story changes, and my mother is the one driving, growing more hysterical with every swing of the car—spinning the wheel with one hand and reaching to hold onto door handles, the dashboard, anything, with the other—while I speak in lulling tones and assure her that she is doing so well, so well, as long as she doesn't hit the brakes. Either way, I am the calm one. I am the one my mother would like to have with her on the *Titanic*.

The story I should have told—the one that reveals more—took place on an August afternoon in northwestern Wyoming, as I was fishing by myself on a spring creek in the Wyoming Range. It had been yet another drought year, and the water level was low: I could cross the creek at most points without topping my green, knee-high Wellington boots. The creek hugged a butte that was dark green with lodgepole pines, rising nearly vertically on my left as I walked upstream. It was a gorgeous, endless-sky kind of day, and the fishing was good. I could walk and cast my lightweight rod at the same time, and in almost every pocket of deeper water I got a nibble on my late-summer fly of choice, a grasshopper. Some of the cutthroat trout I caught were fingerlings, barely bigger than my fly, and when I set the hook I yanked them out of the water and toward me through the air. Others were fatter, shadowy, and sliding out from under the cut banks. I'd flattened the barb of my hook, and after I'd looked over each of my catches and allowed my yellow dog to sniff their fins, I released them.

Perhaps an hour passed before I noticed the clouds. To the west, the sky was turning to iron, clouds thickening as they funneled out from between the higher mountain peaks. And then I heard the soft rumble that could only be thunder: the only road was too far away for me to be able to hear a car, there were no planes in the sky, and the clouds were darkening. I reeled in my line, turned, and ran downstream. My rubber boots were not made for grace or speed. They slapped against my calves, my knees knocked, and my ankles rolled. I ran on the stones for a while, but they slid and I slid and, in what seemed like a practical decision at the time, I decided to run downstream *in* the stream, picking the shallowest parts for my path. Water topped both boots almost immediately, and my dog stayed right on my heels, bumping against the backs of my legs and occasionally tumbling between them. My car was three large cow pastures away, and I was painfully aware of my expensive graphite fly rod trembling like an antenna in the air above my head. I couldn't have asked for a better lightning rod.

Afternoon buildup, as it is colloquially known, is a common weather event in the summer in the Rocky Mountain West. On any given day in June, July, August, or even September, there is likely to be a thunderstorm, possibly with hail. Thunderstorms occur in an unstable atmosphere, and the cumulonimbus clouds that produce them form vertically, growing upward. (In a stable atmosphere, clouds grow horizontally, forming, among other types, the fluffy clouds we call cumulus.) The phenomenon that causes clouds to stack vertically is called forcing, and among the many causes of forcing is mountainous terrain. In Wyoming, the mountains push air up to heights of ten thousand feet or more, and this air rapidly gathers condensation on its way up, forming cumulonimbus clouds, or thunderclouds: the flat-bottomed gray containers of severe weather. Once these loaded clouds pass over the mountains, they are highly unstable, towering, and ready to drop their loads.

Wet and disheveled, I reached my car by the time the wind picked up and sped toward home, water still sloshing in my boots. Did it rain, you ask? Not a drop. Was there lightning? Not one white streak. Another common weather event in the Rocky Mountain West is, of course, the false alarm.

The term for the abnormal fear of lightning is *keraunophobia,* from the Greek *keraunos,* which means thunderbolt. The *Oxford English Dictionary* defines *thunderbolt* as

1. **A supposed bolt or dart formerly (and still vulgarly) believed to be the destructive agent in a lightning-flash when it "strikes" anything; the flash of lightning conceived as an intensely hot solid body moving rapidly through the air and impinging upon something: in mythology an attribute of Jove, Thor, or other deity.**
2. **... Something very destructive, terrible, or startling.**

The rational reader in me accepts that there is no red-hot, god-molded bolt or dart in lightning; we now know that lightning is a giant spark of electricity. The keraunophobe in me feels less willing to accept the definition I've found. I take particular offense to the words *supposed* and *vulgarly* and the decision to put the word *strikes* in quotes. But then I find a citation that I adore. The word *thunderbolt* made its debut in the 1440 *Alphabet of Tales:* "woman was burnyd to dede with a thondre-bolt." I read the citation as justification for running half a mile in waterlogged boots: no matter how you feel about the existence of the thunderbolt, literature's first recorded victim of naturally occurring electricity was a woman. The tale may be fiction, but my fearful self takes it to be factual. How could the author of the *Alphabet of Tales* imagine something so outlandishly, spectacularly violent on his own?

To my dismay, I am not always paddling a canoe or casting a fly rod or driving an old Suburban in Wyoming. My bookish, indoor, other life takes place in a one-bedroom apartment in a city in the Northeast, where I am a graduate student. I spend more time with a laptop computer and books than I do in a tent, and my urban pursuits are the product of my environment: among other nerdy activities, I collect definitions of words I don't know in an unlined notebook of thick white paper. There are words that continue to stump me (abstruse, integument, eidetic, etc.) no matter how many times I look them up, and I write down a definition each time an encounter with the word gives me pause, hoping the meanings will etch themselves into my memory. I've also found that even words you think you know are worth looking up. Hence, from the *Oxford English Dictionary*:

Lightning: the visible discharge of electricity between one group of clouds and another, or between the clouds and the ground.

No gods, no destruction, no mystery, and no dead woman. I must confess I am disappointed, or distrustful, or both. Like much of my reading, looking up words is an endeavor to understand my surroundings, experiences, and myself. I want an explanation-in-print for my fear of this terrible, mysterious, unpredictable force that, if I'm not careful, will destroy me. Perversely perhaps, I like the dictionary because it might be the toughest text to bend to my own subjectivity. Alas, lightning is not mine to define. If it were, I would add

or between the clouds and a person on the ground.

The word *lightning* predates *thunderbolt* by about a century, first appearing in William Langland's fourteenth-century epic poem *Piers Plowman:*

Oon Spiritus Paraclitus to Piers and to hise felawes.
In likenesse of a lightnynge he lighte on hem alle
And made hem konne and knowe alle kynne langages.

(Passus 19)

Nobody gets killed, nary a burned body in sight. Again, I am disappointed. The Holy Spirit graces Piers Plowman's quest in the form of lightning, and the narrator is (rightly) "afered," even though nothing particularly bad happens to him. Lightning, of course, has long been associated with the divine. Jove, Zeus, Thor, and Indra all hurled thunderbolts (or lightning, if we're being unvulgar about things) at those who angered them; in ancient Rome, people who were killed by lightning were refused burial because they had been so obviously condemned by Jove. Even the Christian God may have a bolt of lightning in his holster: in Mark Twain's 1880s short story "Mrs. McWilliams and the Lightning," the heroine, having locked herself up in the boot closet during a thunderstorm, demands of her husband, "Did you say your prayers tonight?"

It must be said that I do not say my prayers very much, nor was I ever encouraged to in a thunderstorm. I grew up in suburbia, and I was taught to run. Get out of the pool and run; drop my tennis racket and run; drop my canoe paddle and run. I was more than happy to run, but it was never clear to me where to run. When I was at the swimming pool, the snack bar awning was a logical rain shelter, but lightning is sneaky. It finds fissures down to the ground. Besides, the snack bar was close to towering oak trees, and I knew they attracted electricity; the snack bar was close to the pool, and electricity is drawn to water; the snack bar awning had metal hinges, and electricity is drawn to metal; I couldn't call my mom to come pick me up in our station wagon because lightning travels through the phone line; and so on. There were so many variables to take into account, and unfortunately, none of my authority figures seemed to understand the way lightning behaved well enough to tell me what, besides running, was the best way to protect myself. I never attempted any research on the subject.

Most likely because there were no boys paying attention to me at that time in my life, my love for Wyoming hit me hardest when I was sixteen. The Wyoming landscape was something I could rely on—for its unquestionable beauty and, perhaps most important, for its availability. In most any canyon, a river rippled toward me, mountain ranges rose up in any direction I looked, and a new trail through the aspens invited me to follow it. Wyoming reached for me as much as I reached for it, and the existence of rivers, mountains, and trails was a consolation and evidence of a kind of love, and this love was unconditional.

The affair officially began when I enrolled in a one-month course at the National Outdoor Leadership School (NOLS) in Wyoming's Wind River Range, which remains my favorite mountain range to this day. That was the first time I saw Wyoming during the summer, and it was the first time I camped out for more than a few nights in a row. Despite the fact that June is late spring in Wyoming, and despite the fact that NOLS issued us ancient snowshoes (I remember them as wooden, which is highly improbable), our group of fifteen or so had been supplied with tarps instead of tents to sleep under. The tarps were the epitome of insufficiency: early in the trip I often woke up unable to breathe because of the snow pressing and molding blue nylon to my face. When this happened, I would have to punch the loaded nylon to dislodge the snow and make it avalanche to the ground. After, I would take deep breaths in the tarp's blue light. I loved this moment: after the panic of near-suffocation, I felt a rush of relief, and somewhere in between those moments of fear and calm, I stepped outside myself. Instead of being an awkward sixteen-year-old (dirty, in a sleeping bag, under a tarp), I became my own observer, and I began to see myself as a character—yes, a heroine—in a story that I narrated:

We have been in the backcountry for five days, and yesterday, in a boul-der field, I saw my first marmot. Wet, heavy late-spring snow fell all through the night, and so much of it fell that it weighed down the tarp, pressing and molding blue nylon to my face. I punched the loaded nylon to dislodge the snow, and it avalanched to the ground. After, I took deep breaths in the tarp's blue light. Even though I'd love to, I do not think I will fall back asleep, because this morning it is my turn to light the stove and heat water for oatmeal.

It may come as little surprise to some that I first encountered adventure literature that summer. By the light of my headlamp, under the tarp, I stayed up late reading Alfred Lansing's excellent book *Endurance: Shackleton's Incredible Voyage.* It had me riveted. Ernest Shackleton's 1914 expedition to Antarctica is perhaps most famous for its spectacular failure (the ship was locked in, and eventually crushed, by ice) and for Shackleton's spectacular leadership, which allowed him to overcome the polar landscape, the lack of supplies, and the eight hundred nautical miles that separated him from the nearest outpost in order to rescue his crew. They all, miraculously, survived. The best part of the story, in my view, is when you think the expedition is over and all is lost, and instead, Shackleton and a small group of his men go off in search of help. Their journey takes them across the Weddell Sea in an open boat and then across the mountains of South Georgia Island. Before that summer, before *Endurance,* I had not realized there were stories like these—true-life accounts of heroic explorers—that also had all my favorite literary elements: narrative, suspense, climax, well-rounded characters I cared about. Being a reader and a writer, I began to think, did not exempt me from a daring outdoor life. I was particularly susceptible to passages like this one, from *Endurance:*

> **Life was reckoned in periods of a few hours, or possibly only a few minutes—an endless succession of trials leading to deliverance from the particular hell of the moment. When a man was awakened to go on watch, the focal point of his existence became that time, four hours away, when he could slither back into the cold, wet rockiness of his sleeping bag he was now leaving. And within each watch there were a number of subdivisions: the time at the helm—eighty eonic minutes, during which a man was forced to expose himself to the full wickedness of the spray and the cold; the ordeal of pumping, and the awful task of shifting ballast; and the lesser trials which lasted perhaps two minutes—like the interval after each numbing spray struck until a man's clothes warmed enough so that he could move once more.**

Trials, deliverance, hell, and wickedness! I believed in all of it.

By the end of June, summer began to creep up on the Wind River Range. As the NOLS course wore on, tender grasses poked up in the higher alpine meadows that had earlier been the sites of our epic snowball fights. We no longer relied on our snowshoes, and a few people had begun wearing shorts. After one particularly mild night, we woke to find a small creek—runoff from melting snow—threading its way between our sleeping bags, and one evening I taught a few people how to fish with an old rod (I remember this, too, as wooden, which is also highly improbable) that one of the instructors had brought. The Wind River Range is famous for its golden trout, but we didn't see any. Two people caught and cooked fingerlings, and I considered my lesson a success.

Would I have changed my summer plans, you ask, had I known that afternoon buildup is a common meteorological phenomenon in the summer in the Rocky Mountain West? It's unlikely, and halfway through my trip in the Winds the answer would certainly have been a resounding no. During those first weeks in the backcountry, I became possessed by the distinct (and largely unfounded) conviction that I was made for outdoor adventure, physical challenge, and tent life. Even though I was reticent, bookish, and a good student, I had certain requisite skills: I could hike, I could fish, I could ski, and I did not cry the fifteenth time my snowshoe postholed through the snow. Looking back, I see now that Wyoming arrived at a juncture in my life when I most urgently felt the need to differentiate myself from the adolescent masses in some small way: I wanted a niche, an area of expertise, and Wyoming offered one. As a sixteen-year-old, I loved the outdoors with a ferocity that, I can see now, was largely the product of loneliness and uncertainty. Though teachers and family members often told me that I was a quiet leader—praising my calmness, noting the way my peers respected me—I had always assumed they were speaking euphemistically, until that summer. I was shy and insecure, until Wyoming.

With the warmer weather that summer, of course, came afternoon buildup, but lightning there was simply another test of my newfound dedication and passion. Lightning made Wyoming slightly dangerous, a brooding loner with a temper, and therefore all the more alluring to a girl who had (and still has) a weakness for rebels. One day, perhaps, I would overcome my fear, but for now it dramatically jacked up the tension and momentum of my ongoing narrative:

Shadows clumped in the meadow, and soon it was dark. We heard rumbling and picked up our pace, looking for a low point to wait out the storm. "Where should we go?" I wondered. "It's getting closer." I pressed my lips together and hail began to fall.

The city is where I have my dictionaries, my books, and my computer: the city is where I do my research. I decide at last to look up lightning statistics and lightning safety guidelines. I would like to know—in print, from a written source—what I'm afraid of, and the *Oxford English Dictionary* can take me only so far. For the up-to-date weather equivalent of the *OED,* I visit the National Weather Service's Lightning Safety website. The third annual Lightning Safety Awareness Week, it turns out, will be in a couple of months, and there is a massive amount of lightning safety information to be had. I begin my reading at the "Outdoors Safety" page, which provides an auspicious start:

> **You're having a picnic one fine Saturday afternoon. The weather is wonderfully warm and sunny. Off in the distance you hear a rumble of thunder. You're having fantastic fun when suddenly—a blinding flash of light—and your life is ruined as family and friends are killed and crippled.**

Now we're getting somewhere, although we're really not all that far from that poor woman who was burned to a crisp in the *Alphabet of Tales.* Even so, this—yet another violent vignette about lightning—enthralls me. I pore over the website for hours. When I visit the same site a couple of months later, after the third annual Lightning Safety Awareness Week, I am crushed to find that the fatal picnic has been excised, and that the passage above has been replaced with a blander warning:

> **The capricious nature of thunderstorms makes them extremely dangerous; however, following proven lightning safety guidelines can reduce your risk of injury or death. You are ultimately responsible for your personal safety. You have the responsibility to act when threatened by lightning.**

What happened to the picnic? The Saturday afternoon? The family and friends? I suppose that the Weather Service wanted to be less alarmist, but it should come as no surprise that I miss the story. Nevertheless, there are some fabulous section titles, including "No Place Outside Is Safe Near a Thunderstorm" and "Lightning: The Underrated Killer." There are also helpful links, such as "Click here to read a story about a motorcyclist killed while riding in lightning." After floods, lightning is the second-leading cause of storm-related deaths in the United States. A single bolt of lightning can be five miles long, measure fifty thousand degrees Fahrenheit, and contain 100 million electrical volts.

Lightning safety means planning ahead and taking precautions, and taking precautions means practicing avoidance: avoid high places, avoid wide open places, avoid wet snow, avoid cave entrances, avoid tents, avoid afternoons, avoid trees (especially solitary ones), and avoid long conductors (metal fences, power lines, phone lines, bridges, even wet ropes). When you've avoided all you can avoid—if you're nowhere near a building, and you're in a ravine, say—you should assume the "lightning position," or the "lightning desperation position": squat, sit, or curl yourself into a ball, wrap your arms around your legs and close your eyes. You should place a foam sleeping pad, if you have one, under your feet for insulation. If you keep your feet together, an electrical current will be less likely to flow in one foot and out the other.

According to the National Weather Service, the odds of my being struck in my lifetime are about one in three thousand. Really, it's not out of the question. My odds are higher when I consider the lightning fatalities per capita when ranked by state: for the period 1995–2004, Wyoming ranked as the number one deadliest state.

Like knot tying, topographic map reading, and wilderness ethics, lightning safety was the focus of one of our many evening classes during the

NOLS course. I remember almost nothing of what I was taught except that, if in danger, I was supposed to look for an L-shaped location (where a cliff meets the ground, for instance) and ensconce myself in the corner it formed, the idea being that a bolt of lightning would hit the top of the L and deflect away from my nook. The L would form a triangle whose hypotenuse was lightning. I suspect, however, that this advice is out-of-date: none of the websites I visited, not even the most recent NOLS lightning safety guidelines, advised this plan of protection.

I want to say that I've tried to follow lightning safety guidelines in order to protect myself when I'm outdoors in Wyoming during a storm. I want to say that knowing how to protect myself, knowing the facts and figures, makes me less likely to end up running in the middle of a stream in rubber boots, all logic and calm tossed to the wind. I want to say that Titanic Girl will appear any moment as the cumulonimbus cloud approaches, and she will lead herself and any followers to an appropriate refuge where they can all assume the lightning desperation position.

In reality, I am not saying those things—because, and by this point perhaps obviously, I can only admit that I must enjoy being afraid of lightning. Why else would I relish gruesome stories, fictional or otherwise, of lightning strikes? I am normally not a sadist, after all. Why else would my brain so easily relinquish the lightning safety tips I learned in the Wind River Range? Why else would I avoid looking up lightning statistics until I reach my late twenties, when it is too late for me to shed my fear entirely? I was telling the truth when I said I wish I could tell a string of stories in which I am the capable, down-to-earth heroine, but I have come to realize that lightning is part and parcel of my relationship with Wyoming—and, believe it or not, though I am no longer that awkward sixteen-year-old trying to find herself and her place in the world, I am still the heroine. I am twenty-nine, and I have grown up with the place that first welcomed me and has since taught me, tested me physically and emotionally, and demanded my full consciousness of what is happening around me. I have capsized a canoe on the Green River, I have hiked in grizzly bear habitat in the Wyoming Range, and I have found myself in the middle of many a snowstorm: Wyoming, as I well know, can be a challenging, even danger-ous, place. Lightning, as I realized in the Winds, is simply another danger in that landscape. And these days, even as it sends me into an idiotic panic, lightning is the constant and dramatic event that makes me an adventur-ess, an explorer, a female Shackleton in my very own Antarctica.

In the city, I am rarely rough-and-ready or even outdoors. My daily challenges include avoiding eye contact on the sidewalk, scaling two flights of stairs during rush hour on my way out of the subway, and mak-ing it to my yoga class on time. The running I do is in a public park, and although I've heard that people fish in the nearby rivers, I am too fearful of hooking medical waste or, heaven forbid, a body part, to try. When a thunderstorm approaches, the news or the Weather Channel has usu-ally warned me it would, and when. I have plenty of time to pop open my pocket-size umbrella and make my way to my apartment, where I retreat, reading on the sofa or writing—but never near a window—on my computer.

In my lightning-safety research, I came across a one-to-ten scale devised by one of the scientists in the National Severe Storm Lab. Ten is the safest, and one is the least safe. Sitting in a modern building, well away from metal, you are at ten. Perching on a steel tower at the top of a mountain is a glaring number one. The way I see it, my city life hov-ers around ten, depending on whether or not I'm waving metal objects on the roof of my building. Because Wyoming ranks number one for lightning fatalities, I reckon that my outdoor life hovers around a two. In effect, I swing back and forth from one end of the lightning safety spectrum to the other. If Wyoming is the state of experience, then the city is the spot of reflection, the place where I process that experience. But if I had to give up one place, it would be, in a heartbeat, the city. Because I believe that Wyoming allows my two selves, the bookworm and the adventuress, the person who experiences and the analyst of that experience, to synthesize, and I feel this most strongly when I am in that moment of beautiful uncertainty—when the trail peters out, when the clouds roll in, when I am so completely out of cell phone range—which is as unpredictable as it is rewarding. If my existence occasionally takes on the characteristics of narrative, and my experiences are both mine and my character's, then Wyoming is the place that allows me to be her, even if only for a moment in time. To this day, she has never appeared in a crowded subway car.

A relationship that I had been in for over three years ended this summer, and I felt the things you typically feel after a breakup: heartbroken, eviscerated, lost. Mostly, I felt deadened. I wandered around the city. I tried to distract myself by running along the river, practicing yoga, dropping a cardigan off at the dry cleaner, visiting museums, seeing friends, but I was only going through the motions of a daily life, and I felt wholly absent from my surroundings and interactions. It was difficult to tell where I was and who I was, and so, naturally, I came to Wyoming, the dangerous state that would always love me. When I exited the plane, I already felt lighter, stronger, and faster in the presence of the mountains, rivers, and sagebrush. There was snow on the tops of mountains; the aspens were turning. The next morning, I stepped my sandaled foot into a spring creek while fishing and its coldness was astonishing; I swore long and hard, but I didn't really mind. This kind of thing, this being outside, I felt, was good for me.

One night after dinner, I went for a walk. I chose a short route that was part trail and part road, saving the road for my homeward leg, when it would be darker. On my way out, I moseyed along the downhill trail, lost in thought (thought, of course, was not so good for me). The uphill demanded more attention and exertion: the road wound through pines at least a hundred feet tall, it was unlit and barely visible, and it was steep. The evening was warm, and I took off my jacket. Soon afterward came the flash of light over the mountaintops, bright and spreading like a tablecloth above me. I heard the thunder some seconds after, and I quickly figured that I had at least half a mile to go, uphill, until I reached the safe modern building that is my Wyoming home. The lightning had been stunning and silent, and in that white moment—two bright pulses—my heart turned over. If I was afraid, it meant I was still living, and if I was afraid, my story had not ended.

I began to run.

Putting In

NATHANAEL JOHNSON

The first rays of sun to reach the guide house illuminated the two of us sitting on the front porch, its green paint peeling up into curlicues, and a tattered U.S. flag hanging from the eaves. I was the seventeen-year-old kid with bleached blond hair who thought he was just about there, just about at the point where he could call himself a whitewater raft guide. And Pat—at twenty-six, with the squint lines and tan already ironed into his face—Pat was the real deal.

I mopped up hot egg yolk with my bread, and Pat took a bag of tobacco from his pocket. He piled the brown hairs onto the paper, rolled it into a cylinder, held both hands to his mouth, drew in flame, and exhaled smoke. We gazed out over the clumps of long grass in the yard, over the rusting fence and gate, over the oil-spotted gravel of the freight yard, up into the pine trees. As the sun rose, it slanted through the trunks in vertical columns, bringing out the yellow in the needles. I finished my egg, licked a finger, and ran it over the surface of the plate, scraping up the yolk that had already solidified on the porcelain. Pat smoked his cigarette.

"You know," he said.

I turned to him, attentive but careful not to spook the moment. "What?" I asked after a few seconds.

"Ah, nothing." He stood and stretched. "No time for coffee. Maybe they'll have some at the warehouse."

Lately, I've been trying to figure out what I was hoping Pat could tell me, what I was doing on that porch, and ultimately, why those summers of running rivers up and down California's spine were so densely peppered by these moments of exaggerated significance. To really get at meaning, it's often necessary to turn the world and look at it from a different angle. That's what I'm doing here with this one summer day, which memory happens to have preserved in sharp, three-dimensional focus—so vivid that I can just about pick it up, like a little snow globe, and turn it over to see what breaks loose.

A little disappointed, I followed Pat back through the kitchen, through the converted sun porch that did triple duty as my bedroom, an entryway, and a laundry room, through the backyard with its overflowing boxes of bottles and aluminum cans, where two clotheslines were draped with a rainbow of drytops and life jackets, and onto the little gravel parking lot. Pat had converted his old minivan himself, making a tiny mobile home with whitewashed cabinets lining its insides. He revved the engine, clamped the cigarette between his lips, swiveled in his seat, and sped backward down the little alleyway, neatly avoiding the parked cars.

"Nice of you guys to show up," shouted Dustin, thumping the van's hood as we drove into the dirt parking lot of the warehouse.

I gathered my gear from around my feet and hurried over to where Dustin stood.

"We've got half an hour to get out of here," he said. "You guys are late."

"Which van are we taking?" I asked.

He jabbed a thumb over his left shoulder at the van topped with two blue boats. "The brown Dodge and the white Ford. Joe and I already threw those 14-Rs on the Ford. We'll be taking a 14-P and the Sotar too."

"How many customers?"

"Twenty-two. The trip planner's on the desk if you got any more questions."

I nodded and turned toward the warehouse.

"Hey, don't move that clipboard," he called after me. "Someone always hides the trip planner right before we leave. Oh, and Nate—"

I turned, still walking backward, "Yeah?"

"Nice hair this morning. You're lookin' slick."

I grinned back at him, "I'll never be able to match your 'fro, Dusty." In the mornings, his wiry black hair stood straight upright. Rather than pay rent, Dustin slept in the warehouse and washed himself under the hose. I'd thought about doing the same so I could have a little more money to feed myself, but realized that the other guides wouldn't approve of my freeloading. As for Dusty, he could do whatever he liked.

Inside the warehouse, the paddles stood in three plywood bins. I counted them out—one for each customer, two extra for each boat—and shoved the blades together into worn canvas mailbags, securing the handles with a camstrap. From the third bin, I selected a paddle for each of the guides. The long-handled green stick for Pat, the big-bladed yellow one that Joe liked, and a small, nondescript paddle for Dustin. Dustin had said the larger blades stress a paddler's shoulders and don't really help move the boat more than the smaller ones. He'd said that big guide sticks were just an ego trip. I took a small paddle for myself as well.

I'm not sure where Dustin fits into this puzzle, only that he was a large part of my teenage crush on river life. Dustin had the whitewater skills, the swagger, the supreme confidence, and the ability to consume inhuman amounts of alcohol or whatever happened to be on the pharmaceutical menu. He could jury-rig an engine, cook a perfect tri-tip, and talk down a hysterical customer. But what impressed me most was the effect of his words on the world around him. When he spoke, everyone listened. When he gave orders, the other guides responded without question. I'd never before seen anyone command such unqualified respect. And I think it wasn't happenstance. The modern world, while overburdened with superstars, produces few local heroes. We usually measure success in dollars—or in power over others. I measured Dustin's success in devotion.

I picked up the two bundles of paddles by the camstraps and waddled out to the vans. Joe and Pat were already standing alongside the van with a raft above their heads. I dropped the paddles at their feet and scrambled up the back of the van as they lowered one side of the boat, then heaved the other side up onto the roof rack. I was up in time to catch the faded black webbing running around the raft and hurl myself backward, throwing every ounce of my weight out, over the edge of the rack. I had done this enough times to be unafraid that the boat would slide over on top of me and that I would tumble off the roof. Even though I tugged with all my force, the raft moved only a few feet. I pulled myself back into a position of balance and bounced the boat into place. Once I had it square on the roof rack, I stepped inside the boat and reached down to haul up the bundled paddles that Joe held up to me.

"Morning," I offered, taking the second bundle. He squinted at me, his ruddy face crinkling up around his hard blue eyes.

"Yeah," he said, turning back to the warehouse. Dustin emerged, a bulging sack of life jackets on his back, the weight bending him double. Pat jogged over and put a shoulder under the bag. Together, they lumbered to the van and rolled the sack up over the railing of the roof rack.

"Watch your back," Dustin warned as I took hold of it and pulled with everything I had. The sack slid into the bottom of the boat.

I scrambled to open valves, letting the air hiss out of the thwarts and floor. I pulled the paddles into place beside the bag of life jackets. I reached down to take the other gear. Pumps, sweep kit, toilet, rolled tables, and helmets. I caught the orange half-gallon water bottles that Dustin hurled at me in rapid succession from across the lot. Joe lobbed the throw bags in with easy precision, making a neat pile in the nose of the boat.

Finally, they lifted the other raft up to me and I tied it to the rack, sealing the gear between the two. The whole process took less than twenty minutes. I stood back in the dirt lot with my arms crossed and looked with satisfaction at the two vans, each neatly capped with two boats.

I was proud of this work, of being capable, of being part of such a crackerjack team—each member knowing his job so well that we could work together silently. I think this was also why I had come to be a raft guide. I was tired of being a student and wanted to be useful. It wasn't enough to be a standout in the gerrymandered, inflated ways all high school kids are standouts. (I once held a "fastest mile" record, which may sound cool until I explain that my track coach managed to make my time come out on top by narrowing the ranks of contenders to freshmen, and then further, to those running their first race of the year. This dubious "fastest-freshman-debut-mile" record fell to a teammate after one week.) It's a rare thing to be truly tested. And at seventeen, I needed to see what I was made of. These days, people who are wrapped up in graduate school and internships can reach thirty before they have the chance to be a professional. I knew that I couldn't wait that long to know.

In the van, on the way to meet the customers, there was always a moment of repose. I lay back on the bench seat, the orange fabric rough against my arms. The upholstery smelled of dirt, sweat, and neoprene. I was already hungry again.

"What's it running these days?" asked Joe.

"Normal," said Dustin. "Three thousand." Then to Pat, "You going to visit your favorite hole today?"

"I'm actually gonna try and avoid the slammajamma this time."

"Where's this?" asked Joe.

"Right below Kanaka," Dustin replied. "You know, it's that big pour-over right in the middle of the river, after it flattens out."

I knew the place. Smooth black rock walls rose out of the water, which resembled champagne there, tiny bubbles still rising from the big rapid. And the pour-over, the fast flow over a submerged boulder, was visible only as a bulge in the surface from upstream. The boulder folded the water back on itself with enough force to slam a drifting raft violently to a halt.

"The thing is," said Pat, "I dropped this guy at the very top of Kanaka. I hit that little 'fuck you' rock at the entrance, and he just lost his balance and blooped out. It was one of those things where it was like in slow motion: he just slo-owly keeled over. I almost had enough time to get to him and grab the front of his vest, but he just fell backward, like he was hypnotized or somethin'." Pat held one hand up and let his wrist fall limp. "Totally helpless. Anyway, he swims the entire rapid and comes up at the bottom with some nasty bruises. But he's all macho and giving his friends high fives, and we're floating right into the pour-over and I call a turn—but he's telling his story and no one really does anything, and we just float sideways into the hole and, badda-boom, there you go, little buddy. Go ahead and take another swim while you're at it."

"He gave you a big tip too, huh?" said Dustin.

Pat pulled at the side of his nose. "Yeah, I got fifty bucks."

Joe laughed. "You gotta tool the customers. I'm telling you, people just don't feel like they've got their money's worth unless they're limping at the end of the day."

I laughed at this and Dustin looked up sharply from the road. "You think that's funny?"

I stopped laughing. "Yeah."

"All right, then."

Joe took a clear Ziploc bag from a white ammo can plastered with stickers (Burton, Wildwasser, K2, Mountainsurf, Sugar Bowl) and handed it to Dustin. "Check this out."

I sat up to see what was in the bag: three tight clusters of dusty-green buds. Dustin held it up to his face. "Wow," he said. He looked up at the rearview mirror, both rows of white, even teeth showing beneath the wraparound sunglasses. "I love that smell."

"That's homegrown Donner Summit love," said Joe. "Nine thousand feet high."

Dustin handed the bag to Pat, who gave it back to Joe, who packed the marijuana into a little glass pipe. Then, gripping the pipe and lighter in one hand, he reached forward and tapped Dustin on the shoulder. Without taking his eyes off the road, Dustin accepted the little package.

"Get the wheel for a sec, Pat?" he asked, and applied the flame to the bowl.

It's at points like this when I can see my comparative youth in highest relief. There in the backseat, enjoying the exchange but lacking the self-assurance to join, I was clearly separated from them by more than age. I'd waved off the pot, which was okay, since the guides were divided on the question of getting high before put-in. Though I wanted their rogue life, the barriers of civilization—the walls of houses, the grid work of roads, and the rules that prefigured the existence of these things—held me back. I still had a bed in my parents' house. I still wanted to go to college.

The other guides glowed with a power I didn't fully possess. A power that came with living life in contempt of all rules but the unbreakable ones, moving with the seasons to places society couldn't get a fix on—winters at ski resorts, summers on rivers—sticking to land unbound by the concrete net of highways.

I lay back on the seat and stared out over the ridgelines. The first canyon was the North Fork: Lake Clementine, then above that, Yankee Jim's, then Chamberlain Falls, Class IV. Above that was Giant Gap, Class V, with no road to the put-in and no way out but down the river. That's where the north fork of the North Fork came in. Then came Generation Gap and the Dream Gap, more severe examples of Class V and even more remote. Above that, the Royal Gorge, one long white stretch of what Pat called "Class-VI-boulder-pile-sieve-death." Beyond the ridges stood the mountains. There, the sun on the snow was making rivulets, which swelled into brooks, one joining the next to rut the talus slopes. The running water would slowly carve away loam and clay and bedrock. It would excavate canyons and leave high ridges, and the rain that fell in the forest would rush down the canyon sides to swell the rivers. As I lay there, looking out over these miles of steeply forested canyons, it seemed profound somehow to recognize that water had shaped it all. Suddenly the world seemed a simple place, where snow would always fall in the mountains, where water would always run downhill, and where the only true laws would follow from those precepts.

The customers, too, were always the same. They milled around their cars, rubbing on sunscreen, tightening the drawstrings of wide-brimmed canvas hats under their chins, locking their cars *(bee-oo-eep!),* then unlocking them again to pull out the gear they'd almost forgotten: towels, water bottles, clothes, sunglasses, water guns, coolers, and disposable waterproof cameras. My attempts to persuade them to leave this stuff in their cars were useless. I handed out liability release forms and pens.

A muscular man in his thirties, whose name I forgot immediately after he introduced himself, asked me what the rapids were like on the river.

"Class four, four plus," I said.

"Any big ones?" He wore a slick pair of polarized Oakley sunglasses and a green-collared polo shirt with the words *Silver Creek* embroidered over the breast.

"I always get a little nervous for some of them. There is actually one rapid rated class six that we walk around," I told him. The white Ford pulled into the lot. I knew I should go help pack the lunch, but he continued.

"No shit? Has anyone ever run it?"

"We ride the boats over every now and then," I said, taking a step away. He was going to be disappointed, I knew, when his guide told him he couldn't wear his sunglasses without a strap.

"You're shittin' me. You've run it?"

"Yeah." I turned to the woman in a floral print hat who had come up beside me. Oakleys stopped me with a hand on my shoulder.

"Class six," he continued, "that's pretty hard, isn't it?"

I held up a forefinger and turned to the woman.

She jabbed at the release form. "What's all this about broken bones and drowning?" She laughed. "I'm not so sure about this."

"That's just describing the worst that could happen," I told her.

"Do people get hurt very often?"

"You ever take passengers down that class six rapid?" interrupted Oakleys. "How 'bout it?"

I ignored him. "People don't get hurt very often," I said, "I've never had a serious injury, and this company has never had a death, but all those things can happen, and do sometimes. You're taking a risk, but I think, at least for myself, it's a reasonable risk. It was probably more dangerous for you to drive here."

The woman squeezed her lips together.

"If you're nervous, you can always try something mellower on another day. I think you'll be fine, though," I said. "You look like you're fit, and we've got a good crew of guides today. If you're really nervous, we'll put you in Dustin's raft. He's our head boatman, and if anyone can get you down this river, it's him."

She took a deep breath and nodded. "Okay."

I held up both hands, "I've got to go get lunch together."

Oakleys jogged after me. "Hey! Any chance that you could take a couple of us down that waterfall you were talking about?"

"No."

"You sure? That's the sort of thing that could be reflected favorably in your tip."

I shook my head.

"C'mon," he persisted, walking with me. "I'll make it worth your while."

More than one guide has since told me that there are two types of people in the world. When I was working in Alaska one summer during college, a guide explained his dualist conception of universal order using the opposing terms *guide* and *wad*. And this sort of philosophy made perfect sense to me. I had already begun to fear that the plasticity of my childhood was disappearing, and that my life was hardening to the form of the lackluster middle-class landscape that surrounded me. I decided that my development in life would lead to one of two possible polarities: either I would break out of the socially dictated realm of possibility, or I would be cowed, buy a tract home, and begin to believe that all the things I owned—my car, my bed, my six-speed food processor, my 401(k), and my platinum, battery-powered, Turbo Groomer 2.0 from the Sharper Image, complete with crevice-illuminating LEDs, exchangeable rotary heads, and six-thousand-rpm nasal defilamentation capability—were absolute necessities. I'd sworn that I would struggle against the forces that would gently prod me down the path to mediocrity. And I knew my time was running out. The mortar was setting.

We all piled into the vans to drive down to the river. As we came around the last turn, I wriggled out the window and pulled myself up to the roof. My pulse quickened, as it always did, at the first glimpse of water boiling down the canyon. We came to a stop, and I untied the boats, breaking open the neat package we'd made at the warehouse, and pushed the top raft down to the waiting hands below me. My body fell into the work, recognizing the rhythm of the motions: throw down the gear, carry the boats, put the pump to work and top off all four chambers, rig in the gear. When we'd finished, the four boats bobbed in the water, with the coolers, drybags, rolled tables, and spare paddles tied firmly in place. The other guides were up in the parking lot, tightening life jackets and handing out helmets. For a rare moment, I was alone and still.

I liked the idea of "putting in." Sailors go out to sea and come into harbors, but for guides the river is *in*. It's home. Sometimes when I'd use the term *put-in,* customers would extrapolate and ask where we were "putting out." "Taking out," I'd correct them. "*Putting out* is something else altogether."

A water ouzel winged through the spray. I slapped a mosquito on my ankle. I could hear Pat's safety talk over the roar of the river.

" . . . if you should fall out of your boat, you may notice that the water is fairly cold and you're instinctually going to want to take a big breath." The customers laughed and I smiled, imagining Pat gasping theatrically. "The trick is to delay that reaction until after your head pops back above the surface. That way it's not so much of a religious experience."

When Pat had finished, the customers filed down to the put-in, each wearing a bulky orange life jacket and a helmet. They picked their way slowly down the hill, not used to walking on uneven surfaces, bending forward and using their paddles for support.

"Are you Nate?" asked a skinny man with thick glasses.

I nodded.

"I think we are supposed to go with you."

I arranged my crew, trying to judge who would paddle hardest, trying to balance one side against the other. I taught them how to brace and how to paddle. Finally, I untied the bowline and secured it in a neat bundle.

In the surging water, the boat tugged at my arms. I pushed out, leaped into the bow, and picked up my paddle. "The first rapid starts right here," I shouted as I walked over the thwarts to the back. "This one's called 'Good Morning, class three.' Forward!" The water tugged at my paddle.

I swiveled the blade and thrilled as the boat responded. We hit the first standing wave square, and the river engulfed us. As we emerged, the customers shouted in a mixture of pain and elation.

"Jesus," said one of my bow paddlers, grinning back at me. "That's cold."

"Yeah, you like that? It comes right out of the bottom of the reservoir here, so it's pretty chilly. Warms up as we get farther down."

"It sure is quiet out here!" someone exclaimed loudly. I looked over to see Oakleys, his sunglasses still on, in the bow of Joe's boat. "Oh-wo-wo-wo-wo-wo-wo-wo!" he shouted, slapping his hand over his mouth.

Once I was on the river and in command of my own boat, everything was all right. The motion of the raft beneath me, the green-forested canyon walls rising up in a V to meet the sky, the warm upstream wind on my face, and the tightening of my muscles on the bigger rapids: it all conspired to make me happy. In the flat sections, I told my crew the story of the river, pointing out the hulks of rusting mining machinery that indicated a time when iron giants had excavated the river bottom. Steam had animated these monsters, and gold had animated the men who carried them here. I had a good group, a family, willing to paddle hard, happy just to be there. They asked me about the trees, and I pointed out the ones I knew: ponderosa pine, live oak, black oak, California bay laurel, Douglas fir, birch, willow, and alder. I told them what I'd learned of tree language—that the twisted digger pines signaled thin soil and a low water table, that slopes covered in manzanita spoke of the passage of fires.

The four boats stayed close together, Joe in front, followed by Pat, then me. Dustin, with the first aid and rescue kit, came last. We were four little ovals tracing a narrow, winding line in the vastness of open forest. On the river, with its cutbacks and turns, I often lost all sense of direction. Not that I cared.

We stopped for lunch at a sandy beach with willows growing in the shallows. Lunch meant pulling coolers and black army-surplus drybags from the bottoms of the boats where we had rigged them and unrolling the little blue river tables, screwing the legs in place, and covering them with a lavish spread. I felt the hunger that I had almost forgotten grow to a clawing urgency in my belly as the customers made their sandwiches. When they had finished, I spread mayonnaise and mustard on my own wheat bread and piled on slices of turkey and roast beef, cheddar, Muenster, avocado, lettuce, and red onion. I sat and talked with my bow paddler about his college plans. Pat waded into the river and wet down the boats, shoveling water with a paddle to keep them from overheating. He nodded every now and then to Oakleys, who talked at him from the shore. After two sandwiches, a handful of cookies, and a long drink of cold water from a one-gallon jug, I was satisfied. We packed the wreckage of lunch back into drybags and tied the gear back into the rafts.

The day lapsed, moving from stupefied noon into evening. The water, alternately darkened by shadow and varnished in the glare of low-angle light, became difficult to read. I had to stand up in the back of the boat and squint into the sun to see the telltale boils and furrows.

Of all the perks of guiding, this deepening of perception satisfied me most. In the time since I'd first come to the river, the rapids had changed from illegible spray and tumult to an ordered set of signs, indicators of the hydraulic forces at work.

This sharp-focus world, so drenched in meaning, stands in stark contrast to what I remember of high school. The terrain of my adolescence was pretty boring. In that world, it was unclear what, if anything, was at stake. There were no constraints, no limits to push against. Technology had freed us from the constraints of nature, providing climate control, cheap energy, and abundant food. As for the constraints of morality, they seemed laughably vaporous given that most of the marriages I'd seen were failing, that my teachers could only note the news of the newest genocide with sad shrugs, that those who understood the origins of their food and clothes were liable to turn ascetic and wild-eyed. Anything could be justified, and the tyranny of this unrelenting freedom left me without anything solid that I could use to distinguish up from down, success from failure. In zero gravity, muscles atrophy. And without use, the senses go dull. Without unbreakable laws there are no needs, and without needs, perception fades.

The river's rules, on the other hand, are absolute. If you mess up, you drown. When I went to the river, I exchanged a world without necessity for one where the need for food, the need to read water, and the need for executing a strong J stroke at just the right moment demanded real attention. And with such demand came a sharpening of perception.

We finished the run, collected the wet gear, and packed it back onto the van roofs. Then the customers piled in, holding cans of beer, telling each other about their close calls. I waited, standing guard at the side door of the brown Dodge so I could be the one to close it. There was a technique to it: pull down the handle, inch the door back slightly, then carefully slide it forward. One false move and the door would fall off entirely. Once I'd sealed the customers inside, I clambered up on top of the van. Joe was already there, wedged low in the bow of the Sotar, a beer in one hand and his helmet tilted over his eyes.

"Riding the roof?" he asked.

"Yep." I pulled myself into the boat.

Joe buckled the helmet straps under his chin. "Get down," he muttered. "It's going to be World War III up here in a sec."

I wriggled into the space between the thwarts as the van lurched forward. The pitch and yaw of the vehicle was exaggerated on the roof. Then came the trees. Branches caught and snapped on my life jacket. I rolled away, looked up, then ducked again as a low-hanging pine bough caught in the roof rack, bent, and whipped across the boats. Needles and bits of bark stuck beneath my collar. When the trees thinned out, Joe and I stood, our legs spread for stability, and gazed back down at the river. It was far below us, gleaming amber in the late light.

Joe drained his beer and compressed the can between his massive hands. "Wish we ran more multiday trips," he said. "Seems like a waste to drive all the way out of here."

"Yeah," I agreed. "I wouldn't mind a few more free meals as well."

The road bent left and the river disappeared.

"Later days," said Joe, and we both sat down.

Back then, I liked to think that my soul was tuned to its surroundings, and that spending my days on the river put me in proximity to absolute truth. I'm not quite so romantic anymore, but I'm still convinced that the river canyons—the rock, water, and pines—formed a landscape that particularly nurtured our little subculture.

At the top of the road, the customers hurried back and forth, carrying unopened coolers and piles of neatly folded dry towels back to their cars. The members of my own boat thanked me and took turns shaking my hand. After all the customers had successfully started their engines, we drove away.

"Thirty bucks," said Pat. "I can eat!"

"I got stiffed," said Joe. "Motherfucker was all pissed off because he lost his designer sunglasses. How long till our next paycheck, anyway?"

"The guy with the Oakleys?" I said. "He knew about tipping, too. He said he'd give me some money this morning if I took him over Rucky-Chucky."

"I told that guy he needed a strap or something." Joe shook his head. "He wanted to run Rucky-Chucky?"

I nodded. "He didn't say anything to you after he saw it, huh?"

"Naw. He fell out on Cartwheel, and after that he was fully terrified."

"How 'bout you, Nate Dog," called Dustin from the driver's seat. "Any luck?"

"No, they were good people; I think they just didn't know."

"Yeah," said Dustin, "it was their first time rafting." He looked back over his shoulder. "Well, good trip, guys. No carnage, everything ran pretty well. I got forty bucks, so dinner's on me."

"Right on," said Pat. "Thanks."

The sun hung low in the sky before us. I scratched at my ankle. I was usually too busy to notice mosquito bites. It was only in the lulls that I felt the itch.

"See this bridge up here?" asked Joe, as we approached a span split into two parallel roads, two lanes in each direction. Massive green beams ran from one ridge to the other, suspending concrete seven hundred feet above the river. "This one time, on the spring trip, Ed Walker was driving, and we came to this bridge and everyone started yelling, 'Run left, Ed, run left! Ed, you pussy, run left!' At the last second, Ed cranked on the wheel and swerved over to the wrong side of the road and just put the pedal down, and the entire van went totally silent. All the way across the bridge, full speed, we weren't even breathing." Joe laughed. "When we got to the other side everyone started cheering. Then we were like, 'Jesus, you crazy motherfucker, what were you thinking?'"

I suppose it's odd that I needed to spend a few years in this tribe of lost boys, among those who refused to grow up, to feel grown-up myself. But then again, growing up usually means conforming to the expectations of the dominant culture. Being a guide meant living for a while in opposition to that culture—not exactly engaged in revolution, but with a churlish middle finger held up in the face of everything hypocritical and dull and conforming in society. It was revolt through drunken valor and acts of brave, destructive stupidity. More than that, it was also a chance to live among people who were certain of themselves and happy with their lot in life.

At the warehouse, we reluctantly slumped out of the van.

"Let's go," urged Dustin. "We're almost done."

We broke down the trip, stacking the boats under the tarpaulin canopy, putting away the paddles and pumps, spreading the life jackets out to dry, washing the lunch dishes, and rinsing the coolers.

"Pack the trip, run the river, unpack the trip," said Pat, tiredly pulling the knots out of a bowline. "Get up, pack the trip, run the river, unpack the fucking trip."

When we'd finished, I was ready to drop with fatigue. On the short drive back to the guide house, I sprawled across the seat and put an arm over my eyes. There is a certain sort of tired that comes from being in the water and the sun all day. The body, from pinkie finger to big toe, becomes a leaden weight. I felt myself sinking into the bench seat.

"No rest for you yet, Nate Johnson," said Dustin. He pulled the van to a stop in front of the little market. The main street of downtown Colfax was a string of shops and restaurants with false-front second floors, facing the train tracks. He handed me two twenty-dollar bills.

"We need two pounds of chicken and a case of Sierra Nevada."

When I got back to the guide house, a paper bag under each arm, the *Blues Brothers* soundtrack was blaring out of Joe's boom box in the kitchen. Oil sizzled in a big frying pan. Pat took the chicken from me and cut it with quick, sure strokes, narrating his work with a singsong string of nonsense: "Slice-ah chim, dice-ah chim, damn, come on back, little buddy. Bidabum, boodabam, badaboom!" With this, he swept the chicken off the cutting board into the frying pan. The oil roared. "Put the chim-chim in the chim." He gathered sliced onions, and cubed squash in both hands and ("Slammajamma!") threw it in the mix. He added the noodles, doused the mixture with soy sauce, then went to the refrigerator and found an egg. "Just to make it special." He leveled a finger at me. "You always have to throw in something different to pull it all together." He cracked the egg and dumped it into the mix, stirred furiously, then slid the frying pan off the flame. "Done!"

Pat's girlfriend, Jen, slid into his arms.

"Smells good, honey."

They swayed to the music together.

Pat had told me that he'd known there was something special about Jen when she rode her snowboard off a twenty-foot jump, landed on her head, and got up smiling. "We've got a good relationship," he told me. "We've stuck with it. The first stage of any relationship is exciting. It's new and it's wet, but sooner or later everything goes to shit. If you get past that, you come to a new stage, the understanding stage. That's what I think we have."

I liked Jen, too. Other than the brief time I spent among the passing female customers, I was constantly in the company of men. Having Jen around made me feel better somehow.

I reached over the counter and took a stack of plates down from the cupboard. The guides clustered around and served themselves.

"You guys want to watch a movie?" asked Dustin. "Zak or Brian or one of those guys rented this the other night."

Zak and Brian were the latest in the train of itinerant kayakers. They'd stay a few days or weeks, run the rivers in the area, then move on. You'd recognize their names in a collection of whitewater videos from the era: B. J. Johnson, Clay Wright, Shannon Carol, Willie Kern, and the Knapp brothers all stopped in at our little house.

"Sure, I'd like to see a movie," I said. "What is it?"

"*First Knight.* Some sort of Arthurian shit. Looks pretty lame."

"Sounds good," said Joe. "Let's watch it."

We gathered around the little TV, sitting cross-legged, balancing plates and bottles on our knees. Pat turned off the music and the lights in the kitchen before joining us.

The movie provoked the guides' derision right from the opening credits, and none of them were going to be upstaged by a bad movie.

Richard Gere, clad in chain mail, looked down at Julia Ormond. "Now," he said, "it's just you and me."

"And that horse," added Pat.

"Pat, please!" said Jen, rolling her eyes.

"Where is your home?" asked Ormond.

"We don't have homes," growled Dustin. "We're raft guides. We live in the dirt."

A freight train, the first of the night, rattled down on us. For a few moments, it drowned out all other noise, and the entire house shook.

"Celebrate railroads!" Joe cheered. We raised our bottles and ironically toasted the train.

On screen, the horses were walking over a small bridge.

"Class two," said Dustin, pointing to the dark water on the bottom of the frame. "There's a sick line, right off the piling and back through that eddy."

I laughed. I was full, tired, and happy. Sitting there, I felt like I was part of something.

Reflecting on it all now, I'm still a bit disappointed that on that morning Pat hadn't passed me some arcane piece of raft-guide wisdom. That was his moment to give me a bit of magic, something that would have triggered my transformation into the kind of river god I wanted him and Dustin and all the rest to be. And when Pat gave me nothing more substantial than a little secondhand smoke, I suppose it was my moment to accept—or begin to accept—the fact that magic of the variety I desired could exist only in the minds of children.

I'd thought growing up would mean earning a place in a sort of riverside Valhalla, where life was full of glory and brotherhood and honor and righteous rebellion. But at some point, I realized that I was standing in the shoes of the men I'd idolized and I hadn't passed into another realm. Instead, I was still looking at the same world through the same eyes. It's a world that offers no godly invulnerability to river runners, but metes out death, alcoholism, unplanned pregnancies, and arthritic shoulders to guides and wads alike. And I'd say guides suffer more than their share of all of the above.

I suffer only from arthritic shoulders, but the river gave me more than my share in return for this offering of pain. The simple joy of those summers would have been bargain enough, but in that time, as water and sun seeped through my skin to cure my hide, a little faith seeped in as well. Even in this age so skeptical of certainty, my time on the river gave me faith in a few undeniable truths: that there's pleasure in work well done, that the universe runs on a handful of simple rules, that most restrictions are self-made and false, that the mind requires contact with the unbreakable laws—those prescribed by nature—and that these laws serve as a whetstone for consciousness.

Most important, the river had sharpened my perception until I could see through my own childhood fantasies. And though this disillusionment wasn't what I'd expected, it was ultimately the thing I'd been looking for all along. The river had shown me how to grow up.

And yet, if I could make that childhood fantasy real, if I could go back to that morning on the porch, if Pat could have handed me the key to that land of youth, I would pass through the portal and never look back.

A Place for All Seasons

CHRISTINE DELUCIA

Sunday, September 28

Late September drizzle soaks the air one Sunday afternoon in Mount Auburn Cemetery in Cambridge, Massachusetts. In a natural amphitheater christened Consecration Dell, leaves carpet the ground and clouds hover above a small pond, the lowest point in the basin. Blanketed by a thick membrane of green algae too brilliant to denigrate as "pond scum," the water blurs, from a distance, into a solid grassy circle. But raindrops pock the pond's surface, betraying hidden liquidity and disturbing a handful of yellowed leaves there. The black mud framing the pond seems placid until I move closer. Out of the muck spring dozens of tiny toads (or are they salamanders?), their backs filmed with algae and their coiled bodies invisible until I rouse them. They plunge pondward in a frenzy of "peeps," the trajectory of their dives obscured by the viscous green.

The hillside above is ringed with crypts and rows of gravestones, all facing the pond in soundless audience. Lacy ferns and moss creep over their feet, and their stone faces darken in the rain-heavy damp. The dell is a precisely calibrated arrangement of the aesthetic and the functional, a marvel of meticulous horticulture and landscaping—yet beneath this carefully cultivated scaffolding pulsates another layer, one of teeming, whirring, bursting activity. I am drawn in by this curious mix of the natural and the constructed, the timeless and the temporal, the living and the dead. This vista evokes at once a sense of the eternal and, as my hand brushes a weathered gravestone, the transient. Founded in 1831, the cemetery is old in human terms, but by the timescale of the amphitheater, these human constructs seem to be tentative and impermanent. As I listen to the muted nearby voices of the Sunday bird-watchers, I am saturated by the increasing rain.

Tuesday, October 7

Binocular-toting bird-watchers weave between the cemetery's gravestones, gesturing skyward; parents tromp across browning grass, chattering children in tow; tourists navigate from one well-known grave to another; and for a moment I'm tempted to retreat to a more secluded spot. With this stream of visitors comes dissolution of the serene stillness, a reminder that the cemetery is as much an item on a *Boston for Dummies* itinerary as it is a sacred place. Yet I seek out, if reluctantly, this nattering parade: I come during the day's peak visiting hours, and I stick to well-trafficked paths within easy view and earshot of park guides and families. For all its seeming tranquility, the cemetery is a place where crime is a distinct possibility; to construct it as an arcadian haven immune to molestation is naïve, even dangerous. Few outdoor places, and even fewer urban wilds, are wholly secure: the land is open to all, and any may intrude.

I feel like an intruder myself. I have no personal connection to the place; I know no one buried here. The inscription "Murray" on the gravestone next to which I sit is a name and little more; "Mother" and "Father" buried a few yards beyond are anonymous. I come to the cemetery as an observer of the land, to meditate upon its striking sweep, its inner patterning. I am here on assignment for one of my literature classes at

Harvard. In the spirit of Thoreau and his devotees, my English professor sent us out into the wilds of greater Boston for a semester. This quirky project entails returning to one place over the course of the fall semester, then writing short essays each week. The cemetery wasn't my first choice. I initially headed to one of Boston's beaches, but the subway ride was too long and the shore too cold at this time of year. Next I visited the Alewife Reservation, at the opposite end of the subway lines. My map failed me, though, and I couldn't find a way inside the reserve without hopping a fence. Mount Auburn, only a twenty-minute walk from my dorm room, was the most convenient alternative. In these early stages of the project, my cemetery sojourns seem a bit silly. What am I doing under a willow tree while my roommates pore over problem sets? How can I pretend to be anything more than a tourist, a passerby with no real investment in this place?

For those who come here to inter someone they love or commemorate the anniversary of a death, the filter of memory must render this a radically different landscape. The dell might unsettle these mourners, because its slopes hold remnants of once-life and reminders of loss; it might also offer more comfort to those with immediate and compelling reasons to seek solace here. This kind of intimacy is far removed from my own acquaintance with the dell, and my feeling of voyeuristic detachment makes me uncomfortable. But neither the mourner nor myself holds better, or any, claim to this land. The mourner constructs in this dell an environmental sympathy commensurate with his loss; I construct in it something less intimate; and independent of all this, the tree branches overhead continue their silent, impersonal swaying.

Monday, October 13

The wind is blowing full force today, buffeting and pummeling me even in the sheltered concave of the dell. This wind is invasive: it penetrates my sweater, blowing straight through the knit, and no matter how I turn or try to shield my face, it rushes into my eyes, my nose, my mouth, forcing a chill. I lean into it, testing its force to see if it will hold me up; it does, for a moment, until its direction abruptly changes and I trip forward. The wind makes its presence known through its effects on all that it batters, strokes, caresses. The lanky trees groan as gusts course through their upper reaches, twisting and creaking in mild protest like the bottommost step in my home's narrow basement staircase. Sporadic *k-k-krack*s punctuate this murmur as fragile branches lose their tenuous holds and fall, ricocheting off other limbs in percussive clatter, to the ground.

I crouch down beside one of the crypts, which deflects the brunt of the gusting fury overhead, and in this pocket of stillness I smell the earth. The morning rain has dampened the soil and its carpet of fallen leaves, and the wet, heavy scent that rises is not unpleasant. Close to the ground, I touch the stone before me. Its face is weather roughened and pocked, and tiny, almost sugary, mineral grains rub off on my palm.

Rising from this corner, I meander off the footstep-hardened path. The ground here is responsive: it gives a little and is resistant and springy in a way concrete will never be. Last night's frost has crystallized the surface of the mud by the pond, and it crunches delicately underfoot like the crust of snow, holding for just an instant before my feet sink downward. The mud clings to my shoes, muffling my footsteps, and I wipe off only a bit. It leaves a greasy residue on my fingers, but I'm in no hurry to rinse away the rich organic sediment trapped under my fingernails. It's the antithesis of my studies, an immersion in a life of the mind that encourages withdrawal from all that is physical. Surrounded by the library's marble walls, carefully modulated temperatures, and fluorescent lights, I don't know whether it is midwinter or midsummer outside, midnight or dawn. This vacuum can breed a certain arrogance: it suggests that we, with our superior intellects, have managed to transcend the dictates of the material world. The cemetery mud reminds me otherwise. This sediment—formed in part, almost certainly, from the decomposed remains of America's great intellectuals buried on the hillsides—is evidence of inescapable grounding in a natural order still beyond human control.

Tuesday, October 21

Since Mount Auburn Cemetery's founding in 1831, little has remained static in these 175 acres of Cambridge. Century-old engravings and lithographs chronicle the land's transformation from dense native forest to carefully landscaped burial ground. In the cemetery's early days, the addition of chapels, fountains, ornamental plantings, and fences gradually checked the land's wild undergrowth. More recently, ponds have been dug, horticultural markers erected, bird-watching guides published, and signs painted to guide auto traffic.

Yet the most significant and ongoing change to the land is less conspicuous than these markers. Over ninety-three thousand people, the equivalent of a small city's population, have been interred in the cemetery; more arrive each day. This vast underground restructuring is only hinted at on the surface by the scattering of gravestones and the even subtler planting of memorial bushes and flowerbeds. What lies underfoot is in constant flux: as decomposition does its slow work, the dead mingle with and return to the soil, fundamentally altering the very substance of the land. The chemical composition of the ground, I realize in a moment of unusual indelicacy, is made distinct by this literal blending of the human and the vegetal, though this distinctiveness remains invisible to the eye (except, perhaps, in plantings like azalea bushes, the coloring of which is influenced by the acidity of the soil).

Beyond physical transfiguration, the most critical metamorphosis has occurred largely independent of the land itself. The lens through which visitors now view this particular plot of land is radically different than in centuries past: 170 years ago, these hills and dells were simply another natural vista; today, they are charged with an altogether different and spiritual import. The gravestones that speckle the hillside, I now see, are only the sparest evidence of the sweeping and often invisible changes that continue to redefine this place.

For all this change, though, much in the cemetery remains stable. More than many outdoor places, the cemetery holds claim to a unique resistance to development. As the final resting spot for thousands, it is accorded a certain respect that will likely prevent the encroachment of condominiums and urban blight. Even so, change, however tightly controlled and monitored, will come to the cemetery as the vagaries of taste alter burial practices.

Constancy in the cemetery, it seems to me, lies not in the fluctuations of the human component, but in the fundamental order and pattern of the natural element. This natural element is itself defined by change: the coloring and dropping of tree leaves in autumn, the dying of grass during frosts, the migration of birds as the air grows cold. Yet these changes are cyclical in a way human-enacted change, though rarely linear, is not. New leaves will grow in the spring; the grass will return and regreen the hillside; the birds will return to the trees in warmer weather. Paradoxically, it is here, in the continuous flux of the natural cycle, that the greatest stability and permanence lie.

Sunday, November 2

Sunday, the day after All Saints' Day and the end of a peak weekend in foliage season, seems a fitting occasion for our excursion to the cemetery. Brendan, my onetime neighbor, knocks on my door early in the morning, and together we rouse our friend Stephanie from her bed, prodding her into the bright sunlight outside. We take a longer route than I usually do, but the two-mile walk feels shorter in the company of friends. I don't notice the surroundings as much as I do on my solitary jaunts; conversation tends to draw my mind from the leaves underfoot and branches overhead.

When we reach the cemetery, I see it alongside two new pairs of eyes. My companions point out much that escaped my notice on previous visits.

Stephanie, perusing an index of famous graves, locates the resting places of Buckminster Fuller and Amy Lowell. Brendan, consulting the *Big Trees* brochure he purchased for a quarter at the main entrance, steers us toward unusual plantings.

Down to the dell I bring them, but not as far as the quiet dip in the land tucked away behind shrubbery on the west side of the pond, the part to which I feel most intimately connected. Eager as I am to share the striking beauty of this place, I am not ready to disclose the secrets of the dell I have come to know only over time; this knowledge, I feel, is earned by devoted observation. I may one day share it. But not today.

Up in the observation tower, I hear an intake of breath behind me as we emerge from the darkness of the winding tower steps into the sun. The foliage, a brilliant quilt of yellows and oranges and reds mingled with the muted browns of trees just past their peak, spreads before us in full splendor. We can see for miles: to Boston Harbor, glinting on the horizon; to the hills of northern Massachusetts, hazy in the distance; and to Harvard's buildings, curiously compacted from this view.

As we lean against the railing, looking together over the same trees, the same diminutive and distant architecture, I am aware that our perceptions of this panorama are distinct. Memory colors my view: I note how this vista has changed since I last visited, exchanging the verdant lushness of late summer for a more mature palette. My New Hampshire–shaped memory also filters what I see. I've grown up saturated by the even vaster foliage of the White Mountains and uncultivated swaths of forest, and I can't help but compare the colors before me to this store of images. Striking here is the proximity of the natural and the built environments. For a moment, I feel the urge to mentally erase all the human elements in the scene before me and imagine the terrain as untouched. But this inclination gives way to a new sensation: I find this intermingling of brick and green compelling. It occurs to me that I can be wowed—and even fulfilled—by other than pristine wilderness.

Brendan and Stephanie, who hail from Pittsburgh and Chicago, respectively, possess different points of reference. Newcomers to the cemetery, they can't know how different this view is in the rain, or when the trees are a monochromatic green rather than motley splashes of color. And, city-dwelling flatlanders both, they are struck by the novelty of this rolling carpet of multihued treetops, murmuring in awe at the sight.

More than aesthetic pleasure emerges from this new perspective. From this height, we need a minute to locate the bell towers of Harvard, which lie within a thick tangle of rooftops and treetops. The university—center of our daily lives—is just one among many patches of color. Gone is the bubble that insulates us from everything beyond the ivied walls. From here we can see the Charles River, which we usually view in mile-long fragments during fall crew regattas, snaking far inland from the harbor. While a ground-level view obscures the river's place in the local watershed, the tower vista highlights connections to places upstream. High up on the lookout platform, it's easy to recognize how the river can affect other communities and ecosystems; how pollution from Boston traffic can taint the atmosphere beyond the city limits; how we move within an interconnected complex larger than we might have imagined.

As I watch my friends scan the contours of the land, squinting in concentration, I'm reminded that their perceptions of this landscape remain, on some fundamental level, as inaccessible and foreign to me as mine are to them. If we can be said to share a collective memory of this time and place, it is hardly a consistent memory; the physical reality of the wind and sky and land may be constant, but individual consciousness molds these elements into the distinctive, personal form that is remembered reality.

Monday, November 10

The leafy indentation at the center of the cemetery's dell might surprise a newcomer. Such a visitor might blithely begin to walk across this carpet of leaves only to find himself ankle-deep in water. In September, water peeked through the pond's coating of green algae. Now, as the leaves stop falling, accumulated strata of organic debris render the pond deceptively solid in appearance.

Of the cemetery's four bodies of water, this pond is the smallest; an acorn can easily be thrown from one edge to the other. Wind gusts never quite tidy this corner, shielded as it is on all sides. Climbing down to the very edge of the water is tricky, because the banks slope downward in a slick, muddy slope. I always step carefully, wary of losing my footing and tumbling into the muck.

The pond is noticeably quieter than it was earlier in the fall. In September, I loved circling the pond's perimeter and watching tiny peeping toads spring away from me and into the water. I was privy to a secret, I felt, a curiosity known only to those who tread within a foot or so of the pond's edge. Now I hear only the vague sucking noise of near-frozen mud squelching underfoot at the perimeter. Perhaps the toads are decomposing in this mud; perhaps they are only lying in torpid half-slumber deep under the water, awaiting the springtime thaw that will warm them back to activity. Life still burbles beneath this surface. An underground spring feeds the pond and will bubble throughout the winter; and though the water may freeze at the surface, its insulating coat of algae and leaves may warm it just enough to keep its core uncrystallized.

Tuesday, December 2

Last night's snow has dusted parts of the dell with a shimmering white, lending an air of purity to the frozen amphitheater. This apparent incorruptibility is illusory, though; beneath this flawless snowy coat, I know, lies a damaged land. Natural forces place considerable stress on this environment. Water freezes in rock crevices during the winter, expanding in the cold and sometimes splitting the stone; lightning chars, from time to time, the most prominent trees on the hilltop. Rain and wind wear down exposed surfaces, fell tree limbs, flatten plants; in winter, snow and ice make tree limbs bend, strain, and snap under their weight. Downpours erode the soil on the steep hills surrounding the dell.

Many of these stresses are exacerbated by human influence, which transforms the natural cycle of decay and regrowth into irreversible degradation. The cemetery's landscapers have thinned trees on the hillside to make room for graves, diminishing the root network and rendering the topsoil more susceptible to erosion. Unrestricted foot traffic from visitors, including myself, flattens grass on the paths and tramples small plants whose roots also hold the soil in place. Visitors' vehicles cloud the air with exhaust. The rain that beats down on the cemetery is hardly pure water, since the cemetery is situated so close to urban Boston and exposed to the acid rain caused by the city's pollution. The tombstones' pockmarked stone faces bear witness to the effects of this caustic precipitation.

The cemetery is most certainly a working landscape, and some of the most significant environmental degradation results from its function as a burial ground. The phrase "ashes to ashes, dust to dust" is hardly so simple in an ecological sense, because corpses leave a toxic trail. Embalming agents injected into arteries and body cavities before burial leach into the soil. Once-common but now-banned agents like arsenic still seep into the ground from bodies buried long ago; still-legal solutions like formaldehyde—listed as a probable carcinogen by the Environmental Protection Agency—are added to this poisonous mixture with each new burial. Several gallons of such chemicals are used in preparing a single body; multiplied by the ninety-three thousand people buried in the cemetery (minus those cremated), the total amount of chemicals that have soaked the ground amounts to hundreds of thousands of gallons. Microbiological contaminants from corpses add to this toxic stew: traces of viruses, bacteria, pathogens, and the by-products of decomposition can permeate the soil. Materials surrounding the corpses can also leach deadly (though inorganic) residues, such as the lead used in old caskets.

In addition, the herbicides, pesticides, and fertilizers sprayed to keep the cemetery in immaculate, photogenic form seep into the ground.

Much of this contamination is filtered by the soil, nature's version of an immune system. But soil can filter only so much. Unfiltered elements eventually percolate through layers of earth, making their way down to the water table; tainted runoff flows directly from the cemetery grounds into the nearby Charles River. While gravity initially pulls these contaminants downward, tree and plant roots thirsty for liquid also absorb them, carrying them skyward. It seems unlikely that fluids used to embalm the dead and to kill insects can be healthy for vegetation.

I mull over this toxic saturation. Are the bare tree branches overhead made brittle by the chemicals coursing up their xylem and down their phloem? How much of the opaque slime on the dell's pond is organic, and how much is some corrosive compound produced in a laboratory or industrial plant? The primary concern with this cemetery seems to be its ability to soothe and heal the grieving spirit; less attention is paid to health of the land. Yet is it possible for a cemetery to be both a spiritually healing and an ecologically healthy place?

Monday, December 8

The brick sidewalks leading up to Mount Auburn's gates are more familiar to me than the grounds within, even after all my treks to the cemetery. I spend far more time outside the gates, since the greater fabric of my life is urban Boston and Cambridge; when I graduate and move elsewhere, my relationship with Mount Auburn will likely conclude. But I don't think I'll forget this place. The actual time I spend in the cemetery may be the least significant aspect of my engagement with it. These few acres of land have come to speak to me after I exit the gates; they rouse me to reimagine all my surroundings and to reconsider my place within them.

When I first arrived on campus after leaving my home in New Hampshire, I ached for open green space beyond the manicured grass of Harvard Yard fussily roped off for months at a time and colored aqua-marine with fertilizer. I empathized with Frederick Jackson Turner, the renowned historian of the American frontier who moved east to Cambridge in 1910 to teach at Harvard. He reportedly felt so ill at ease in the city that he often lived in a tent on the porch of his house. The mass of brick and glass and concrete seemed a wholly artificial world to me, too, a thing apart from the land. Four years of college in this setting might be tolerable, but after graduation I planned to seek out a less citi-fied existence.

In the course of my visits to Mount Auburn, though, my aversion to the built environment has eased. The cemetery, which makes visible the ties between nature and culture that underlie virtually everything on this planet, has compelled me to reconceptualize these urban environs. Its grounds make problematic the easy distinctions that have historically been drawn between these two elements; they dramatize an intertwining, a symbiosis. Cambridge is less divorced from the natural world than it ini-tially appears to be, in the sense that it remains in large part unmanaged. Natural are the crows that loom in massive congregations on the rooftops; the rats that scurry through the streets and courtyards, especially after a wet night, following routes ingrained in their rodent minds; the squirrel perched outside my dorm room window, gnawing on a buffalo wing dis-carded from the dining hall. Natural, too, is the crushed and half-chewed body of a bird in the middle of tony Brattle Street's sidewalk, victim of a fall or a collision or a predator; the fat, bold pigeons strutting in Harvard Square; the crying geese migrating to and from the banks of the Charles River. And natural is the row of trees surrounding the university faculty club, carefully placed and pruned and fertilized but changing colors and shedding leaves on their own timetable; and so is the weather, asserting itself in winter snow, in rain and wind and electrical storms that can shut down the city within minutes. All are reminders that we're still living within nature, for all that we build and pave.

As I pass the Citgo station and apartment complexes directly outside Mount Auburn's gates, so fixed in mortar and brick, I'm reminded that cities are here to stay for the foreseeable future. It makes sense, it seems, to find a better way to know them and to live in them, since an environmental sensibility that feels at home only in the few untouched reaches of the earth is going to be thwarted again and again. I still need green space. But it can be the lesser urban oases of wildness—such as the cemetery grounds of which I've grown fond, protective—rather than Ansel Adams's country. Here in the streets of Cambridge, and in the myriad other cities I've yet to encounter, I just may be able to feel anchored. I may be able to call these places home.

Thursday, December 11

I'd planned to walk only to the corner mailbox, but the late afternoon sky's streaks of gold, brilliant against the ground's cover of snow, stir me to continue on to the cemetery. The air is chilly, but not yet at the nose-numbing stage. When I arrive at the cemetery, feet partly frozen, the hillside seems to have been reduced to a black-and-white photograph; only the gold-tinged sky and the odd cluster of berries break the starkness of white snow against dark branch and tombstone.

The path down into the dell is unshoveled, and I'm delighted to climb over the snowbank at the entrance to the now-buried path, tromping in and immediately sinking up to my knees in snow. It fills my shoes and socks. I stop for a second—this will be unpleasant later—but two sets of tracks leading pondward grab my eye, and I can't resist. I gingerly step ahead, trying to keep my feet in the larger set of tracks, made by a pair of snowshoes. Almost parallel to these tracks snakes a much smaller set of prints. Squirrel prints? They're delicate, fronted by tiny claw marks, and they make only inch-deep impressions in the snow. I'm envious as I stumble through the deep drifts, ungraceful in the thick, soft accumulation of flakes.

A dozen other sets of animal prints stamp the hillside of the amphitheater, all drawn, as if by a magnet, to the pond. One set is an uneven spacing of elongated pawprints—the trail of a bounding snow hare? Other prints are shallower, far apart—maybe a running fox? Three sets of animal tracks traversing the surface of the pond tell me the water has frozen. There's no sign of hesitation, no suggestion of tentativeness at the edge of the water, only ruler-straight lines of tracks spelling some instinctual knowledge, some blind animal faith that the water is safe for crossing. Two more sets of tracks ring the edge of the pond, crisscrossing, veering, and backtracking before swinging up the hill in a wild tangent. Evidence of an energetic courtship dance or of a frantic tango of predator and prey? The snow conceals a great deal, but it also makes visible these mysterious romps, or at least their vestiges; no intrusion into the fresh snow cover can be hidden. It seems the snow has frozen time: the squirrel's delicate dash, the pond-circling romp, the ice-crossings lie before me all at once, motion forever arrested in the swirling, intersecting tracks.

Enchanted by this play of tracks and time, I stand still for a moment at the bottom of the dell, all sound muffled except the quiet crepitations of the melting ice. The shadows on the snow are lengthening as the sun rolls behind the upper rim of the amphitheater, and I soon trudge back up the hill toward the pavement and exit. During the walk back, I notice that one squirrel, no respecter of persons, has bounded around and around a gravestone and finally on top of it, scrambling in its cap of snow. Other tracks cavort between the spaces in the wrought-iron fences guarding some markers. I wouldn't mind, I think, to one day have a fox or hare frisk atop my grave. Pausing before a sugar maple, I find myself within arm's length of a squirrel midway up the trunk. We stand, for an instant, in terrific stasis, I exhaling frozen clouds, he quivering with tiny rapid breaths, sleek sides vibrating. Then he darts skyward, claws scrambling.

Before stepping outside the cemetery gates and toward the rushing traffic, I look back at the silent hillside. The spare silhouettes of trees against the snow, the stark black of gravestone against clean white, the simple play of sky and land: there's something clear and sharp and elemental about winter that resonates with me, drawing me beyond the slushy city streets to this place of uncorrupted wintry binaries. I may one day move south, to places where seasons slide into one another with little change. But I have a feeling I'll return, in the end, to New England, where the winter snow startles the mind and the senses in its radical transformation of landscape. Where life persists even in that frigid season, in a cemetery. Where I can stand eye to eye, for a moment, with the fat squirrel chattering and gamboling atop a snow-capped gravestone.

It's All Downhill from Here On Up

McKENZIE FUNK

Objectively speaking, being lost in a wilderness of shirt-tearing, skin-scratching, path-obscuring ten-foot-tall rhododendron bushes is pretty miserable. And two hours after we lost the trail, wandered into the thicket, and started crawling over all those logs—just before the wasps stung Lisa six times—Jim even went so far as to admit it. "You know," he said, "this is pretty miserable." His tone suggested he was merely noting an established truth about hiking in rhododendrons—personally, he wasn't all that flustered. But he did say something, and for that we were grateful. We kept moving.

At eighty-one years of age, Jim Harrang walks just like he walked at seventy-one and probably fifty-one and probably twenty-one: deliberately and relentlessly, taking long strides on long legs, silent except for periodic bursts of good cheer. ("Say, this could be the world's longest bushwhack." "These rhodies are a good reference point—after this, most anything's gonna seem easy." "Well, Mac, there's always next weekend.") Soft-spoken and pathologically optimistic, he's the subject of a cult of personality in our hometown of Eugene, Oregon. Get to know him or know of him, and you realize all his adventures follow a basic pattern: First, he leads a group of people half his age on what is promised to be an "interesting" trip. "Interesting" is Jim's word for "grueling." Next, they run into adversity, perhaps in the form of rainstorms or blizzards or ten-mile uphills. But Jim doesn't acknowledge any of it as a hardship, and they slog on for hours and hours and hours. Somehow, a day trip becomes an epic, and his legend grows.

Jim had been his typical hopeful self when he proposed our hike a few weeks earlier. He and his wife, Nadine, had strolled across the field that separates my parents' house from theirs. Nadine brought a homemade cobbler, Jim a half-baked plan. "We've got some serious business to discuss," he said when he arrived. Over dinner, he described the Oregon equivalent of a buried treasure: a forgotten trail, unmaintained since World War II, that climbed into the wild heart of the Cascade Range. The trail didn't appear on modern maps, he said, and he was one of the few people alive who knew of its existence. He spoke of waterfalls, meadows, and old growth. He promised we would pass through four distinct biozones. He described blazes, left on trees by long-dead U.S. Forest Service workers, that would help us find our way. When the Harrang kids were kids—they're now in their forties and fifties—this was the family's secret route. Jim had decided it was time to show it to another generation.

He failed to mention that the last time he'd hiked the trail was in 1987, but that, no doubt, hardly seemed relevant at the time.

When I was growing up, Jim's role in my life fell somewhere between guru and grandfather. He drew my parents into his orbit soon after they bought the farmhouse next door in 1976, the same year I was born, and I was raised not only with Jim stories but in the presence of the man himself. It was Jim who introduced my parents to what would become the family passion, river rafting. Some of my earliest outdoor memories—cross-country skiing at Santiam Pass, floating the McKenzie River, my namesake—include a hazy recollection of someone my dad referred to as "Old One-Stroke." It was a nickname for Jim, whose raft was always so perfectly aligned in rapids that he seemed to glide through with a single stroke of the oars.

Once, on a trip down the Middle Fork of the Salmon River in Idaho, my parents, sister, and I watched from camp as Jim, then in his sixties, bouldered on a rock above the water. He fell in, lost his eyeglasses, and, for the next four days, had to run the river half blind. This, my parents explained, was inspiring.

Until they moved on to my more dependable sister, the Harrangs called on me to watch their house and feed their dogs when they were away. It was like sitting in port, watching the ships come and go. They rode off with bikes or boats or hiking gear, returning days or weeks later. The destination might be the three highest peaks in Africa, or maybe Alaska, which required rafts but also rifles in case of a bear attack. Or just somewhere in Oregon. In down periods, Nadine worked in her garden while Jim was in his gear shed, saddling up, or downtown at his office. (He heads one of the state's top law firms.)

Jim never gave me advice, but every now and then he'd give or lend me a book: an *American Alpine Journal* chronicling the year's boldest mountaineering ascents, for instance, or the biography of the famous Oregon outdoorsman Prince Helfrich, who'd spent a lifetime exploring the Cascades. By example, Jim showed that going out into nature was a completely normal thing to do—even a necessity. "A night indoors is a night wasted," he told me. He had structured his existence around the idea that the outdoors wasn't an escape from real life but the basis for it.

But Jim's support was as much logistical as it was spiritual. My first self-led mountaineering trip, a spring climb with two classmates up 8,744-foot Diamond Peak, was possible only thanks to Harrang gear. His ancient crampons and unwieldy glacier axes featured heavily in our photos; his orange climbing rope, which we never needed, made us feel tough. I began asking to borrow equipment so often that he instituted an open-lending policy at the gear shed. I liked to walk over late at night after last-minute planning sessions with friends, using my headlamp only once I'd entered the shed to avoid waking anyone up.

The furtive trip became second nature: slip behind barn, step over blackberry bushes, undo wire securing gate, tiptoe through the Harrang yard, open shed door at a snail's pace lest its squeak set off the dogs. The rope, crampons, and axes were hanging to the right, just inside the door; paddles were knee high, lying flat with the oars; the inflatable kayak was in another room altogether, along with the two big rafts.

The essay I wrote to get into college was an ode to my then-seventy-year-old neighbor. "In the house next to mine," it began, "a few hundred yards off, lives one of the people I admire most. His name is Jim Harrang and he has the distinction (along with his wife, Nadine) of being one of the few neighbors I truly like. The fact that Jim didn't cut down the forest I grew up in, or doesn't practice with his band until three A.M., like other neighbors, is not reason enough to respect the man as much as I do. I respect Jim because he is living the life I hope to live in the future."

When I ended up wanting to defer college for a year, winter in the Tetons, and earn money for a spring trip to Europe and its Alps, my mom tried to enlist Jim in her all-out war to keep me on track. To her dismay, he was one of my few adult allies. "That sounds great," he said. I took the year off.

About sixty miles east of Eugene, the old McKenzie Highway branches off the new McKenzie Highway and starts winding up into the Cascades. These days, people drive it less to reach civilization on the other end than to see the wilderness areas—Mount Washington and the Three Sisters—that lie on either side. There are lava flows and glaciers, black bears and brown trout, huckleberries and stands of Douglas fir. My parents, who briefly lived in these parts before moving next to the Harrangs, like to joke that I was named after these thirty-seven miles of two-lane road. Thanks to climbing trips and fishing trips, I saw a lot of the old highway growing up, and it was odd to think that Jim's secret trail lurked on such familiar ground. Yet that's where he steered his minivan when it came time to sniff it out.

It was late October and the days were already colder, shorter. We camped just off the highway, then got an early start, hiking due south from a parking lot, a cement outhouse, and a sign that had welcomed us to the Willamette National Forest. Within minutes, Jim had us on track. The trail started out as a spur off the popular Proxy Falls loop—drive-by tourists' favorite mile-long hike—and at first it was a veritable autobahn. But after fifteen feet, the space narrowed and nearly disappeared. Our five-person hiking party kept going, clambering over a downed tree and following the faint path into a fern-filled ravine. The forest darkened, a headwall rose above us, and suddenly there it was: a blaze, the first of hundreds, seared into the trunk of a trailside fir. Jim had told us what to expect, of course, but nevertheless I felt a strange rush of discovery. The trail was underfoot. The blazes were real. Even as the forest crept to reclaim it, the treasure was right here, just yards away from discovery by the rest of the world.

Early on, we learned to distinguish blazes from natural scars: if there was only one—not a matching mark on the other side of the same tree—it was probably just a scar. We peered at tree trunk after tree trunk whenever we got off course, quietly fanning out in a dragnet until someone yelled, "Hey, I've got one." Also early on, Jim began assuring us that the hike was going well. When we crested the first pitch and came to a narrow granitic fin jutting from the earth, he advised me to "fix this in your mind, Mac." It was an ideal landmark. When we spotted a forty-foot plume of water that cascaded onto the mossy rocks below, he declared confidently, "Now that might be the waterfall." We hadn't known we were looking for one. When we hit a streak of obvious blazes a half hour later, he sounded a triumphant note: "I think we're on it," he said. "Here's another one." Then, "Yeah, there's one here." Then he yodeled, calmly. Then, "I think this is it, Mac." When the streak ended below a broad lava field fringed by yellow and orange vine maples, he was more pensive. "This is kind of like life itself," he reminded us. "The future is uncertain."

At camp the previous night, I'd stayed up late with two of Jim's latest young co-conspirators, Lisa and John Manotti, poking fun at his inability to say anything negative. I shared my dad's story of a Christmastime cross-country ski trip with Jim and family. Deep, heavy snow had hidden the trail to the Cascades' Burley Lakes, and they started to get off course, inadvertently climbing the steep flanks of an eight-thousand-foot volcano. When the clouds cleared and they realized their mistake, they headed back, my dad falling over and over again. Frustrated and exhausted after the twentieth face plant, he was again struggling back to his feet when Jim said, "Golly, Dave. You sure are good at getting up from falls. That's quite a talent."

More recently, in the canyons of Utah's Escalante, Jim was spotted dipping his hiking boots nonchalantly in a water pocket. Someone asked what he was doing. "Well, I think I might be having a little bit of a toe problem here." Two toenails had turned completely black; to even brush them must have been enormously painful. They cut the big toes out of some running shoes, and he donned them and a full backpack and hiked out twelve miles the next day.

Lisa and John told me about their first Cascades climb with Jim, a successful ascent of Mount Washington, when his insistence that they park at an obsolete trailhead condemned them to a postsunset bushwhack back to the car. (Followers soon learn to carry headlamps at all times.) When they finally got back, Jim's only comment was: "Well, that certainly was a full day, now wasn't it?" The Manottis still employ that phrase all the time, just as my parents and I say "interesting" when describing hell. We've taken to repeating an apparent Harrang family motto, which Jim's kids must have come up with during a walk with Dad: "It's all downhill from here on up."

Somewhere in all this, it seemed, was a blueprint for how to commune with nature: Be bullheaded. Never let the fact that you're having a horrible time of things get in the way of the good times. The wonder of your surroundings always outshines the specifics of your difficulties. Never admit that you're cold, lost, hungry, or hurt. Never admit that you're discouraged. Never admit that something sucks. Ignore adversity. It'll go away. Hardship, it turns out, is the spice. With sufficient underplanning and a good dash of stubbornness, a jaunt in the Cascades can be every bit as life changing as a Himalayan expedition.

As far as Jim has ever gone—the Andes, the Alps, the Caucasus—he has always seemed most content in the state where he was born, exploring the mountains where he grew up. After his tour with the army's Tenth Mountain Division in World War II, he returned to found the University of Oregon's ski team with some army friends and some army skis. (They competed in all four disciplines—downhill, slalom, cross-country, and jumping—on the same seven-foot, government-issue wooden planks.) In the 1940s and 1950s, with a cadre of climbers that included Willi Unsoeld, who went on famously to conquer Everest's West Ridge, Jim pulled off a number of first ascents in the Cascades—but he never joined his buddies in the high Himalayas. For his eightieth birthday, he summited the tallest mountain in Oregon, 11,239-foot Mount Hood.

His connection to the home state rubbed off on me. During summer breaks from college, when many of my friends stuck around the East Coast for this or that impressive internship, I made a beeline back to Oregon and worked as a rafting guide. The first time I ran a river with my boss, Jim happened to be along. She watched in silence as I botched the run down Pinball, the trickiest Class IV rapid on the Umpqua River, missing the entrance chute and getting sucked all the way to the right. I bounced sideways over rocks and holes just inches from the bank. But Jim knew just what to say. "Wow, Mac, I hadn't even noticed that slip route. What a great idea to save yourself all that maneuvering."

Even now, after living in Jackson Hole; Philadelphia; Washington, D.C.; New York; Seattle; and again New York, I've clung obsessively (and probably illegally) onto tokens of Oregon identity: driver's license, vehicle plates, and mailing address for anything important. I still spend at least a month there each year. Any opportunity to go home, I take, and the visits invariably revolve around some epic ski trip, trek, climb, or paddle in the Cascades.

Jim had neglected to bring a topographical map on our hike. So had I. It didn't matter much, he'd reasoned—the trail wasn't shown on it anyway. Thankfully, that wayward disciple John Manotti had been overly cautious, and it was his map that we all huddled over once we were good and lost in the rhododendron thicket. The topo showed lots of valleys and creeks and ridges, and I think we followed one of those ridges for quite a while. The rhodies made it hard to tell. We wandered for two hours, maybe three. Lisa informed Jim that she was ready for another biozone. We ate a snack. But the trail never reappeared, and eventually John's map—and the swarm of wasps that beset Lisa as we descended a brushy hillside—persuaded us to turn around.

By the time we hit the car, Jim was calling our hike an "exploratory mission." By the middle of the next week, he'd dismissed the wasps as "kind of a fluke." Meanwhile, Nadine had instructed Lisa on how to make a meat-tenderizer poultice to reduce the swelling from her stings (somehow, Nadine had had occasion to master this remedy), and I had become obsessed. I spent my days poring over historical maps in the University of Oregon library. My studiousness, though certainly not my stubbornness, may have been a break from Harrang tradition; I lack his ability to make things look effortless. But the real hike, not the mere exploratory mission, was planned for the coming weekend, and this time I wanted to be fully prepared.

The oldest Three Sisters map I dug up, a topo drawn in 1925 by a geologist named Edwin T. Hodge, didn't show Jim's trail. Nor did any subsequent U.S. Geological Service quadrangle, from the first one, made in 1932, to the current one, printed in 1997. However, on the 1930 Forest Service map of what was then called the Cascade National Forest, a weak dotted line climbed the headwall next to Proxy Falls, switchbacking its way to the base of the Sisters. In 1940 the line was stronger and more obvious. In 1967 it was even drawn in red. After that, though, it vanished. The maps all showed the same important detail: not far past the lava field, where we'd gone straight uphill and found rhododendrons, the trail cut left and forded Proxy Creek. We'd missed the crossing, simple as that.

The paper trail intrigued me. Why had it been mapped and official for only thirty-seven years? Had the Forest Service simply lacked the resources to maintain it, as Jim supposed? My calls to the McKenzie Ranger Station finally led me to Jim Drury, an eighty-eight-year-old former fire ranger who still lived up the McKenzie River. On the phone, Drury could hardly hear me and I could hardly hear him. He wheezed proudly about the days of trail building and twenty-six-inch rainbow trout—he'd started with the Forest Service in July 1934—and about the fires he had fought and the fires his father had fought. Drury said the trail was a "way trail," one designated as a way to get from A to B in a time when recreation wasn't a priority on public lands. Trappers used such trails, hunters, too. If the Forest Service worked on them, and sometimes it did, the maintenance was done so firefighting crews could quickly access the high country. Though Jim Harrang remembers it as a leveled, clearly marked thoroughfare, Drury couldn't tell me much about this particular trail: it was already there when he entered the Forest Service, and he had hiked it only once. When the recreation boom happened in the 1960s, the outdoor enthusiasts usually stuck to more hiker-friendly routes.

I liked that the trail was a relic from another era, but more than that I liked being reminded that the era wasn't so long ago. For me and my peers, none of us having been alive long enough to see America's changing relationship with its wilderness, going outside for the sake of being outside has never been an alien concept. It's eye-opening when you realize that backpackers and river runners weren't ubiquitous when our parents were born—that the culture of outdoorsiness ushered in by pioneers like Jim Harrang is still spreading.

Jim assembled a strong crew for the final assault. My dad, infected by my obsession, came along, as did our longtime friends and fellow Jim groupies Carrie Gagen and Dennis Smith. Neyo León, a Venezuelan mountaineer who'd recently moved to Eugene and had taken English classes from my mom, was there, too. And John Manotti. But not Lisa—she was still convalescing at home, sprinkled with meat tenderizer.

We bristled with maps. I had photocopies of the one from 1930 and the one from 1940 and the one from 1967. I'd also bought some 1997 topos for good measure. Dennis had found a 1957 Forest Service map that showed the trail; using it and computer-mapping software, he and Carrie had made everyone customized topo printouts marked with the approximate route. John had the map that had saved us earlier, plus an altimeter and a compass or two. I carried a GPS and, at the trailhead, took the unprecedented step of turning it on.

We started out early, just as before, and we found the spur, just as before, and we climbed the headwall, just as before. When it came time to cross Proxy Creek, we crossed it. And there, on the other side, was the trail, just where it was supposed to be. We couldn't believe we'd missed it the first time. The path—sometimes faint, sometimes clear as day—traversed the slope and climbed up a mossy creek bed and gained a ridge where nary a rhododendron grew. Up and up we went in the open woodlands, passing a beautiful clearing where frost had flattened the long yellow grass and where red huckleberry bushes still bore fruit.

Farther along, we filed through thin slots in a forest of Christmas trees, the dew on their branches soaking through our clothes, and followed riverine channels of matted grass toward the cloud-covered Sisters. Jim walked up and over the dozens of logs in our way with such ease that Neyo's curiosity got the better of his shyness and he asked me, in Spanish, how old Jim was. I told him. "Increíble," he said. Rain started to fall, intermittently. We lost the trail, then found it again, twice in quick succession. We looked often at the maps and altimeter and GPS, and even marked a few waypoints, but we never really needed them.

Lunch should have been a victory banquet, since we ate it at our goal: Eileen Lake, with its views of the Three Sisters and its fiercely cold wind. But we didn't have time to savor our success. A storm was brewing and it was getting late. So we devoured our sandwiches and, for a change of scenery, headed back via the next drainage over, Linton Creek. Our way down was marked by mud, meadows, forty-five-degree slopes, three-hundred-foot waterfalls, and, mysteriously—wonderfully—more blazes: the remains of yet another forgotten trail, one that, I later determined, doesn't appear on a single map between 1925 and 1997. We were too rushed to investigate. When darkness hit, we were separated from the car by more than a mile of fallen logs and slippery rocks. We fumbled for our headlamps. Jim led us onward. "Well, guys," he murmured, "at least we can say we made use of all the available daylight."

A little over a year after our triumph, I went back for a third attempt on the trail. It happened to be the weekend of my ten-year high-school reunion, but three friends and I decided our time would be better spent climbing the Middle Sister. Matt, Natsu, Simon, and I piled into a car and headed up the McKenzie, and halfway there, I had a thought. "Do you guys know my neighbor Jim?" I asked. They did, at least by name; they'd all used his ice axes and kayak over the years. "Well, he showed me this secret trail." I convinced myself that we could walk it to the base of the mountain, camp, climb to the summit, camp again, and return. Then I convinced them. By the time we were on the trail, it was four P.M.

At first I was proud of myself for being able to find it, and my friends were impressed. The waterfall was especially beautiful in the afternoon sun. Despite our loaded packs, we made good progress. But when sunset came, we were still in the thick of the forest, denied even a glimpse of the Middle Sister. When it became totally dark, it was revealed that Simon had forgotten his headlamp. For some reason, I gave him mine. We lost the blazes almost immediately. I pulled out my GPS and found that the nearest waypoint I'd marked was named "Mid-bramble"—and Matt and Natsu began to complain. Channeling Jim, I pretended nothing was wrong—which, friends say, has been a pattern of mine since high school. For three hours we stumbled in darkness through the same rhodies and head-high firs, zigzagging up and down a ridge. I kept assuring them we were close. We ran out of drinking water. The hiking ended nearly at midnight at a non-descript flat spot in the forest, where I tried to press the group to go on and Natsu screamed at me in an expletive-filled breakdown.

The next day, having given up completely on the Middle Sister, we got lost again trying to make our way down to Linton Lake. Monsoon rains soaked us the next night and the morning after that, and we reached the car wet to the bone, barely talking to each other.

I sent Jim an e-mail when the trip was done, telling him I'd be in town and offering to give a full report. But he and Nadine were preparing for some adventure in New Mexico, and the gist, no doubt, he already understood. "Any time before our departure that I catch a glimpse of you," the eighty-one-year-old replied, "I'll be bounding across the fence."

The Road Already Taken

NICOLE DAVIS

i never intended to be a copycat. If someone had told me that I would retrace the path two men had forged a hundred years before, I wouldn't have believed him. I'd seen *Thelma and Louise,* read Jack Kerouac, listened to enough Bob Dylan to know that road trips could involve many things—adventure, love, double suicide—but they did not involve dead men's travel itineraries. Then I read about an unfathomable cross-country journey that predated, by at least a half century, every book, song, and image about back roads and blue highways. More people would want to know about this legendary trip, I imagined, and I decided I would be the one to re-create it. Which is more or less how I ended up in a place called Winnemucca, Nevada, studying ghost towns on yellowed maps.

I found Dun Glen on one such antiquated map in the public library in Winnemucca. The former mining town was nowhere to be found in my own atlas, but the librarian assured me that I would see an exit for it on the interstate. Sure enough, I found the sign and, following its arrow, turned south at the end of the ramp, toward a dirt road that picked up where the asphalt left off, then snaked through a silvery carpet of sage.

"You think this is it?" I asked my friend Kristen at the first clearing.

We stopped on the sandy track and examined the possibilities before us: a weathervane, beating in a breeze we couldn't feel, and a trough of water. Not likely. After a few clicks of Kristen's shutter, I suggested we keep going.

On the horizon, a moving cloud of dust nearly obscured a beat-up truck approaching us. When it caught up with our tiny red hatchback, I asked the driver if this was the way to Dun Glen. He leaned out the window and shook his head.

"Aw, there's nothing there," he said.

I realized this—the town boomed and went bust a century ago—but I still wanted to see what was left. He shrugged and admitted that we might find "a couple of ruins" a few miles up. We thanked him and drove on, bumping across the desert until the first crumbling stone wall came into view.

"I'll wait here," Kristen said. Just a few days into our re-creation, she was already losing interest. Not that there was much to sustain it: we had no historical placards or GPS coordinates to guide us, only a book filled with black-and-white photographs that proved the two men we were trailing had once been in this general vicinity.

Outside, the Mormon crickets reveled in the furnacelike heat, hopping in and out of doorways separating nothing but air. I peered down stairs that led to the remains of a cabin's foundation and tried to imagine the place Thomas Fetch and Marius Krarup stopped on their cross-country road trip a hundred years ago. Perhaps they bought some kerosene, or filled their canteens with water, or maybe, like us, they just drove on.

"Exploranography" best describes this trip I took in the summer of 2003. The writer John Tierney coined it a few years earlier to explain "the titillation of exploring without the risk of actually having to venture into terra incognita." He was talking about re-creations in still-unforgiving places—the Congo, for instance, or Antarctica—but the first men who drove across the country, in 1903, were not unlike the Livingstones and Shackletons of their day. Even their names sounded heroic: Horatio Nelson Jackson, accompanied by his mechanic, Sewall Crocker. Together they spent two months battling sagebrush, muddy roads, and repeated breakdowns, one of which left them stranded in Wyoming for thirty-six hours—without food. (A sheepherder ultimately saved them.) Whenever they found themselves without gas or stuck with a flat, they slept in whatever open field they happened to be parked in. Though they didn't have a word for it then, they were essentially car camping, well before our deluxe gear and modern campgrounds made this style of travel so tame.

Their packing list was also expedition-worthy. To get from San Francisco to New York, they had to bring firearms, compasses, camping gear, and a block and tackle—a towing device they hitched to a tree if they couldn't find a horse to tug them out of the mud or help them ford a stream. In those days, the animals still outnumbered autos, and the lucky few who did own cars rarely took them on anything longer than a five-mile spin. You couldn't really go farther, as there were no signs, no gas stations—there were barely even roads.

A century later, Kristen and I had thousands of miles of smooth asphalt to choose from, all clearly mapped on our glossy road atlas. We knew exactly where to camp (by the little green triangles), where we could pilfer condiments (from the multiple golden arches), and where to gas up (according to the familiar logos looming over the highway). We knew that much of the pure, unadulterated America these men covered had since been blasted, steamrolled, and staked with mile markers, but we would make do with the remaining wild places. After spending three years at the same travel magazine, a tough job to stay with considering the subject matter, we were ready to hit the road—along with the other copycats.

As it turned out, I wasn't the only one fascinated by this forgotten first cross-country trip. A year after I'd begun my scheming, I learned that Ken

Burns, the award-winning filmmaker, had a documentary about the first cross-country road trip already in the works. Then came the news that a retired orthodontist planned on retracing Jackson's route in a replica of his original 1903 car. I was clearly out of my league, and I considered calling off my re-creation—until I learned about the second road trip across America. One month after Jackson left San Francisco for New York, Thomas Fetch, a Packard Motor Company mechanic, and Marius Krarup, a New York journalist on assignment for *Automobile* magazine, tried to beat Jackson to the punch. Their drive didn't exactly have the same cachet as the first trip (second place never does), and it didn't seem nearly as rustic. There were no tales of near starvation, and though they packed 150 pounds of camping gear, it's not clear that they used it. The two took "the most central and direct route," Krarup wrote, following the railroad whenever they could, staying in towns or at station houses across the country. But it was also "the most problematic," particularly in the West. After sharing the Sierra's steep grades with pack horses and mule-drawn wagons, they faced the trackless Nevada and Utah desert, which had stymied other drivers, then crossed the Rockies at ten thousand feet—a much higher elevation than Jackson reached. They continued through the I-states—Iowa, Illinois, Indiana—then on to Ohio and north along Lake Erie before arriving in New York City, a full sixty-four days after they'd begun.

We planned on taking our sweet time, too. Using Fetch and Krarup's itinerary as our guide, we would try to recapture the spirit of those early road trips, back when car camping was a rugged way to travel.

A milk-white fog still shrouded San Francisco when we arrived at the Cliff House, a historic restaurant overlooking the Pacific. It was here that Fetch and Krarup dipped their tires in the ocean, as if to christen their car for their coast-to-coast trip, and we copied them as best we could. The parking lot at Ocean Beach was empty on a weekday morning, so Kristen reversed our car onto the concrete sidewalk, just inches from the seawall. She cursed the low light before taking a few parting shots of me grinning on the hood of our tiny Ford Focus, as if this were a car to be proud of. And in truth, I was proud of it. For months I'd pleaded with Ford to lend me a car for the centennial drive, and a week before we left they granted my audacious request.

There was only one wrinkle: the car had a stick shift. "You know how to drive one, right?" the company rep asked me over the phone.

"Sure," I said, my telltale heart pounding in my ears. "But I'm more comfortable driving an automatic. Aren't there any in stock?"

There weren't any, at least none the company was willing to give up for a month. I panicked until I learned that Kristen had learned how to drive on a manual transmission.

She put me behind the wheel immediately on our way to Yosemite. As we twisted around the mountain road cut out from the bald granite above, I listened for cues from the engine like a doctor monitoring a faint heartbeat. "Am I okay or should I be in third?" I asked.

"You're fine," she reassured me. How quickly our roles had reversed. Only a few weeks earlier, we had been mere acquaintances working in a steel box in midtown Manhattan. I gave notice first, and then Kristen asked to tag along and take photographs. At the time I thought I was doing her a favor. Now I couldn't get home without her.

◎   ◎   ◎

A year after Krarup had returned from his trip, he doled out travel advice in an article, "How to Tour in an Automobile." Packing tip number one: "Women are always to be considered baggage—very pleasant baggage, but so far as usefulness in the transportation plan is concerned, nothing more." If only I could have introduced him to the highly capable women now stuffed into the pockets of our backseats. Together with Fetch and

Krarup's itinerary, I'd packed a 1920s travelogue of Winifred Hawkridge Dixon, arguably the original inspiration for *Thelma and Louise,* and the letters of a young Nora Saltonstall, who, along with some friends, embarked on a road trip of the West's national parks in 1919. Yosemite was her first extended stop.

We were headed into the valley with only a day to spare—the park was slightly off Fetch and Krarup's route—so when the ranger told us we were lucky to get anything on such short notice, we believed him. Behind a train of cars crawling along the valley floor, we ogled El Capitan and Bridal Veil Falls, amazed to see these icons of the American West in real life. Then we entered the dark, designated camping area and passed an armada of RVs. Beyond these great white ships, tents popped up like suburban sprawl. Smoke from portable grills rose through the ceiling of ponderosas and mixed with the toxic smell of bug spray. In the eighty-four years since Saltonstall had visited, things had gone from bad to worse.

"We thought we had chosen a rather good spot," she wrote home to her family. "And were quite pleased with ourselves when we discovered twenty-five yards away from us another family of campers and then again a little further on some more." Even in her day the crowds were spoiling the view.

As early as 1900, writers had prophesied that the car would make us see more of our own country "out of beaten lines," though park officials knew better. The "devil machine"—so called because it scared the bejeebers out of horses—had no place in the wilderness. But when the railroads began transporting fewer and fewer visitors, Yosemite begrudgingly admitted cars, starting in 1913. The mobile campers soon began arriving in droves, outfitted with more gear than a Patagonia catalog.

"We are carrying on the Pierce two tents, our sleeping bags, food and cooking materials, each one a duffel bag for immediate use, a small trunk for town clothes, extra gasoline, water, etc.," wrote Saltonstall. To set up camp, they needed only to raise the hood of the car and fasten the tents to it. "From the front view, it looks as if the auto were emerging from a canvas garage."

The beauty of these proto-SUVs was that the driver could park anywhere she wanted: on a bluff overlooking Yosemite Valley; beside a stream; underneath the redwoods. Basically, they went everywhere trains could not go and hikers had already been. But the car did backpacking one better: it allowed us to travel farther and wider without straining our backs or corralling packhorses for the effort. We were nomads all over again.

As Saltonstall explained in one letter back home, "We just pitch tents when the spirit moves us. . . . Very gypsy like, don't you think?"

It was a description she'd probably seen before. At the time, newspapers and magazines were calling this new kind of camper the "motor hobo" or, more often, the "auto gypsy." By 1921, the *New York Times* guessed that of the 10 million cars on the road, half were used for camping. Wrote one "auto tourist" that same year, "Camping is all the rage. I suppose we'll see tents and wood fires in Central Park if this keeps on."

The craze never reached that kind of frenzy, but it certainly went unchecked at Yosemite. Visitors crowded the trail to Vernal Falls, and not a space could be found in the lot outside the Village Store. I shook my head in wonder as Kristen paused in the deli section and debated whether to buy tofu bologna or turkey—who knew they had this kind of selection in the woods? We returned to our site stocked with fake meat and microbrews and, over a cold dinner, toasted the beginning of a great road trip. Then Kristen pulled out the road atlas and began paging through states that were off Fetch and Krarup's route, places we had no business being in. Before she could even say the words *Grand Canyon,* I was shaking my head. "There's no time," I insisted. Without a replica car, the only way we could approximate the experience of our ghost drivers was to visit the same places, around the same date. Straying too far from their past, I thought, would render our present trip a bust.

◎   ◎   ◎

Within a week it became clear that more of this coveted past that I was trying to resurrect was preserved not outdoors but inside public archives. Flipping through microfiche at the Winnemucca library, I learned about the crowds that had formed around the Packard when it rolled into town, as if the one-cylinder car were a traveling sideshow. Whereas the desert had proved insurmountable to other drivers, Fetch and Krarup had had the sense to put strips of canvas beneath their tires to "avoid sinking in the quicksand." In addition to some Milwaukee beers "packed in ice and wrapped in wet gunnysacks," the men brought twenty-four-foot-long cloths to spread across the sand and give their tires purchase. They rattled across this movable track in the sweltering June heat, with only a parasol to shield them and the boom-chick, boom-chick, boom-chick of their engine as a soundtrack. A century later, their original route in Nevada essentially is now Interstate 80, and as we whizzed by with the air-conditioner cranking, the sagebrush beside us blurred into one silvery hedgerow.

Because he was never quoted, Fetch, I imagined, was quiet during the drive, focused tensely on the land unfolding in front of his goggled eyes. Krarup, on the other hand, was probably the same wisecracking raconteur he was in print. "Say," he told one reporter. "Don't spell my name the way I've seen in other papers. It gives me the Kra-reeps."

I knew that my weakness for news fiche was driving Kristen crazy, so I tried to redeem myself in particularly scenic places like Lamoille Canyon. The guidebook had touted the Ruby Mountains as the Alps of Nevada, which was as good a description as any for this out-of-place oasis. Inside the mountains, the desert quickly changed from a mind-numbing brown to an electric sage green. Fluttering aspen surrounded a quiet campground at the heart of the canyon, where we found a spot beside a rushing stream. In the morning, we hiked up to a series of vivid green alpine lakes, and there we met our first true character on the road.

Butch found us beside an emerald tarn. We were sunning ourselves on the surrounding rocks when he appeared, his gray shirt drenched from the ridgeline hike he'd just come from. He let his pack fall to the ground and smoothed back his silver hair.

"This thing was so heavy I had to burn my clothes before hiking down," he announced.

"You burned your clothes?" Kristen asked.

"Well, it was better than leaving them there," he reasoned.

He was weak, he said, because he'd spent the past year on his couch nursing a knee he'd hurt while skiing. It was perhaps the only time in his life he'd been grounded. On the hike down, we learned that he had skydived in New Zealand, worked the gas pipeline in Alaska, got himself appointed captain of a Sri Lankan cricket team, and sipped kava kava with the natives in Indonesia, and that afternoon he was planning on running with the bulls—in Elko.

"You should come," he said, inviting us before we parted ways at the trailhead. We told him we would see him in town, then debated whether we would just watch or become a part of the spectacle. Kristen chickened out immediately. "Who would drive the car?" she pointed out, supposing she got hurt. I sat firmly on the fence, reserving final judgment until I'd had at least one drink. We ducked into the Tiki Hut in downtown Elko, a dark bar decorated with black velvet paintings, where I ordered a beer and weighed the consequences. The course was not that long—measuring just fifty feet, it wrapped around the Stockman's casino parking lot. But I'd seen footage of Pamplona.

"Has anyone ever been hurt?" I asked a regular. He explained that normally no one did, except for the year before, when they had to medevac a boy to Salt Lake after he'd been gouged. That settled it. I liked my body puncture-free.

In Utah, Fetch and Krarup often drove at night. Without a roof, much less air-conditioning, it was the only way they could avoid the desert heat, which was all the more unbearable considering the state they were in.

"Nevada is awful but Utah is the worst I ever saw," Krarup told a reporter once they reached Colorado. "We carry a pick and a shovel along, and we found it necessary in more than one instance to use them when we have to build roads ourselves, cutting a way along the sides of hills. We have also had to build three bridges across gullies and places where the roads have been washed away."

I missed one treacherous stretch of theirs called Soldier Summit, a hill that took them two hours to climb. We'd passed it in a matter of seconds—a mistake I didn't realize for a good fifteen minutes more. Kristen sighed and rolled her eyes when I asked her to turn around and drive back. It was the first time my friend Jody, who had joined us in Salt Lake, witnessed just how obsessive I'd become. As we backtracked, I tried to rouse their interest in the place, reading aloud from a magazine called the *Packard Cormorant.* Soldier Summit, Krarup noted, was the site of "the only wax mine in the world."

"Wax came from mines?" Jody asked. Actually, the mine at Soldier Summit—along with others worldwide—produced a waxy, coal-like substance called ozokerite, which was used at the turn of the twentieth century to seal phonographs. But whatever interest Jody had mustered was lost by the time Kristen stopped the car. I got out, alone, and stared at the Indian paintbrush poking through the foundations of the old mining town. Deep down I knew this historic tour was losing its steam, but I was still trying to compare the country Fetch and Krarup might have seen with the one now in front of our eyes. It was like flipping through a photo album of someone else's road trip, except I was the only one reminiscing.

"Did you see everything you wanted?" Kristen asked derisively when I climbed back into the car. I lied and told her I had, aware that I wasn't the only one contributing to our car's sour mood. So far, Utah itself had been a disappointment. Instead of the Jacuzzi and clean accommodations

the guidebook promised we'd find, our Salt Lake City hostel turned out
to be a decrepit, wood-paneled pit run by a man named Socrates. We
thought we would fare better the second day, as we headed into the Uintah
Mountains. White fluff from the cottonwoods drifted silently as we followed a meandering stream to a primitive campground, peaceful for
the Fourth of July. We set up camp beside the musical brook and set
about preparing a patriotic barbeque, when three dirty-kneed kids came
crashing into the stream. Their mother followed, and then the father,
and then the friend, and soon we had dinner guests who offered a slew
of conspiracy theories involving everything from the chloroform in tap
water to the covert cameras sanctioned by the Patriot Act. By sundown,
in front of a flickering campfire, we were deemed worthy enough to join
their backwoods commune. They already had the perfect plot of land
picked out. All they needed was for us to buy it.

We fared better in places like Goblin Valley, where the wind had
sculpted the red sandstone into funky animals, human faces, and tall
mushroom caps (or phalluses, depending on your perspective). A ranger-
led hike through a section of Arches National Park—appropriately called
the Fiery Furnace—led us to open-air cathedrals of smooth pink stone.
But the heat was stifling. The only way to avoid it was to submerge ourselves in a swimming hole on the edge of town, a pool of sapphire blue
water that remained refreshing only so long as we stayed underwater.

Colorado came as a relief. The red rocks and blazing heat had finally
given way to alpine air and mountains that dominated every vista. The
Grand Mesa greeted us first, a stone plateau so massive it looked as though
it were plotting to slowly smooth over the town of Grand Junction. Next
was Glenwood Springs, where we soaked in the same hot baths that Krarup
relaxed in after arriving in the state looking "like one mass of gray dust."
We passed through Glenwood Canyon, a natural wonder Coloradoans
thought of so highly that they funded one of the most expensive highways in history to keep it intact. (A breathless hike to Hanging Lake, an

iridescent pool high above the interstate, explained why they went to the trouble.) We drove over the Rockies without a hitch—a feat that took Fetch and Krarup two days—then hiked in a yodelworthy mountain valley before a night of dancing in Aspen. And whereas our counterparts had driven along the Arkansas River, we hired a whitewater rafting guide who took us down a Precambrian pinball machine called Brown's Canyon.

These were not exactly the exploits Fetch and Krarup had had time to pursue, but at night we did our best to approximate what the early road-trippers might have experienced on the road, staking out sites on public land far from established campgrounds. We came close along one oxbow of the Colorado River, where we found a plot overlooking the foothills of the Flat Tops. Our only company was a hippie bus painted with a thick coat of green, and even it looked vacant, save for the two totemic owl eyes painted on the windshield curtains.

It was the kind of roadside site the women in *Westward Hoboes* might have cleared for themselves. In this travelogue written by Winifred Hawkridge Dixon, she recounts her 1920 road trip along the Southwest's emigrant trails with her best girlfriend, Toby. They, too, spent most nights sleeping just a few feet from the road. "We coasted down a surprising little canyon to emerge into a long dark road tangled with mesquite.... When we almost despaired of finding a suitable camp, we came casually upon a snug little grove, and heard nearby the rush of a stream.... The lamps of the car gave us light to stow away our belongings, and its lumbering sides screened us from the road."

As more and more people slept willy-nilly around the country, towns began erecting free municipal campgrounds to corral them. Savvy businessmen sniffed a goldmine, so they started building cabins with more creature comforts than tents offered. By the 1930s, motor courts had arrived, along with better roads and faster cars. As one writer rationalized in a 1933 issue of *Harper's*, "We are not a knapsack, open-air people. We like nature, but we must have our roads straight and smooth, and we want to view the scenery through the windows (usually closed) of a two-door sedan."

We were always happy to be out of ours. Though it sat not twenty feet away, off a desolate two-lane highway, we felt utterly alone as we snacked on smoked salmon and sipped wine before our campfire. The Colorado drifted silently in the dark, and aside from snaps and pops from the smoldering embers, the night was pin-drop quiet. Then a freight train passed and called all the coyotes in the surrounding hills into chorus. We listened intently to their howls, trying to gauge whether they were near or far away, or more important, whether they liked to eat humans.

"Their teeth are, like, this big," Jody said, holding her fingers impressively far apart. Soon after, a truck crunched onto the gravel driveway to our site and the hippie bus, then circled back toward the highway and stopped, illuminating the dark hills in an eerie spotlight.

"What's he doing?" Kristen wondered for all of us.

"Maybe he wanted to camp here," I offered.

The truck sat with the motor running for an interminably long time—long enough for us to imagine the worst. Finally, it circled back and pulled into the site.

"I've got the knife," Jody said. Kristen grabbed her mace. I held onto the corkscrew. We sat together, ears perked, as two truck doors slammed and footsteps disappeared inside the camper. Whoever they were, they didn't come to visit us. Kristen poured us each another cup of wine to calm our nerves. It helped us sleep, but as soon as I felt myself sink into a deep snooze, Jody grabbed my arm.

"Nicole, do you see that light?" she whispered. "What is that?" I took one look at the low-hanging orb, blurred by the walls of our tent.

"That's the moon," I said.

We city girls continued to adjust to life in the country—and all the open-air people it still attracted. The more we camped out, the more I coveted the sites furthest from roads, cars, and other campers. My own private nirvana was a hike-in campground in the Collegiate Range, where we crossed paths with just one other couple, who barely left their tent. By nightfall, they were invisible to us, and we were left alone to admire the sparkly white glow the moon cast on the surrounding peaks, which looked covered in snow. The only sound was the thunderous stream coursing below us like a spray jet, and as we walked through a grove of pines to gather ice-cold water for our pots, I felt stronger and healthier than I had been in ages. But just as I was getting into my backwoods groove, it was time to move on.

In Denver, Jody joined another friend traveling through the Rockies, and Kristen and I continued east, back to our homes. It wasn't until Ohio that we heard from her again. We had just finished a load of laundry and were about to crawl into our tents when she called us from Ten Sleep, Wyoming, two time zones and a world away. She and Jan had met some cowboys, who'd taken them horse packing in the Bighorn Mountains.

"He was the real deal," Jody said of her guy. "He even made his own spurs." Afterward, literally back at the ranch, the cowboys had cooked them dinner. Kristen and I cupped our ears to the cell phone, fawning over every word.

"What about you guys?" Jody asked. "Where are you?"

"We're in a place called Mosquito Lake," I told her. It hurt just to say it.

You could say that that was the proverbial last straw. For over three weeks, we'd followed the trail of Fetch and Krarup almost to the letter, but there was only so much of their past we could simulate. Slick roads had dominated their thoughts in Rifle, Colorado, while we passed our time in the same mountain town on a real, live cattle drive. In Mechanicsville, Iowa, Krarup had pulled a gun on an irate man after the car spooked the man's horse; we spent a half hour talking to a good-looking mechanic, tickled by the coincidence. And while mud had made Fetch and Krarup's drive across the plains nearly amphibious, we found a sea of corn and clear blue skies.

Our trip had begun to mirror theirs in only one, unfortunate regard. After the violent episode in Mechanicsville, Krarup noted that "the traveling, as such, was devoid of all incident and interest from Wheatland, Iowa, far into New York State." That was it—a road trip just isn't a road trip if it's devoid of incidents. We lacked a great adventure or some tragic misfortune. After all, Thelma and Louise ran from the law, right into the Grand Canyon. Nora Saltonstall's tour of the national parks ended tragically when she died of typhoid fever midway through in Portland, Oregon. And before those Westward Hoboes arrived safely home in Boston, they nearly sank their car while crossing a river.

By now, Kristen had endured every excruciating moment of my road trip redux, so when she suggested we visit the world's longest bar, on South Bass Island, I threw caution to the wind. We would go off-route for a while in favor of raucous pontoon boat parties and a local singer known as "Ohio's Jimmy Buffet." Both sounded incredibly scary to me.

The ferry dropped us off at a knob of limestone so far from the shore that Lake Erie resembled the sea. We found a site at its state park, set on a cliff above the lake, and set up camp with the kind of efficiency that comes from spending a month on the road. We were now connoisseurs of campgrounds and RV parks, accustomed to every variation and amenity possible: hike-in, drive-in, hot showers, no water, WiFi, pool. With our tents and sleeping bags in place, we fled the barbequing families and explored the cedar-shaded avenues on rented bikes, only to find that, with its mix of quaint Victorian inns and stadium-seating bars, the island resembled a cross between Martha's Vineyard and Hooters. When the sky began to darken, we headed back to camp, where we found a picnic table overlooking the lake and fired up our stove. As we prepped for an uninspired pasta dinner, a fisherman took pity on us and offered us fresh-caught perch, which we fried and ate as fat water droplets began to hint at something more violent. He offered two more, and then the rain sent everyone running. Back at the tents, Kristen and I did a quick swap, cooking gear for purses, and then sat beneath the public restroom awning, waiting behind a curtain of water for a taxi to circle through the campground and take us into town.

We found the world's longest bar at a place called the Barrel of Beer. Inside, a Commodores-style funk band, glitzed out in silver lamé, played to a gargantuan crowd. Barmaids with blinking barrettes sold Day-Glo Jell-O shots in syringes. Meatheads gathered on every square inch of the looping, 405-foot bar, waiting to hit on something moving. One asked if he could buy me a drink.

"I've got a boyfriend," I warned.

"That's okay," he said. "I'm married."

We accepted more drinks from strangers and danced to songs with words I'm embarrassed to know. Then we waited for another taxi to bring us back to our campground, where we discovered my soggy and misshapen tent, pushed aside by another twice its size.

"How dare they shove into our site and move your tent!" Kristen yelled. For reasons I now regret—mostly drunken rage—we took out a few key supports of their nylon condo and then crashed into our tents before promptly passing out. We awoke to a witch-hunt. Our neighbor, whose eyes I could barely meet, asked me if I knew what happened to his tent, as soon as I crawled out of mine. ("It was like that when we came back," I lied.) Then he inquired about a missing tent pole, something I honestly knew nothing about. Soon the park patrolman arrived on a mountain bike and again brought up this mysterious missing tent pole. I denied everything a second time, then found Kristen, washing off her tent in the bathroom, and mouthed to her my plan: "We have to leave now."

Once we were safely out of the park, Kristen admitted that she had put one pole beneath their tent. I was amazed at her pluck, then hit by a sharp pinch of guilt. Car camping may not be as rugged or romantic as it was a century ago, but it's still the way many people vacation, and we'd just ruined a perfectly good one.

What bothered me more, however, was the possibility that I'd spoiled our own trip. By hewing so closely to someone else's path, we'd missed a lot of stunning places and squandered our time in humdrum towns. But the payoff had been great, too. Had I done it any other way, I would have never learned how a few pioneering drivers put an entire nation on the road and, ironically, into the outdoors. It was a mental arm-wrestle I couldn't win, not then or now.

I kept quiet about my regret, trying to make the most of our last days. We'd come this far on Fetch and Company's trail, so we continued in their tire treads, north along the coast of Erie to Niagara Falls, where we admired the thunderous show along with tourists from Peru, Sri Lanka, Japan, and Poland. And then came another bout of rain. Like the Packard people before us, we suffered through a downpour on an all-night drive into the city, deciding to bypass a stop in the Adirondacks and brave the heavy rain and blurry taillights to reach New York. While our counterparts arrived caked in mud before an expectant crowd in midtown, Kristen and I headed home in secret, hoping to surprise our significant others.

After a brief reunion—in which I nearly gave my boyfriend a heart attack—he fell back asleep while I stayed up and stared at the ceiling. I could still feel the vibration of the engine running through me, an entire month of driving across the country now brought to a standstill inside a quiet New York apartment. I was excited to return to my own life; I'd been following someone else's for far too long. But after weeks of camping out, I suddenly felt caged. Painstaking as my re-creation had been, with all its stops and lack of spontaneity, it had also forced me to slow down and reset my inner clock. Staring out at the artificial glow of the city, I realized I'd grown accustomed to setting up camp by dusk, preparing dinner by firelight, and dozing beneath the stars. As much as there is to lament about what the car gave birth to, for better or for worse it is still our means to the outdoors, and the reality of this fact saddened me as I lay awake, knowing I would have to return that devil machine to Ford.

Eelian Thinking

JAMES PROSEK

> We have not attained to the full solution of the exceedingly
> difficult eel problems, but the steady progress of the last twenty
> years is full of promise for the future. . . . Altogether the whole
> story of the eel and its spawning has come to read almost like a
> romance, wherein reality has far exceeded the dreams of fantasy.
>
> *Dr. Johannes Schmidt, 1912*

My early encounters with eels were awkward, confused. My friends and I caught them by accident while fishing for trout or bass with worms. We never stopped to admire them; we were too shocked by their energy and frustrated by our inability to hold onto their slimy bodies, and we just wanted our hooks back.

One December in Italy eight years ago, I stood at the edge of a lake next to my friend Larry Ashmead. Slender poles stuck out of the water in a line along the shore. A man nearby said the poles marked traps for catching eels, and I began to tell Larry what little I knew of the life history of the freshwater eel.

Like those slender fish on the other side of the Atlantic, the eels in this lake were hatched in the middle of the Atlantic Ocean, somewhere east of the Bahamas, maybe several thousand feet deep. The discovery of the eels' spawning place was made in the early 1900s by the Danish oceanographer Johannes Schmidt, who caught thousands of specimens of the larval stage of the eel in fine mesh nets in an amorphous region of the North Atlantic, several million square miles, called the Sargasso Sea. Observing these larvae, only a few millimeters long and a few days old, drifting at the surface of the ocean currents, Schmidt concluded that the adult eels had recently spawned somewhere beneath his nets. News of the find, one of the most exciting in marine biology in the twentieth century, was published widely in popular magazines such as *National Geographic,* in 1913, and the journal *Nature.* But it soon became clear that, although Schmidt had solved a part of the "eel problem," he had also stoked the fire.

Before the twentieth century, scientists both amateur and professional had concocted numerous explanations of how eels reproduced, many of them harebrained: they believed that they were generated from horse hairs or drops of dew, that they mated with snakes on the banks of rivers, or that they emerged from the carcasses of dead animals or the mud. It was not even known whether eels were asexual or had gender and reproductive organs until Sigmund Freud, as a young medical student, published the first paper on the location of the eel's gonads. As it turns out, the reproductive organs are virtually invisible until the fish begins its journey in the sea. The larval stage of the eel—which looks nothing like the adult itself, but more like a leaf-shaped fish with fangs—had been known for centuries and named as its own species, *Leptocephalus breverostris.* But until two Italian biologists in the late 1800s observed these fish metamorphosing into eels, we didn't know the eel had a larval stage at all. Schmidt was determined to find out where these larvae, caught in the open ocean, came from. But despite Schmidt's discovery of the general vicinity of the Atlantic eels' spawning place, to this day no one has witnessed an adult eel spawning in the sea or seen adult eels much beyond the river mouths on their way to the spawning grounds. His findings merely opened a larger can of eels.

"After the young are hatched in the ocean as little leaf-shaped fish," I said to my friend Larry, "they are spread randomly by ocean currents to the coasts of the Atlantic. After twenty years or so in freshwater, the adults return to the ocean to spawn and then die."

The eel is one of the few fishes that are catadromous—that is, it spends its adult life in freshwater but reproduces in salt. This life history is the opposite of that of the salmon, for instance, an anadromous fish, which spends its adult life in the sea but reproduces in freshwater. There are several other populations of catadromous eels around the world that spawn in other oceans but live lives very similar to that of the Atlantic eel.

Larry found all this hard to believe. Until his moment of doubt, I hadn't really stopped to consider what the eels went through to get to and from the small brooks and lakes where they spent their adult lives. The place where they would reproduce, and probably die, was thousands of miles away.

Some weeks later, Larry came across a 1941 story by Rachel Carson from *Under the Sea Wind,* called "Odyssey of the Eel." It is a tale seen largely through the eyes of a female eel named Anguilla (the genus name for catadromous eels) and was inspired by Schmidt's discovery. The story begins with a description of juvenile eels swimming to a small body of water called Bittern Pond, two hundred miles from the sea, looking "like pieces of slender glass rods shorter than a man's finger." One dark rainy night in autumn, many years after she first entered freshwater, Anguilla leaves the pond, beginning her long journey back to the Sargasso.

Anguilla is drawn almost magnetically toward that place of warmth and darkness hundreds of feet below the surface of the ocean where she hatched. Beyond that, the author imagines the rest, because once Anguilla leaves the mouth of the river, her life in the ocean is entirely a mystery:

"No one can trace the path of the eels that left the salt marsh at the mouth of the bay on that November night when wind and tide brought them the feeling of warm ocean water—how they passed from the bay to the deep Atlantic basin that lies south of Bermuda and east of Florida half a thousand miles."

We don't know much more of the eel's life history today, nearly a century after Schmidt's discovery. What remains consistent about the eel is its ability to avoid our gaze. That ultimately was what attracted me to the eel.

It's not easy to get to like, or to know, the eel. It is dark and slippery and not particularly beautiful at first glance. For me, the eel began as an idea. The idea was of the unseen journey and the eel's intangible determination to reach a destination, a destiny that ends with death, and life. I'm still trying to figure out what to do with this idea and to determine whether trying to make sense of its ethereal qualities would somehow diminish the beauty of its incomprehensibility. In the course of my time spent with eels, I have met other people as interested in eels as I am, people whose lives cross paths with the eel. Anglers, scientists, slippery lovers of darkness themselves, whom I began to call, in jest, "eelians."

Many eelians live lives like that of the eel, unseen, quiet, under the radar. For me, the unexpected paths that led to these people became wrapped in the original idea. One eelian, Ray Turner, an eel fisherman in the Catskill Mountains of New York State, became a kind of prophet to me. He spoke in aphorisms that appeared alternately meaningless and prophetic, depending on the circumstances and delivery. "It's not the journey, it's the road," he once told me. Or: "Art is reality out of proportion." The elusiveness of the eel was its beauty.

All around the world, the eel inspires fear, awe, and respect. Humans seem to have some visceral reaction to this minimalist fish, as they do to the snake, a tempter of the innocent and virginal, an erotic symbol, a food source, a god. In some cultures the eel fills both the well of human spirituality and the stomach. The mystery of the eel's spawning areas and catadromous life history may be, as the indigenous people of New Zealand believe, best left unsolved. But it would be unfortunate if the opportunity to know the eel became lost. All around the world, catadromous eel populations are in serious decline. The causes are many and not always easily defined. If we were to lose the eel before we witness its spawning or learn more about what fuels its determination to make the journey or how it navigates in its migration, then this would mean, as the poet Wallace Stevens wrote, "farewell to an idea."

I began my work on eels around 1998, and, as is the case whenever I dig into a topic, I mentioned my interest in eels to anyone who came within talking distance. I brought up eels in conversation with family, editors, artists, therapists, my barber, and a friend named David Seidler, a screenwriter in Santa Monica. David asked me if I'd heard of the sacred eels of New Zealand. I had not, nor had I read anything about how important eels are to the culture and traditions of the Maori, the native Polynesians of New Zealand. There was, I would discover, a reason for this—Maori stories and traditions are passed on orally, and they are shared primarily between Maori.

As I had found out on my first visit to New Zealand a few years before, a postcollege trout-fishing trip with my friend Taylor, the Maori are genial but don't go out of their way to share anything. Taylor and I saw Maori men in bars after their long days at work in the sawmills or slaughterhouses, but not much more than a grunt or nod passed between us. We trekked on Maori tribal land, hiked trails through old-growth forests, fished crystal clear rivers with tall fern trees shading emerald pools, caught trout species introduced by the British, and hung out with naturalized British people. But overall, the experience, though visually and physically fulfilling, felt superficial. I left New Zealand feeling empty, knowing that I was glimpsing only one small part of that country and little of its soul—in other words, I'd learned little of its people. It was the first time in my travels that a pretty landscape was not enough for me.

As David told me more about the giant eels in New Zealand, I remembered a moment on that first trip with Taylor. While we ate lunch on the bank of a remote river, a slender dark shape, five feet long and as big around as my arm, had come out of the shadows to eat a piece of the sandwich that I'd thrown in the water. I saw it so briefly that I wasn't sure I'd seen it at all. But as David spoke, I registered the fact that the big dark fish had been perhaps the only native one I'd seen on that trip, an eel.

David told me that it is a tradition of the Maori to keep ponds with sacred eels. The Maori feed the eels and protect them, and in turn the eels protect the *iwi,* or tribe. The eels can be huge—six, seven feet—and will feed right out of one's hands. The Maori say some of these eels are over three hundred years old.

David, who grew up in America, knew the land of Kiwis from his years living there while married to a Maori woman named Titihuiarangimoana, whom he met while working for a television company in Australia. His marriage gave him access to a world usually closed to *pakeha,* or white people. His introduction to the New Zealand wilds, or bush as it's called, came while he was fly-fishing for trout with a Maori man named DJ.

"I've seen some huge ones while trout fishing, mate," David said. "I was fishing in this mountain lake one day, wading through the shallows, and went to step over this big log when . . . the log moved! It was a giant eel, big around as the fattest part of my leg. There was no stream running out of the lake, so I don't know how this eel would get to the sea to spawn, but they say that some small eels get up to high lakes when there's a typhoon, and they'll stay up there, sometimes over a hundred years, until the next big typhoon comes and washes them down the mountain."

David sent an e-mail to his friend DJ on the North Island in the autumn of 2002 inquiring about eels on my behalf. DJ said he knew only a thing or two about eels, and would try to find someone who might have more to say than he did about the importance of eels in Maori culture. Eventually, it was decided that the best person to lead me around New Zealand in search of eels was a twenty-three-year-old half-Maori woman named Stella August. Stella had just finished her graduate work at Waikato University in Hamilton. The subject of her thesis was the spring migration of glass eels on the Tukituki River, which flows to the eastern coast of the North Island, near her family's tribal land in Hawke Bay.

A few e-mail correspondences later, Stella agreed to set up an itinerary for me and to be my eel guide on a trip around New Zealand. Our trip was scheduled for February of 2004, summertime in the Southern Hemisphere.

In the meantime, I came across some Polynesian myths that involved eels, in the work of Joseph Campbell. Campbell explains in his book *The Masks of God: Creative Mythology* how the creation myth in India involving the snake made its way through Indonesia and was eventually inherited by the Polynesians. In their version of the story, Polynesians replaced the snake, which was unknown in the islands, with the indigenous eel.

In several stories throughout the region, particularly in Samoa, a small eel is taken as a pet by a girl named Sina. Sina raises the eel in a coconut shell until it becomes too big, at which point she lets it go in a spring but continues to feed it. One day when she's bathing in the spring, the eel tries to pierce her vagina with its tail. The eel is killed and the head is buried, where a coconut tree grows. The nut of the coconut bears the mark of the eel's eyes and mouth. The story of the eel as a creature both loved and feared, and as a kind of detached phallus with a mind of its own, is consistent throughout the region.

Another Polynesian story, of which there are many variations, concerns a monster eel called Te Tuna and the seduction of the god Maui's wife, Hine. Campbell likens Maui to a kind of Hercules of Polynesia. When Maui finds the giant eel Te Tuna in bed with his wife one night, he cuts off the eel's head with a hatchet. In the story, the head of the eel becomes all the saltwater eels of the world, and the tail becomes all the freshwater eels of the world.

It is not surprising, perhaps, that in the South Pacific region the word for eel, *tuna,* is a synonym for *penis.* There are many variations of stories of eels seducing women in their sleep or while they are washing clothes by a spring, as well as stories of eels as monsters, but I found nothing specifically about the Maori and eels, or about sacred eels at all, until I stumbled onto the works of Elsdon Best.

Best was born in Tawa Flat, New Zealand, in 1856, the son of British immigrants. He is considered to be the foremost ethnographer of Maori society, which was diminishing rapidly even in the late nineteenth century. His work makes clear that the eel was once the greatest inland food source for the Maori. Best listed over two hundred local Maori names for the freshwater eel in his *Fishing Methods and Devices.* If the number of different words used to describe the nuances of an object in a language—for example, the words for snow among the Eskimo—is evidence of its importance to a culture, then this fact alone, for me, confirms the importance of eels in Maori life.

It was also in Best's work that I first read about the Maori monster called the *taniwha,* which most commonly takes the form of a giant eel. In part 2 of *Maori Myth and Religion,* Best describes how Captain Cook, on his third voyage to New Zealand in 1777, gave us the first written record of taniwha: "We had another piece of intelligence from him, more correctly given, though not confirmed by our own observations, that there are snakes and lizards there of enormous size. He described the latter as being eight feet in length and big around as a man's body. He said they sometimes devour men."

Best, commenting on Cook's account, points out that the Maori man telling the story to Cook would certainly have known a lizard—though no eight-foot lizards exist in New Zealand—but would never have seen a snake. What the native described to Cook was the longfin eel of their freshwater rivers, *Anguilla dieffenbachii,* capable of growing to eight feet in length, reaching well over eighty pounds, and living a hundred years. Best also wrote that large eels were sometimes tamed and regularly fed. Offerings were sometimes made to these eels, and, thought to be sacred, they were respected like gods.

Though these works of European writers are interesting, as they relate to eels, I found them dry at times. I think it was because the people who recorded the stories were not the authentic tellers of the tales. There was no Polynesian Homer to write them down. The soul of these stories was yet unwritten, was still in the minds of Maori elders in seaside and mountain villages in New Zealand. Because the stories are nature-based, they feel deflated and pale when told in any context outside the environment they came from. On my return to New Zealand, I would learn of the dangers that face the so-called pagan faiths. If nature was endangered, New Zealand culture and ideas were as well.

Stella August was twenty-four years old when I visited New Zealand in 2004. Her mother is British, and her father was Maori. Stella's mother left home when Stella was nine, and Stella lived with her younger sister, Wiki, and their father on their tribal land on Kairakau Beach, a remote, windswept coastline at Hawke Bay. Stella learned of her affinity for the sea and rivers through her father, and it was the sea that took him in a boating accident, when a rogue wave overturned his skiff. He drowned just off the beach near their home. Stella was sixteen at the time.

When her father died, Stella contacted her mother and asked if she would return to their tribal land to live with her and Wiki and help out on the farm. Her mother had not set foot there since she'd left years before. She agreed to return and has lived there ever since, tending to a herd of sheep and cows with her boyfriend, Ray, and with the help of cigarettes and cold Lion's Red beer to pass the time. Drinking was just another part of living out there, a good hour and a half from the nearest supermarket.

Because of her love for the sea, Stella studied marine biology in college while on a fellowship awarded by her iwi, Ngati Kahanunu. When I met up with her, she had just handed in her master's thesis, was working part-time in a coffee shop, and was organizing for me what she'd termed an "eel adventure" throughout New Zealand.

Our scheduled meeting point was a Burger King on the second roundabout in Hamilton, about a two-hour drive south of Auckland. She was wearing board shorts and a sweatshirt with surfer logos and would not look directly into my eyes.

"You brought the sun," she said.

It had been raining for three weeks straight, and New Zealand waterways had experienced some of the biggest floods in a lifetime. It was good weather, I supposed, for an eel.

We talked briefly about our itinerary there in the parking lot. "We should sit down and make sure we both know where we're coming from," Stella said, with slight severity. "About what you're going to write."

The Maori people had a right to be wary, even protective—the English colonists had lied to them, stealing their language, customs, and land and replacing their spirituality with Christianity, with mixed results. In the eyes of some Maori, the latest assault was the success of the film *Whale Rider,* about a young Maori girl learning the indigenous customs from her grandfather. Hollywood had made all kinds of money on what Stella called Maori "intellectual property," and her people hadn't received commensurate compensation. It was clear that Stella was conflicted about being my guide. She seemed happy that I'd shown interest in learning about her culture and sharing it with whoever cared to read about it, but also reticent about making known what was sacred and very personal, and being paid, though not much, to do so.

Whale Rider, Stella agreed, was actually a realistic portrayal of modern Maori life, especially in the instance of a young girl inheriting the culture from her reluctant grandfather, who traditionally would have passed that oral knowledge to a boy. The boys in modern Maori culture had no patience, had attention problems, were fidgety, and more often than not got into trouble with drugs and alcohol. It was young women like Stella and her sister who were inheriting the faith and staging a cultural revival.

"I'm here because of a genuine fascination for a very strange and fascinating fish," I said, repeating sentiments I'd shared in numerous e-mails over the previous months.

She paused before answering. "Well, you and I are alike, then," she said. "But I didn't always like them. Eels. When my father brought them home, I wouldn't go near them. But my interest in fish is definitely because of my father."

A lot of people were suspicious of me, Stella told me, when she rang them up and told them she wanted to bring an American by to do research on eels in Maori culture. "The first thing they said was, 'Why does he want to know?' They've got a lifetime of experience, which traditionally is shared with those in their *hapu,* or subtribe, within the iwi. They're suspicious of science."

"I'm not a scientist," I protested.

She knew that, she said, but there was something she wanted me to understand about her culture. "I went to this big eel conference where the leading eel experts in New Zealand had gathered. Don Jellyman, a pakeha, probably the most famous—he's at NIWA [National Institute of Water and Atmosphere]—was delivering a paper on his attempts to track eight large migrant eels from the river mouth to their spawning grounds with radio transmitters. He explained that all signs of the radio transmitters had been lost once the eels reached the edge of the trench off the east coast of the South Island. When Don sat down, Kelly Davis, who I hope will be available to see us, got up to represent the Maori. He addressed Don directly, saying, in front of everyone, 'Why do you need to know where they go? The juvenile eels come up the river in spring, the adults migrate out in the fall. My people have known this forever. What good will it do the fish to find the house where they breed?' Don was speechless."

I listened. And I learned not to assert too much, not to ask too many questions, and to listen as best I could to what the individuals on our eel adventure had to share. Not an hour went by that Stella did not remind me that we would be meeting with the people most knowledgeable about eels in all New Zealand, and that I was privileged to have time with them. As she advised, I had brought *koha,* or personal gifts, to give to them all—small artworks I'd made and signed books.

Over lunch at her flat, Stella told me more about her love of eels and about the time she spent with them. "Why do we have to try to understand everything that isn't understandable? Everyone wants to unlock everything. I'm conflicted because I'm Maori: I don't want to know where they go, and yet I've studied their movements in the rivers in a scientific way."

Our conversation returned to the idea of the taniwha, that important element of Maori stories. In the *Reed Dictionary of Modern Maori,* the translation of *taniwha* is "water monster, powerful person, ogre." It can make itself known at certain times to certain people, sometimes to warn them of danger. Stella pointed out that the most common form in which a taniwha shows itself is that of an eel. Usually a large eel.

"If you spear an eel that's a taniwha, or catch it in a net, it will cry like a baby or bark like a dog, or even change colors," Stella said. "If you killed a taniwha, you'd have a *matuku,* or curse, and start going crazy, like you're possessed." In that case, she added, it meant you had broken *tapu,* something sacred or off-limits.

Three weeks later, Stella and I were huddled in a tent, stranded in the bush with DJ. He had taken us up a small tributary of the Mata River he called Stony Creek, in the northeast corner of the North Island, so we might fish for trout and search for the big eels that often live in the head-waters of streams. The creek was in a remote piece of tribal land thick with *punga,* the New Zealand fern tree, the fronds of which hung over emerald plunge pools inhabited by large trout and eels. A helicopter had dropped us off four days before. In a driving rain, with the river in the canyon rising, we waited for the weather to clear so we could be picked up at the appointed time. A day later, we were still in the tent, wet as water rats, hoping for a break in the rain so we could try to start a fire.

After four days in the bush, DJ was just starting to get comfortable enough with me to tell me what was really on his mind. He was, like all Maori I had met, a little reserved at first, even intimidating in his silence. His stature was imposing: he was tall and thin, but strong, and had dark skin like a Native American cowboy. He had a long, sage nose and a casual swagger and wore a silver pocket watch in a leather sack on his belt. The rain let up and, toward evening, the sky began to clear. Relieved that we'd probably fly out in the morning, we slipped from our tent, stretched our legs, and after some effort, got a fire started.

DJ pulled out his skillet to cook the two remaining steaks we'd brought. "I've seen some crazy things out here," he said, poking the fire with a stick, making a spot atop the coals for the skillet. "But it's more the things I've felt and haven't seen that stick with me." He started to talk about the skillet and its history. I asked DJ if he had any stories of taniwha. I was eager to know more. But, as I was learning, he wouldn't be rushed.

"This was my dad's skillet," DJ said. "Most of the places I take people fishing and hunting in the bush are places I went hunting with my father as a boy. If I'm in an area I don't know, I ask local people in the pub, the bros, or I have a yarn with the publican. I never take my white clients along, 'cause if I do, the bros won't talk. They won't even move their lips, mate." DJ stoked the fire with his stick. A cool wind blew down the river valley.

One time, he said, he was up in the bush with friends on horseback, pig hunting. "We'd camped under this permanent shelter that had been there forever. We'd had a long day of hunting, and we were cooking a big feed, and all of a sudden the bush went silent. You normally hear all these noises, the crickets and that, like now. Well, it all went quiet, and then the horses started acting up, and then the dogs went ballistic. We're told, you know, don't ever camp on the track, you're never supposed to, but we did, we were set up right on it." DJ flipped the steaks.

"I'm always trying to reason, and I thought: There's a logical reason why the horses are acting up. An experienced horseman could ride up in the dark and spook the horses. People do it all the time. It's possible. I waited for that horseman, but he never came."

Stella asked if he had grabbed a gun.

"What good's a gun?" DJ asked. "I was in my sleeping bag with the top pulled over my head. And then come this roar. I don't know how to describe it, and I've never heard it since, and I'm not superstitious, but I have no way of explaining it. It was like a jet engine, and loud, like, deafening. I don't know what to call it, like, a taniwha or what."

DJ split the steaks three ways, and we sat on logs and ate. We made the fire bigger and were soon dry. To hear a personal taniwha story from DJ made me think. This wasn't a dead story told by a European ethnographer; it was a live account told in the element from which it was derived. And the impact of the experience on me was as loud as the monster in his story. It was more powerful than a ghost story at a campfire, because I knew from his tone and seriousness that DJ had experienced it and had no logical reason to explain it. In his Maori spirit, he believed it was a taniwha.

DJ knew I'd come to New Zealand to learn about eels in Maori culture. He'd been waiting for the right moment to tell me his version of things.

"The way I see it," he said, salting his steak and taking a bite, "there are three players in a New Zealand river: the rainbow trout, the brown trout, and the eel. The eel is the cultural factor. The eel is the Maori factor. The trout is the British colonist. Everyone forgets about eels because you don't see them. They're out at night mostly. You don't see the eel, but he's there, and he's relentless in his efforts to catch the trout. He's always stalking them. He can take the other two out any time. He might wait years to catch them. Till they get old and weak. The eel's got time. The eel's been there since long before the British put the trout in the rivers." DJ threw the gristle from his steak in the fire. "And he'll be there after. We call that *morehu,* the survivor."

DJ's was a common sentiment among Maori in the early twenty-first century. The culture, buried underground for the better part of a hundred years, was reemerging with a vengeance and, sometimes, with resentment for the descendents of the British colonists. The eel, I would come to find, is not only sacred but also one of the most important creatures in Maori culture for a host of reasons—the lubricious creature seducing the wife of gods, a symbol of the penis, a protector, and the main traditional food source for the inland Maori. But most important, the eel is a symbol of what is being lost the world over: nature. The loss of nature amounts to a loss of culture, especially indigenous "pagan" culture; a loss of connection to the earth; and a loss of soul.

This new world was not one I wanted to live in. And I began to rethink the assumptions I'd made about indigenous people from the things I'd read in the works of Joseph Campbell and Elsdon Best. I'd treated the stories about taniwha in the way that they were presented, as myth. But from the conversations I'd had with Stella and DJ and others, I was finding out that what I'd perceived as mythology was in fact very much a part of the spiritual reality of the Maori. And eelian thinking about nature—as an idea that couldn't be, and didn't need to be, pinned down, as something that would persevere long past humans—began to make a lot of sense.

It occurred to me that the Christianity myth has been successful partly because it is much more portable and versatile than the core of any nature-based faith. Its story can be understood by any human in any environment in the world, and its concepts are promoted both in buildings built by people and in the open air. But with nature-based faiths like those of the Maori and other indigenous peoples around the world, once you lose the nature that the spiritual system is based on, you are also in danger of losing spirituality. If the eel is endangered, isn't the Maori sense of spirituality also endangered? If a young Maori boy does not see a giant eel, is not awed by that six-foot, writhing length of muscle, can he have faith, truly, in a taniwha?

For the Maori, the end of the eel will be the end of an idea. So was the end of the kiwi. It is precisely what happened to the American Plains Indians, when the Europeans slaughtered hundreds of thousands of bison. I wonder if there is a connection between the loss of such natural wonders in New Zealand and the disillusioned youth of the Maori, especially the young men, who turn to drugs and mischief instead of nature. When their energies and aggressions aren't spent running around fishing and hunting, do they turn to hostility? Toward their spouses, toward the government, toward everything?

Although it's harder to imagine myth as a spiritual reality in the twenty-first century, I think we do need some form of this eelian thinking to survive. In New Zealand, when I let my reason fade, I could imagine a giant eel living in a deep pool, one that warned children away from a dangerous current or that protected the surroundings of a place. When I heard stories of areas of forest that were sacred, where there was a spiritual silence and "no birds sing," I felt whole, and motivated. I felt human.

Building Home

JAIME GROSS

I was born and raised in New York—in Queens until I was eleven and thereafter in a Westchester suburb. But I grew up, really, in the shade of three oak trees in the Berkshire Mountains of Massachusetts. When I was six, my parents bought twenty-four acres in the southwest corner of the state, and over the next decade my father built, by hand, a vacation home. There were things I didn't know that might have made the place feel less wild: that the man who sold us the land had let a logger troll through the forest and fell the oldest, most valuable trees; and that, if you headed northwest half a mile, you'd come upon the backside of a popular ski slope, well populated in winter with loud, red-faced families. But my sense of it was that the forest stretched on endlessly, and it was all ours, and I could explore it at my leisure. I assumed that sooner or later I'd cover all the ground there was to cover. I assumed I'd continue to get braver, more adventurous, as time went on.

We had no television there, so I spent most of my weekends and summer days on tentative treks, making gradual inroads into the woods. There was one spot that interested me the most, and I came back to it over and over again: a small grove of oak saplings not far from our house, where the branches arched over each other to create a little shelter. The earth beneath was mounded and peaty; it seemed to embrace my body when I lay upon it. The more time I spent there on my belly, picking through the dirt (relocating earthworms, wondering at the bugs that curled up under my prodding fingers), the more distinct the spot became from the surrounding woods. It was mine: I defined its borders with my fanned-out arms and legs. I see now that its greatest virtue was its proximity to my family's house—just far enough away for me to establish a private world separate from that of my parents and brothers, but close enough to keep home in sight. Wild, but not too wild.

I was eight then. The natural world was kaleidoscopic, malleable, and infinitely layered. I re-created my own version of home. The small dip in the earth: that was my bed. Those roots breaking the surface of the soil: those were my front steps. The changing sky was my ceiling. I traced a winding pathway to my "front door" with gravel pilfered from my parents' newly laid foundation. I lined a hole with black plastic garbage bags, filled it with water—carried bucket by bucket from the house, fifty yards away—and called it my pool. I worked relentlessly, domesticating the wildness, until winter drove me inside.

That makeshift hideaway sustained me for several years. But one summer something gave. The little grove began to look like what it was: a group of scraggly trees surrounded by scattered gray gravel. I suppose I got bored. I was eleven years old. My family was in the process of moving to a suburb an hour north of Queens; I was about to be uprooted, and I wanted something with more structure, more opacity—walls, a floor, a roof. What I wanted, I told my father, was a tree house.

I became obsessed. As if I were planning a real house, as if I had a serious grown-up budget, I began poring over photographs from magazines and catalogs. I saved one of those pages, ripped out from an old Ethan Allen catalog—a sunny, barnlike space full of florals and cheery country touches, a pitcher of lemonade on the pine table. I thought I could see what lay beyond the frame: a fragrant herb garden, a sleeping cat, a stable life laced with logic. Nothing of that style actually materialized in my tree house, outfitted as it was, in the end, with a cheap rag rug and beanbag chair from Kmart, a milk crate piled with my favorite books, and some photographs of the school friends I had left behind. But I clung to that promise of everything-in-its-place adulthood.

I spent months sketching, then presented my father with a plan: a triangular tree house bridging three oaks, directly above the old hideaway. We began gathering materials, most of them salvaged—aluminum storm windows and corrugated fiberglass snagged from the street on garbage day, floor planks from an old attic. I accompanied my father on his next trip to the lumberyard. We returned with six sheets of thin mahogany plywood, a material that is both inexpensive and virtually indestructible—bugs don't eat it, and it never rots.

A few weeks later, my father finally stalled work on his own house to build mine. It went up over a single weekend in September. First we bolted three two-by-eights around the perimeter of the trees, to form a triangular base. On top of this went shiplap floor decking; similar to tongue-and-groove flooring, it prevents buckling and forms a tight seal to keep animals out. We framed the three walls on the ground, one with a window in its center, then hoisted them up and nailed them into place. We topped the structure with the corrugated fiberglass sheeting: my roof. The following weekend I bought some paint and covered the front of the house with a blue, cloud-filled sky.

To my surprise, the structure turned out to be tiny, most of the floor space rendered unusable by the triangle's corners, but that didn't matter much. I was four-foot-three and fifty-three pounds, and it was plenty big for my purposes. I liked to lie on my back, picturing myself at the bottom of the ocean. The sun-dappled shadows on the fiberglass roof flickered like waves, and the whole thing gently swayed in the wind. And it was large enough for me to sit cross-legged with my battery-operated typewriter, a birthday gift from my parents, and write. The first document I churned out was a *Tree House Contract* packed with thesaurus-dependent prose that effectively forced my brothers to sign away their right to enter it, ever, without my permission. I curled my hand around my four-year-old brother's hand and helped him scratch out his first initial on the line. Moreover, I added a clause promising: "And once I learn to read, I will follow these rules too."

Soon after, I recruited a friend to spend the night with me in my new hideaway. We lay side by side in sleeping bags, squeezed into the center of the triangular floor plan. I had intended the structure to be a shelter from the wilderness outside, but come sundown it seemed to have the opposite effect, inviting the spooky outdoors in. Branches scratched violently against the roof, and the darkness outside our candlelit room seemed to stretch on forever. Hoping to dispel our suspicions about circling, hungry mountain lions, we opened the trapdoor and peered below, seeing only blackness and hearing the whoosh of the wind. Our imaginations spiraled further and further out of control, until we finally dropped down the ladder and ran, hearts pounding and pajamas flapping, for my family's house.

Daytime was a different story. In the sunlight, the house was a home base, a place to return to, something to keep in sight, to glance backward at as I ventured deeper into the wilds. Having domesticated this spot, I became braver wandering farther from it. There were new frontiers to explore. I descended my ladder and surveyed the landscape. I discovered new areas in the woods, and for each one I conjured a different dwelling. A rocky outcropping suggested a Japanese teahouse, similar to one I'd seen on a San Francisco postcard; a knee-high field of ferns suited a woodsy A-frame. I found a rotted-out tree trunk, the perfect place to wait out a storm. Fashioning shelters in the woods made me more confident in moving through nature. What had been anonymous (trees, more trees) became familiar, points of reference on my journeys. I could find my way back.

I suppose this was my first notion of architecture. I began to under-stand the dialogue between a good building and its site. Certainly, build-ing a shelter brought me closer to nature—after all, I may have been too chicken to venture beyond the original outskirts of my family's home without it. It expanded my sense of the landscape and made a wider swath feel navigable. But at the same time, it furthered my dependency on roofs and walls, buffers between myself and the land around me.

These days, the landscapes that move me are those beyond glass; they scroll across car windshields and shiver through dusty living room win-dows. Framed as such, they are manageable and full of promise; I invent them and move through them confidently. Take away that boundary, drop me solo into a foreign landscape, and my heart pounds. I have no faith I'll find my way.

Three years ago, at the age of twenty-four, I moved across the country to Berkeley, California, where my boyfriend, Calder, had decided to pursue an advanced degree in landscape architecture. I was ready, I thought, to leave the East Coast. California had always appealed to me. My mother grew up in the Bay Area; to this day she remains perplexed as to why she's no longer there ("You married a Brooklyn boy," we gently remind her). I'd grown up hearing about the bridge, the fog, the contented citizens. They scared me, a little, but part of me longed to know whether or not I could be one.

In the months leading up to the move, I reimagined myself, an ideal-ized version of myself, with qualities I now suspect I'll never possess. I bought athletic clothes in improbable colors and high-tech materials and hoarded hiking gear. I saw myself tan (I'm never tan). I figured I'd love California, adapt easily. "What's not to love?" I'd say—in what now seems distinctly New Yorkese—to anyone who asked.

I meant to revisit the tree house—its paint peeling and plywood warp-ing—before I left, but in the madness of the move, I didn't. I thought I'd

sit there in silence, like a girl at her grandmother's deathbed, and hold
my breath while hoping for a sign, something to indicate who I was and
whether I was on the right track. I hoped that the space would have some
knowledge to impart—something about growing up, and slowing down,
and priorities. But I didn't find the time, and the moment passed. I packed
up and left New York City.

Our apartment in California was a former carriage house, with trees
close around our bedroom window. At the right times of day, the room
glowed green. From our deck off the kitchen I could see the tops of palm
trees, a constant reminder of where I was. Berkeley embodied a poem by
Denise Levertov that I loved in college, "O Taste and See," about everything I could hope for—a rich, bounteous, saturated life.

> The world is
> not with us enough.
> *O taste and see*
> the subway Bible poster said,
> meaning The Lord, meaning
> if anything all that lives
> to the imagination's tongue,
>
> grief, mercy, language,
> tangerine, weather, to
> breathe them, bite,
> savor, chew, swallow, transform
>
> into our flesh our
> deaths, crossing the street, plum, quince,
> living in the orchard and being
>
> hungry, and plucking
> the fruit.

A few streets from our apartment, a plum tree bore a sign urging passersby to help themselves. Persimmons hang heavy above front lawns. They dropped to the ground and rotted there. The aisles in our local grocery store were stocked with fruits I'd never heard of before I moved here: pomelos, pluots, cherimoyas. At times, the bounty seemed unreasonable, even perverse.

While living in New York, I carried a compass to find my way through the sea of high-rises. Without it I was hopelessly disoriented, blinking blindly at every street corner, losing track of my lefts and rights. I get lost more rarely here. Directions are given in relation to visible natural features—you're either heading toward the hills or toward the bay. I eventually began to find these brackets immensely comforting; they were my first glimmerings of groundedness, offering a sense of scale and orientation. But for a long time I felt adrift.

Early in his first semester, Calder learned to identify local plant species for a class. He would tell me the names of the trees we passed, as if to root me in our new landscape: *Eucalyptus sideroxylon, Pinus radiati, Melaleuca ericafolia.* I watched his mouth but retained nothing. I tried to learn a bizarre new schedule of seasons: snowless winters, summer days that begin and end with fog, spectacularly hot autumn afternoons. I took walks through the neighborhood. But each day it felt like starting over. All it took was a deep inhale and I was blindsided. I blamed the eucalyptus trees that scented the air. I blamed the orange blossoms. The land felt wrong.

A few months after the move, an old friend came to visit me. In a beer garden strung with lights, he leaned in to tell me, "You used to laugh more. Where's your sparkle?" I promptly burst into tears. Later, trying to soothe me, Calder asked, "When was the last time you really felt like yourself?" Like an internal compass finding north, my mind turned to an image of the tree house. The world unfurled around me, beckoning with possibility. It'd been a long time since I felt that way.

After a year in Berkeley, I went back east to see my family. I was itchy for Massachusetts, where I knew what to expect in June: white-and-pink bursts of mountain laurel carpeting the hills, the mounting buzz of insects, grass so green it glows. (In California, summer means yellow fields and dry grass that pricks you when you sit.) I was eager to see my tree house, the memory and significance of which had grown larger than life in the intervening year. My parents warned me against visiting it. "I think you'll be depressed," my father said. I was intrigued.

I grabbed a large stick on my walk to the site. The house slanted slightly away from me. As it turned out, our bolt-through-the-heart-of-the-tree approach was more than one of the oaks could withstand: it had died of dry rot. My father took it upon himself to save the structure—"I couldn't bear to lose it," he tells me now—and quietly replaced the tree with a sturdy wooden post, set atop a large flat stone to keep it dry.

I stood beneath the gaping trapdoor and banged at the opening with my stick, warning away any inhabitants. Praying that nothing would scurry over my head, I climbed up and hoisted myself inside. It took a minute for my eyes to adjust to the dim light, but when they did I was shocked. Half-chewed acorns blanketed the wood plank floor. Some creature had methodically undone my rag rug: cloth strips lay in a rhythm of parallel lines, an incomplete project. The curtains and tapestry I had hung so optimistically more than a decade earlier were chewed and draped in furry chrysalises. My heart thudded, like a book closing. Disappointment drove me back down the ladder, and I stepped gingerly from rung to rung, eyes cast firmly to the ground.

And just like that it was over, or almost. That night I lay in bed and wondered. Tried to feel something new. It was still just me, a day older, still searching for something to build. Something to hold on to. I went back to California. In the air, on the flight there, I thought about my world: now contracting, now expanding, natural as breath. Later Calder curled around me in our bed, his body shaping mine. I began to understand: there's no place to go but forward. The land isn't going to claim me.

The next morning I bolted awake at sunrise, still on East Coast time. Outside, the fog had rolled in; the air was cold and wet. The cherry tomatoes were out in full effect, little red bombs dotting the yard. Walking to the mailbox to get the paper, I reached up to pluck a lemon from my neighbor's tree, barely on tiptoes. The fruit fell into my hands. I pierced its electric yellow skin with my fingernail and held it to my nose. Then I turned for home.

Trespassing

JONATHAN KIEFER

In Wadsworth, Nevada, the issuer of my $142 speeding ticket had straight, white, Erik Estrada teeth. As a highway cop, he was perfectly cast. A Paiute, he was in good shape, alert and lively, and the job of peace officer seemed to agree with him. He behaved officially but not officiously, letting me see the teeth without grinning or snarling, and calmly explained that today—the Saturday before Memorial Day—was historically the deadliest in the whole state of Nevada. He let that sink in. There are plenty of open roads, he said, nodding outward, scanning the horizon, but here it's more densely populated, and we're in a school zone, where children might be playing.

On the highway? I thought. On a Saturday? But I kept my mouth shut because of course he was right; I was busted, fair and square. In these parts, anything more than one person per ten square miles is what passes for "densely populated"; think of how rotten you'd feel if you managed to run over that one person. Plus, his suggestion about the other open roads seemed like a gesture of goodwill. Either he hadn't been around or he'd been looking the other way on the previous day, when I had my generic American-made rental car up to 120 on the road down from Gerlach.

But today he asked if I had a lawful reason for doing 42 in a 25 zone.

I couldn't think of one. To tell you the truth, I was taken aback by the question. I've been pulled over once or twice in my life—call me a lead-foot if you must—but I don't think anybody has ever asked me that. A lawful reason? It occurred to me to have a look at the penal code sometime, just to see what's allowed. The question of lawfulness has always been more existential than administrative in Nevada, home over the years to such tourist attractions as precious ores, nuclear weapons tests, Sinatra, neon-lit scale-model dioramas of world landmarks, instant weddings and divorces, extraterrestrials, loose slots, loose women, wide open highways. We weren't far, as Nevada distances go, from the flat void of the Black Rock Desert, where wheeled vehicles on the ground have broken the sound barrier—traveling upwards of 750 miles per hour—and children rarely play, unless you count Burning Man. None of which can easily be rendered explicitly lawful.

I looked at my traveling companion. Her face was stilled in mild annoyance. For a moment, I considered a dramatic bit about her being in labor and in immediate need of a hospital, but that wasn't about to work with Ellen. Her low threshold for bullshit is one of the reasons she wears this place so well. And besides not looking pregnant, she is my stepmother. I almost tried a philosophical line—the landscape itself is so arresting that it defies you to remain aggressively in motion—but couldn't work it out quickly enough and guessed it would spoil the officer's goodwill. No, I said. No reason.

After confirming my residency in urban California and asking where we were headed (he didn't say "in such a hurry," because we all knew that would be too much), he advised that I was free to contest my citation at the local courthouse. He didn't need to tell me that, either, but I was glad to consider it. Wadsworth's recently refurbished courthouse is a diminutive thing, and it seems more like a set piece than a functional building. It is conspicuous in its context—many of the buildings here are like the trees, dried up, rotting, left for dead but apparently still hanging

on. Busted I was, yes, without a lawful reason, but strangely intrigued by
the prospect of coming back with a prepared defense. In Wadsworth, even
the most mundane of legal wrangles might feel like an authentic round
of roughing it. The little courthouse looks so proud in this town, where
the largest building is the volunteer fire department and the Family Toy
Store advertises "GUNS!"

"Nevada is a state of small population but numerous courts," A. J.
Liebling wrote. Well, for such an implicitly hurried city slicker as myself, curiosity alone is no reason to contest a speeding ticket, and from
the looks of the place, it could use the 142 bucks. Ellen told the officer
that we were headed home, to her house in Palomino Valley, half an
hour away.

Released and under way, we were greeted with a series of increasingly
tolerant speed limit signs. The farther away from that school zone we got,
the faster we were allowed to move: fifty-five, sixty-five, seventy-five, then,
for a while, there was no posted limit at all. The officer had mentioned
that I'd be seeing a lot of cops this weekend, so I kept it reasonable the
whole way home. We cruised smoothly, crossing with a *whump* over the
occasional cattle guard.

The trip allowed me enough time to begin loathing myself, not for the
speeding or the getting caught, but for making another lame and predictable contribution to Native American–Anglo-American relations—for
being almost exactly the young white city-brat carpetbagger he'd been
waiting for. And here the guy had been so gracious, extending to me the
same courtesies he would to a local, by taking me for a libertarian.

Today, I told myself in some ironic, half-scolding narrator's voice, the
Paiute teaches the white man to calm himself, to slow down, to loosen
his too-firm grasp on the idea of getting somewhere, and to pay better
attention to the environment through which he's been allowed to pass.
The Paiute exacts a toll for the white man's arrogance and reminds him
that, lawfulness aside, a place can also be governed by a kind of inherent

authority, the transgression of which, however innocent, can at once make a visitor into a trespasser.

I cannot bear to feel like a trespasser here. This place means as much to me as a place can mean. When I want to get away from it all, or from most of it, this is where I come—this swath of the Great Basin between the Rockies and the Sierras that was once a lake of about eighty-four hundred square miles, called Lahontan. The lake existed during the last ice age, and times have changed, but not as much as they've changed in other places. Most of the lake is gone now, dried up, but you can still find its remnants, the smaller northern Nevada lakes, Tahoe and Pyramid, the latter enclosed by a Paiute reservation, and the Truckee River connecting them. If you're inclined toward civilization, Reno is the best you're going to get. The rest of it, with due respect to Wadsworth and Gerlach and Nixon and Fernley and Fallon and Sutcliffe and Susanville, is raw, rough desert. This is what I'm after.

At an elevation of a mile above sea level, give or take a thousand feet, the sky seems unlimited, and the air is dry and quiet and perfumed by the ubiquitous sagebrush. There isn't much else around in the way of vegetation, just junipers and cottonwoods here and there and—on a few of the many, many rocks—a vivid lichen in shades of rust, yellow-green, and peppermint. Stop moving for a minute and the stillness will clobber you. If you think the city can be pitiless, you should try the desert. Such beauty and indifference combined can consume souls. It encourages total self-absorption but absolves you of the attendant guilt by making you feel very small. Nevada's high desert will make you believe in geologic time. You can feel its impossibly gradual exertion, feel it grinding your bones into the topsoil. Somehow, it feels good. It's quieting, and therefore a relief. There aren't many better ways to make yourself at home in a place than letting it swallow you.

Logic dictates that, on first glance, you may take this place for dead. Actually, it does okay, lifewise. There are networks of California quail, chukars, hummingbirds, eagles, vultures, phoebes, snowy egrets, black-crowned night herons, great blue herons, gulls, and pelicans. There are ground squirrels, pack rats, wild horses, lizards of various ancestry, gopher snakes, rattlesnakes, bobcats, jackrabbits, mountain lions, foxes, coyotes, marmots. There used to be imperial mammoths, American lions, saber-toothed tigers, and even camels. Seriously. They think camels originated in North America. They've found bones.

But that was before the people got here. Not surprisingly, the people are problematic, even in the less-than-densely-populated areas. If you venture onto the nature trail off Highway 447 just north of Nixon, for instance, you'll see a modest sign declaiming the ecosystem's "Ribbon of Life." It's riddled with bullet holes. That is, unless they've replaced it, which I'm sure they haven't. The traffic signs, too, have their share of rusty gunshot wounds. In general, people tend to ruin things, and in Nevada they tend to let them stay ruined. Just by being here—visiting, trespassing—I am ruinous in my way and prone to feeling rotten about it.

The place never fails to move me, in more ways than one. Usually, not long after I arrive here, I get a bad reaction. Something to do with the altitude and dryness, or the aesthetic assault of Reno's slapdash gaud-mod architecture, or the sudden switching on of whatever synapses, formerly dormant, are required to function out here. It comes on as a headache, like a migraine or a horrible hangover but also worse, as if some metaphysical thing inside me has become petrified and must be cracked into pieces and expelled. Most times I'll throw up and feel better. This feels transformative, so I romanticize it into a kind of deliverance, a conversion into some mode of wildness essential for local survival. Then Ellen will pour me a Pepsi or a sauvignon blanc and we'll sit on the deck with some cheese and crackers and talk about books we're reading, or how expensive San Francisco has gotten, or whatever.

It's not going home again, exactly, because you can't do that, and because I didn't grow up here. I got to know the place only after the end of my childhood, though I expect it to keep me young for the rest of my life. Ellen and my father came out from the East Coast in 1988. He died a few years ago, and we buried his ashes, with only the most insouciant of ceremonies, on his own land. Dad loved the hell out of this place, and turning me on to it may be the best gift he ever gave me. But it was also a gamble. He wasn't a gamer, and the only reason you'd ever find him in one of those casinos was to get lunch at the reliably cheap, enormous buffet. But with the desert and me, he chanced it, played the odds. I might have missed the appeal entirely, found it barren and boring. It might have really spooked me. It is a place, after all, where solitude is magnified; my parents' house is four miles from its own mailbox. Worst of all, it might have irreparably pissed me off: You left me in Connecticut for *this?* But sure enough, it took. In the silence I could hear the music. When I came, I made claims, and when I left I always looked back. Being closer, keeping this place in range, has a lot to do with why I finally replanted myself on the West Coast. Its gravity has me.

Now I wonder if it's okay that I have this impulse—after the headache and the vomiting have cleared—to stay here indefinitely, to forsake my urban life once and for all. At my age, would I be weak for making that choice, or strong? Wise, or stupid? The fantasy of holing up here and catching up on reading, writing, and contemplation is not so easily actualized. And there's more to it than the fantasy. It has thrown my rootlessness into relief because it seems so rooted. Whenever my Bay Area friends make the trip across the Nevada border, it's with some Tahoe time-share as the destination. They pile into their Volvos and Subarus, indulging in snowboarding and partying, sophisticatedly recreating in sizable packs. I never want to join them.

Instead, I nose around alone in Ellen's old Toyota pickup with the cracked windshield and the coat-hanger antenna, exploring the dramatically less-crowded environs of Pyramid Lake, the gem of the desert. The notion of a time-share could apply to Pyramid Lake only as an ironic euphemism for the standing arrangement between Nevadans and the Paiutes, whose 475,000 acres surround it. That arrangement allows me the satisfying privilege, completely innocent of urbanite chauvinism, to describe this as a strangely backward American place—here, the Indian reservation is where people go to get away from the casinos.

It is easy to feel as if Pyramid Lake is all yours. Historically, this has been a problem. In 1859, several millennia after the locals had settled in, the American General Land Office decided to earmark the area around the lake for a reservation—but the land wasn't surveyed until 1865 or officially reserved until 1874. In that crucial meantime, there was bloodshed and the beginning of a cooler, more protracted conflict. Whether it has been resolved remains a matter of interpretation.

Before the reservation was formalized, a handful of white ranchers managed to set themselves up on several acres of the area's most agriculturally viable land. Confounding their pioneer-spirited neighbors, however, the Paiutes weren't especially inclined toward agriculture themselves, because, first, they lived in the desert, and second, until their fish supply was decimated by a dam on the Truckee River (Pyramid Lake's only tributary), they hadn't really needed agriculture anyway. So there's always been some tension.

The marina's visitor center has a good exhibit of Paiute history. It explores the legacy of the area's initial discovery by the explorer John Fremont in 1844 and the development that accompanied the California gold rush, four years later. When I saw the exhibit, its poignancy was heightened by the fact that ceiling speakers were blasting Survivor's "Eye of the Tiger."

Scored by the band's suggestions of hangin' tough and stayin' hungry, a placard on the wall read, "In less than twenty years from Fremont's visit, we went from being the richest people in the Great Basin to some of the poorest." Against the tuneful thrill of the fight, the rise to the challenge of a rival, the taking of prey in the night, another placard explained: "We were forced to depend on the white people for our survival. They had destroyed our food sources and taken away our land."

The voice in my head said, Trespasser! Why don't you just buy your soda and Slim Jims and get the hell out of here? Congratulate yourself for spotting the irony, get back on the road, get pulled over, and get that you-probably-think-you're-not-part-of-the-problem look from the Paiute cop, and deserve it.

Okay, I know it wasn't me destroying the food sources and taking away the land. But I'm a product of the culture that did those things. The culture that then went on to produce that God-awful music that I grew up with. So it's no wonder that, when I finally show up here, it's as a reluctant tourist, a fetishist of natural spaces, desperately starved for the better music of dry silence.

When I wrote about this place for a big metropolitan newspaper, it awakened an unsettling possessiveness. Come see this, I implied, it's gorgeous; it'll amaze you. It was a version of what my father had said to me, what I had said to close friends and girlfriends over the years. Ostensibly it was a loving gesture. But I had misgivings. Isn't describing something so purposefully just another way of staking a claim on it? Didn't this make me just another grasping developer? Before long I was fighting hard not to write, "No, stay the hell away from this place. It's mine, goddamn it." Well, here I am, at it again.

I think these places to which we turn for nameless solace will, in the final analysis, gauge our impact on the world more truly than the places in which we live. It doesn't matter if we're here less often and don't know as many people, if we consume fewer resources or make less waste. Even if it's only to make sure the place wasn't a dream, to see what's become of ourselves since the previous visit, we come to be nourished. We make profound demands. Why is it the land's responsibility to keep me young for the rest of my life? Hadn't I damn well better do something for the land in exchange? Maybe telling you about it, bearing witness, is the beginning.

My parents' Palomino Valley house is filled to the gills with rocks, arrowheads, animal bones, fossils, plants, shells, buffed glass, and other stuff gathered from hourslong expeditions of combing, sifting, prospecting. It's a hobby, merely; we search not for the bones of people who killed and died for the sake of owning this land, and not for the landscape's mineral riches, as earlier generations did. Just for the little earthen treasures that strike our fancy on a given day. I've never gone out with a metal detector or anything. It isn't like that. I'm not looking for something in particular. I'm looking for whatever I might find or whatever might find me. I'm looking, in essence, for nothing in particular. A pattern of color, maybe, a pleasing shape. I know it when I see it, and can be almost religiously grateful for that clarity. Sometimes I pick stuff up, turn it over in my hand, carry it for a few paces, and toss it back. Very, very subtly, you understand, *I am rearranging nature.*

If you're a beachcomber, you get it: In so expansive an environment, when you can see to the horizon in more than one direction, and you choose to focus instead on what's right in front of you, what's right at your feet, it may be an act of aggression against your evident smallness in the scheme of things, but it is also inevitably a way of staying connected. And what constitutes the difference between self-imposed myopia and finely honed meditation? Well, when I'm in the city staring at my computer, I get myself all worked up over stupid rhetorical questions like that. When I'm in the desert, I have a good time looking around for interesting rocks.

You could say collecting is a way of converting the exotic into the familiar. There's so much of this stuff at the house, actually, that it's become unreasonable. It's an arbitrary, unregulated collection. It threatens to engulf the furniture, implying that these imported natural elements will soon outnumber and dominate the human-made, and then what will be the point of collecting them? On a grander scale, geologic time will achieve the same end by burying, eroding, reducing objects to rubble. Have we been trying to bury ourselves? The mantra of ecologically responsible outdoorsmanship is Leave No Trace. It becomes a kind of self-erasure. How but by actually being made of its elements can you really call a place yours? How but by being swallowed?

In the final decade of the twentieth century, Nevada's population grew by 66 percent, more than any other state. I saw it. The forty miles between Reno and my parents' house, once empty by anybody's definition, sprouted a new, sprawling development with every visit I made. And they keep coming. Years ago, when a new house went up a few hundred yards away from our backyard deck, my father groused that it was much too close, and I told him he was spoiled. Now I take it back. A lot of the new neighbors are retirees. They've decided to make this place the end of their line. I can understand that, and in a way I'm heartened by the apparent wisdom of their priorities. But I'm alarmed by their numbers. It's still a place of purity, of beauty in roughness and life defying the presumption of lifelessness, but how long will it be before the emptiness, the patience and permanence, is gone—before the cops can't tell you to go find another open road nearby if you want to drive too fast?

I should know better than to think, I was here first. I'm a slow study, but I'm learning. We have too many ways of laying claim to the land. We try to own it, to develop it, to farm it or rent it out to tourists, to collect its detritus or mentally internalize it, to describe it on paper. We point our cars into it and go, unveil it for our friends and lovers, get buried in it. But we're always trespassers, at its mercy, because it never was ours to begin with.

Dad was a naturalist and lifelong teacher of biology. Foremost, he was a bird guy, and something interesting happened on the day we put him in the ground. We came back in the house and gathered solemnly in the living room, saying nothing—until we noticed, one at a time, a golden eagle hovering outside. It swooped and circled and let us look. Ellen said she'd seen a few before but never this close to the house. It had come out of nowhere. It got closer, arcing gently, spreading its enormous wings—kind of showing off a little, actually, now that I think about it—and finally sailed right over the apex of the roof. My cousin Jeremy grabbed the camera and rushed outside, but somehow the bird was already gone. You can see for at least a quarter mile in any direction from this house, and you can count the nearby trees on one hand. It doesn't make sense for such a conspicuous creature to simply disappear from the sky, any more than it made sense for it to simply appear. But around here that seems like the only way to travel.

God in the Cannery

LILITH WOOD

Scenery didn't give me trouble until the day my first pair of Coke-bottle eyeglasses came in the mail. Until I was about five, my parents were under the impression that they were raising an odd and slow-witted child with no interest in planes flying overhead, wildlife, or the stars. My mom would later say, apologetically, "We just thought you were, you know, average. *Real* average." After my kindergarten teacher discovered that I could hardly see, my mom and I took the ferry up to Juneau, because an eye doctor wasn't scheduled to come through Petersburg for a couple of months. A few weeks after our return, a pair of brown plastic-framed glasses arrived.

My mom took the glasses out of their packaging and handed them down to me. We were standing in the kitchen near the iron stove, which had chrome detailing. The sun was glancing around the room, leaving big unruly puddles of light in its wake. Light was a tricky thing for me then, the way it bulged and leaked, but I understood that to be the way of things. I guided the stems of my new glasses over my ears and the shine off the chrome snapped into place. The puddles of light evaporated. The kitchen windows organized themselves into rectangular panes. A picture of what was outside stayed put within straight lines and right angles. My

[223]

uncle's fishing boat was there, tied up at my grandpa's cannery. Beyond the cannery, on the other side of southeast Alaska's Wrangell Narrows, Petersburg Mountain loomed over everything.

Until the day I got my glasses, the mountain was a large, custodial blur. I knew about the little things that I could crouch down to get near or bring close to my eye. I had studied the horsetails, male and female, that grew on the shoulder of the road, and I knew about the forget-me-nots in the ditches. I had examined the mixture of moss, fish scales, crushed mussel shells, and bits of knotted twine that accumulated on the docks in my neighborhood. But I thought that where the mountain ended and the sky began was something no one could be too sure about. I wasn't sure how far away the mountain even was. It was just a friendly, undefined bulk.

With glasses, I saw that hundreds of individual trees grew on the mountain, and they were not all the same shade of green. Some were just dead gray snags. The sky was a concentrated, flat blue screen somewhere behind the mountain. It was very far away, and lines separated it from other things that had other colors in them. Everywhere I looked, then, lines contained and separated things from other things.

Once I could see the mountains, they demanded constant attention. I had trouble concentrating on schoolwork. My eyes always turned toward the windows. I could never get used to the mountains around me because they were always changing. The light shifted throughout the days and the year, the tide sucked in and out, and clouds moved overhead in new ways. It was somehow my job to appreciate all that beauty, and I wasn't equal to the task. I felt unworthy. The mountains were big and majestic. I was small and messy.

By the time I got to junior high, I had noticed that the natural world around me—whales, icebergs, waterfalls, mountains, very large and old trees—showed up often, and suspiciously so, in the standard-issue inspi-

rational posters that my math teacher tacked up around her classroom.
I hated those posters. They were so cheesy, so earnest, and there I was,
trapped inside one. The only thing missing from our scenery was a positive affirmation written across the sky.

The mountains on the mainland were the worst. They were on the
other side of Frederick Sound and had been too far away for me to see at
all without my glasses. They were jagged and icy and caught the alpen-
glow at sunset. It was so Technicolor, so over-the-top, so show-offy. My
sister put it into words one night as we were out walking after dinner.
We rounded a bend in the road and were suddenly presented with that
glowing, toothy skyline. My sister flinched and muttered, "Jesus Christ.
Are *those* still there?"

I got up close to those mountains once, in high school. My surveying class went over to the mainland to measure the face of LeConte
Glacier. LeConte is the southernmost tidewater glacier in the Northern
Hemisphere, and its terminus recedes and advances in a long fjord. It
was a chilly spring day, and the wind blew so hard that one person's job
was to crouch next to the tripod and hold it steady. When we finished our
work, the teacher took half the kids home in a boat. The rest of us went in
a helicopter with a guy named Doc.

In our headphones, over the engine's roar, Doc said, "I'm going to
show you something." We wove through a series of barren peaks before
Doc lowered us down onto a pillar of rock. The pillar rose a thousand feet
above an ice field that was itself two thousand feet above the water. Doc
told us to hop out and take a look. A good chunk of the helicopter's skids
hung off the edge. Everyone piled out. I knew I was getting away with
something magnificent, something someone would have put a stop to
if they'd known about it beforehand. I stepped down onto a flat surface
that was smaller than our classroom. The air was warm and windless,
like nothing we'd felt since the past summer. Not even the thrum of the
large ships below disturbed the quiet. I had to lie down to look over the

edge, because it was too scary to stand. We were the same distance from the ice as the observation deck of the Empire State Building is from the street below it.

Only there was no protective glass or metal in this case, just a sheer drop. And instead of tiny yellow cabs and antlike people, all we saw down there was white. One of the boys dropped a rock, and we watched it disappear. I backed away from the edge and stood in the middle, looking out. Far below us, the islands and channels of the archipelago were laid out like a map. The forested mountains looked peaceful compared to my more immediate surroundings. The bright ice and rocky nunataks against the empty blue sky set off something panicky in my gut. It was more hysterical than holy. I felt like I was trying to stifle a nervous bark of laughter in the most somber moment of a funeral. I felt like I was in a staring contest with God, and if I lost I might just step off the edge and let myself fall. And whether I fell by accident or on a whim, it wouldn't really matter in the larger scope of things.

So when it was time to go, I hurried to get back inside the helicopter and let the engine's drone close in around me. We skimmed down over the beaches and flew back to town alongside the curtain of trees that came right up to the water's edge. The clouds closed in before long and brought with them a measure of relief. It was as if someone had put the roof back on, and I could relax again.

When the clouds came in low, we couldn't see the mountains. Sea, land, and sky were a continuous gray blur. By contrast, my parents' house was small and brightly lit inside. To boats in the channel, it must have looked like a little glowing lantern on the beach. The worse the weather got outside, the cozier it was to be inside. We curled up with books and enjoyed the company of man-made things.

It rained a lot. Alaska is not like Seattle, with its sprinkles and sun breaks. After days or weeks of rain, a listlessness settled in that was nearly as bad as the uncomfortable jangle of beautiful days. My grandma once said, "Alaska is like war. It's either dull as dishwater or way too exciting." During rainy stretches, we adjusted to the dreariness until we didn't know that we were moping anymore. We forgot we were waiting for sun until it finally came out and cracked our moods wide open. Those days spilled over their allotted number of hours and blazed across the gray days on either side of them. We saw our own giddiness reflected on everyone else's faces. We packed whole summers into just one of those long, bright days. I was overwrought, like a little kid on Christmas morning. I knew I didn't deserve so much splendor, and I would have to pay for it later.

But the town existed for fish, not for scenery. People in Petersburg were supposed to work hard and not worry too much about how pretty everything could be. Some kids went out on boats with uncles and fathers, where they were at the mercy of all kinds of weather. Sometimes it rained sideways, and they were seasick and miserable. Sometimes the sun came out and tanned their skin, lightened their hair, and made them squint from the glare off the water. I escaped the weather altogether—and with it the scenery—by hiding inside a salmon cannery.

I grew up with the noises and habits of my grandpa's cannery next door. I knew how it sucked fish from the holds of boats and spun them into cans. My brother and sister and I were tolerated in the cannery as long as we minded the forklifts and stayed away from the machines that could pulverize and slice children as well as fish. From the cannery's central breezeway, we watched bloody carcasses slide by on conveyor belts as cans zinged along overhead on tracks that twisted and turned like little roller coasters. The mouths of long, cylindrical retorts opened and shut with the turning of big metal wheels. Steam hoses belched and hissed. The clincher whirled, keeping a fast beat as it sealed lid after lid. For a few seconds at a time, we flirted with this factory world. Then we'd be on our way back out to the sun and rain, back into the presence of the mountains.

My grandpa died when I was fifteen, on the day that his cannery shut down both for the winter and for good. For the next several salmon seasons, my sister and cousin and I rode our bikes into town every day to work at one of the bigger plants. We disappeared inside the machine from seven or eight in the morning until past midnight, seven days a week, for a long stretch of weeks in the summertime.

I spent a lot of time out in the can-cooling warehouse, where forklifts brought steaming buggies of cans out of the retorts and lined them up in rows. Each wheeled metal buggy carried half a ton of canned salmon. My sister and I trotted up and down the rows of cans waiting in their metal buggies to be stacked on pallets, shrink-wrapped, and loaded into a shipping container. We were quality assurance technicians, the last line of defense before cans left the plant. We had to test the integrity of the seams by running our fingernails around the edges of the lids on the top layer of cans in each buggy. There were no windows in the warehouse, but daylight filtered in through the industrial fans high up on the wall. When the fans were still, early in the morning, I could see a few hemlock trees on the hill across the street.

Sometimes my sister and I worked together, moving in time with each other, lifting, rotating, spinning, and returning each can in one fluid motion. When I worked alone, I left the lids turned up so my sister would know which cans had already been spun. The lid was the only part of the tin that was not covered in dull green enamel. In the dark warehouse, the bare, gold-colored lids lit up like coins in the shafts of sunlight that came in through the fan. Sometimes I fell asleep standing up, leaning against a warm buggy of cans. I was so tired that even when I was awake I was dreaming. Sparrows flew low to the ground ahead of me between the rows of buggies. Sometimes I saw a child perched up on top of one of the retorts, near one of the holes where steam came out. Sometimes I saw a pair of gloved hands resting on the rusted metal rim of the buggy. When I looked up, no one was there.

The inside of the cannery proper was a controlled area, with sanitizing foot and hand dips and air curtains to keep flies out. The workers wore hair and beard nets, and a cleanup crew worked constantly to wash away blood and viscera. Everything was food grade. On breaks, the machinists came in with grease guns and put dollops of gray grease on the joints of the machines. One grinned and brandished his grease gun at me, yelling over the steam hoses, "You could butter your toast with this stuff!" At night the machines were rinsed in a liquid that was described to me as heavy-duty orange juice. I tested the water for contaminants, collecting samples from the cooling water that spilled out of the retorts, from the gush of water that washed salmon eggs into a flume that delivered them to the caviar room, and from several of the hoses inside the cannery. I also had to check the water coming from a spigot around the back of the warehouse. It was just around the corner from the concrete yard where people stood outside and smoked on break. I waded through fireweed and salmonberry bushes, ferns and horsetails, to get to the spigot. Rainwater ran down the corrugated sides of the building and disappeared into a mat of creeping mosses. If it was nighttime, I stood in the weeds a few seconds longer than necessary. Hidden by darkness and the roar of the cannery, I felt like a kid who had been forgotten in a game of hide-and-seek. I breathed in the smell of the ocean and the creatures that lived on the beach. If it was day, I kept moving. I squinted in the light and avoided the gaze of passersby on the road.

The cannery had the habit of stripping away everything but itself, as neatly as its machines stripped a fish of its insides, head, tail, and fins. The plant was a big world, from cold storage to crab alley, from the machine shops to the reduction facility where the odds and ends were turned into fishmeal. Across the street, the mess hall and bunkhouses stood. These things were real, and everything else was suspect. Outside was outside, and inside was inside. Being inside gave us the right to ignore everything that happened outside.

When the can lines finally shut down around midnight, most of the workers shuffled across the road to the bunkhouses and Quonset huts where they slept. My sister, cousin, and I rode our bikes home to my mom's house. If it rained, we almost forgot how rain worked. It seemed as though the drops might not be falling, but just hanging in the air waiting for our bodies to strike them. Our leg muscles were happy to bicycle after a long day of standing and walking on concrete. At home, we gathered around the kitchen table, suddenly alive at the end of the day, talking shop and wolfing down whatever was in the refrigerator. We laughed until our voices brought my mom stumbling downstairs in her nightgown, yelling us all into our little dormers.

In the morning, I would wake up crying because my feet still hurt, and I had to go back. I felt like a rusty, creaking machine that didn't want to start up again. But once I got to the plant and eased into the day a little, I started to smile at everyone again. I smiled almost against my will. It was like a religious calling to smile and laugh and accept the hard candies that the machinists fished out of the breast pockets of their coveralls. But for every glowing, heartening, human thing about the cannery, it also had more bleakness and exhaustion than any other place I've ever been.

Sometimes, around the beginning and end of the salmon season, I had to work at the slime tables in the cannery fish house. This was the hardest work, and it made everything else seem manageable by comparison. I don't know how people did it all summer. Pain shot up and down my body from standing in one place on concrete, and my hands stiffened into claws from gripping a knife in one hand, the cold body of a pink salmon in the other. Coffee breaks were every two or three hours. There was no way to know how much time had passed, and the machines were so loud that we couldn't talk. If we did try to yell over the machines, a lead supervisor would notice and separate us. A mist of pulverized fish blood hung in the air, and some of the workers would be coughing with fish lung by the end of the season.

We wore cotton gloves under neoprene gloves, which were themselves tucked into elastic neoprene sleeves that went up to our elbows underneath our raincoats. If my hairnet itched or my nose ran, there was nothing I could do about it because my hands were bundled up and dripping with gore. I was clumsy with a knife, and if I nicked my neoprene glove just after a coffee break, that hand would be wet and freezing cold for the next two hours, and my next coffee break would be wasted standing in line for a fresh pair of gloves. Just before breaks, the lead supervisors filled aluminum troughs with steaming hot, soapy water and long-handled brushes. Because there was no clock, this was the first indication that a break was near. When the lead made a motion with both hands in the air like he was snapping a twig in two, we all crowded around the basins, sloshing the hot water down our rain-geared bodies, washing away all the blood and guts. Even after I was clean, I doused myself a few more times just to feel the heat run down my body.

I usually took my breaks in the break room with everybody else, but sometimes I found a spot in the hollows of the cannery where I could sleep for fifteen minutes. I rarely sat out on the unloading dock, because it was crowded and busy with forklifts, dock crew, and fishermen. Once I did sit out there, deep into a salmon season. By this time I was a college kid and planning to go back to New Jersey in the fall. It was a pretty day, with less activity than usual. Petersburg Mountain was right there, across the narrows. I didn't have time for scenery, the same way I didn't have time for noncannery acquaintances I saw on the street, the ones who looked clean and well rested. I sat down on the wooden curb on the edge of the dock with my back to the mountain and the narrows. My skin crawled and then relaxed in the sun. The cup of coffee in my hands was giving me some hope of waking up, but not much. I was so tired that I felt like throwing up, and the coffee was bitter and awful. But I liked the feel of it warming my hands through the paper cup, and I liked the smell of it. The sleeves of my sweatshirt had gotten damp sometime in the last shift, and I'd been living with an uncomfortable cold wetness against the inside of my wrists.

I rested my elbows on my knees and stared blankly down toward my coffee and my neoprene-booted feet. I breathed in and out a few times. I rolled my shoulders. I took a swallow. A crack between the dock's rough, creosoted planks ran between my feet. The water of the harbor was directly below me, about twenty feet down. I could see it through the crack. Sunlight slid in beneath the dock and lit up the water so it shone an opaque mint green like beach glass. Small black fish hovered near the surface, barely moving. They were perfect and still, hanging there, surrounded by light. This image filtered up through the gap between the dark, ugly planks and diffracted outward until it filled the space between my feet, sliding into focus. It was a blessing I hadn't asked for, but I knew it was rightfully mine. Finally, I received it gratefully, like warmth.

Looking at this little slice of the picture, I felt in my weariness that the mountains were not separate or majestic. The sky was not far away but near. My feet throbbed inside my boots. I wiggled my toes a little. The wind kicked up, counteracting the sun's warmth. Break was almost over. I knew life was going to start nibbling at this newfound peace almost immediately, but it was all right. I thought, "I'll never tell anyone about this." Then I got up, walked inside, dumped out my coffee, and faded into the next shift.

Courting

ADAM BAER

Some people feel whole, part of the natural order of things, alive, when they see large, hilly swaths of hunter-green grass peppered with pine trees and wildflowers. For me, it's open and flat fault-ridden sheets of pale green concrete, faded red clay, or dusty olive hard-tru imprinted by the zigzagging treads of rubber-soled low-tops. I am a writer, not an athlete. My father is a pianist and businessman, not a coach. And at five-foot-ten and a meaty two hundred pounds, I am nowhere near the level of fitness it would take for me to serve as the casual hitting partner of the last-ranked man on the senior pro tour. Which is why it's so wonderfully bizarre that it's the tennis court—any one, situated anywhere in the world—where I feel most at home.

The fault rests squarely with my father. God bless him.

Crocheron Park, Queens, New York, 1981

Every relationship between two people has to begin somewhere, and—though the history of my conversational relationship with my father can be traced back to story sessions with the *New York Times* on Long Island beaches, Wiffle ball lessons in urban lots, and kid-seat bike rides as he traversed the coastal paths of eastern Queens—the tennis courts of

Crocheron Park, on the edge of New York's Little Neck Bay, are where I remember learning my first lessons in male communication.

Developed in 1935 on a rocky waterfront site that housed the hotel where Boss Tweed hid in 1875 after fleeing Ludlow Street Jail, Crocheron was once a political meeting spot, where smarmy Tammany Hall power mongers cavorted through picnics and clambakes among formidable American elms, sycamore maples, black Japanese pines, and honey locusts. Now a nearly fifty-acre swath of preserved nature, Crocheron was one of the first casual buffer zones between blue-collar Queens and Long Island. It was a naturalist retreat for urban soldiers, where thoughts could be shared, chewed on, and dissolved like cigar smoke into the dewy air without the consequences that might await in more aggressively inhuman city environs.

I met Crocheron when I was just four years of age. To me the grounds were Xanadu, and I was too young to grasp their societal role. I was simply elated that we lived a few blocks away from fields that bore a resemblance to the Smurfs' cartoon landscape. Riding the elevator down our six-story midrise for weekend picnics was a fantastic descent to a natural wonderland unlike the pavement and pigeons and pollution that awaited my friends who lived in crummy wastelands like Brooklyn or the Bronx. There the best nearby parks a four-year-old could see were bumpy asphalt courts, crusty orange swing sets, and brown, uneven lawns.

Crocheron had enjoyed significant buildup in my young, overactive mind. I had seen my father ready himself for trips to the park early each Saturday. He wasn't headed there for picnics without us. He had to wear white, pants-style shorts, thick socks, and a white polo shirt. (He often shouted cryptic questions at my mom like: "Karen, where the hell are my Wilsons?") He had to carry a special bag that held his tennis racquet. (Were there weapons in there?) And he always seemed juiced and just mildly nervous before stepping out the door. (Who would he play with? Would he have to give up my new baby brother if he lost?)

So, that one Friday evening when he returned from work with my first junior-size racquet—a copper-hued spoonish thing with a reinforced throat and a black vinyl cover—I bounced off the walls. The next morning, I skipped my cartoons and woke my mom up early, asking for my whitest outfit (a Star Wars T-shirt and red Adidas runners would do), later zipping down the hall to get the elevator before my dad and I could say good-bye. I had been picked to do battle beside my father. To defend the family. I would not let anyone down.

Riding over to the park was a superhero adventure. We moved through the normal channels of urban life before taking a secret passage into a private world. First, we hit average Queens Saturday traffic, with families buying groceries and Orthodox Jews walking to temple—nothing unusual. But our environs changed as we neared a seemingly exclusive entrance-way, a road from which I could see the tennis courts: the green-tarped, chain-link walls; the Swiss-style stone tennis house where players met each other; the pro shop where priceless weapons of steel and graphite were offered only to the most worthy gladiators.

In an essay called "Golf Is Vile," Thomas Beller writes, "A golf course is nature in stiletto heels. It is nature in stage make-up, nature strapped down and held in place. And at the same time the space feels boundless. To walk out onto a golf course, even a fairly unkempt, unspecial, unleg-endary one, is to imbibe the freedom of an open space, a vista, a sense of unclutteredness, the feeling of simplicity and the earth's bounty, even as one understands that it is a man made creation, highly vigilant towards the natural forces of decay."

A tennis court, however, isn't nature dressed up: it's nature objectified, manipulated, pounded flat by bulldozers and will. It's nature processed, colonized, and elegantly packaged. On a tennis court, space doesn't feel infinite as it does in the rolling hills of a golf course so expansive you can't see its boundaries. A tennis court, explicitly manufactured—grass courts don't look like grass, chain-link fences offer views of what's outside—feels open and closed at once. *You can often see a tennis court's limits and setting at the same time.* It's an honest construct.

In fact, while a tennis court doesn't evoke a traditional feeling of freedom, it evokes the freedom of form. Like a modernist's midcentury home—simple squares and rectangles made of straight lines and clean angles, placed on a desert hill or green flatland—a tennis court reminds you that you're part of a society that has been creative and determined enough to literally make something original out of the land it inherited, while remaining respectful to it.

A tennis court placed in the outdoors is as much a way to think about your place in the world as it is a space to think about your place in the service box. You can look at a tennis court as an example of how man has taken too much freedom with this planet, or you can see it as a beautiful structure, like a mathematical theorem or Mozart sonata—an instance of how man has chosen to express a vision of nature. Except that just like the earth, a tennis court will develop cracks: it will buckle and, without proper care, become a wasteland, a reminder of what once was. A tennis court is a metaphor for humankind's progress and the limits of that progress: it's a product of the industrial, and yet it's most useful to people interested in accessing their primal selves.

Outside Crocheron's main court gate—the absolute boundary between real life and sport fantasy in my introduction to tennis—numerous men in get-ups like my dad's stretched their calf muscles, teased their racquet strings, and swung vicious air forehands, sizing each other up, hopping from leg to leg, and adjusting their sweatbands. These were preparations necessary to enter a defined outdoor space reserved for specific action. An elegantly dressed man called Sid, who looked to be about the age of my grandpa, approached my dad. How was he? Was the elbow holding up? Did he catch Connors in Paris? (When was my dad in Paris? Where was Paris?)

Sid owned the biggest sports store in Manhattan; I could thank him for giving us a deal on my racquet. Dad met Sid by simply coming down to the courts, looking for a game, and talking to as many potential partners as possible. The same way he had met Ira, a lawyer who told my dad how to handle his money when he wasn't shouting at TV criminals like the Joker (that's what lawyers did, I was positive), and Artie, one of Manhattan's most notable restaurateurs (to me, the guy who brought us free ice cream when we went for dinner in the city).

I would later learn that both Artie and Sid gave my dad advice about how to start a company, buy real estate, and just generally deal with adult life as a New York City patriarch. "You have to learn how to get along with other guys, in life," Dad said. "A good way to do this is to play tennis in the park. After a while, you start to make friends, and who knows, you might even meet someone you can do business with. Be a good talker. Start conversations. Don't be afraid to talk to new people. You never know who's on the courts with you."

It doesn't strike me as strange, exactly, but I now suspect that nowhere else in this park—not on the baseball diamond or the soccer field—would my father, a hungry thirty-one-year-old self-made businessman, have been able to enjoy the friendship and counsel of such prominent, learned, and generous men. Which is not to say that these guys didn't play baseball or soccer—or that tennis is (or was) a more elite sport. After all, the entire park once belonged to Tammany Hall, and you can still hear whispers of the controversial discourses that were held there in the far corners of the picnic grounds, the walking paths, the tough-guy football fields.

But there was something cosmically fraternal—paternal, even—about the male-mentorship dialogues that the Crocheron Park courts staged for determined men of various generations pursing aggressive, entrepreneurial lines of work. This much I could pick up, at least in a very abstract, simplistic way, as a preschooler sitting on a bench too high for my feet to hit the ground, sipping sugary Gatorade out of a giant water bottle, and watching the animated, joy-infused body language my dad exhibited as he conversed with his senior colleagues. "Don't slouch when you meet a new friend," he said. "Give him a firm handshake. Look him in the eye. Make some jokes. You might get invited to a doubles game."

Observing these postures and behaviors, I could have been a young lion learning how to attack. Soon enough, a mysterious bell rang and it was my turn. I might never grow old enough to talk about buildings or cars or stocks with Sid and Artie, but I could visit their private, special box. I had my dad with me.

The scene inside the squeaky gate looked like a war zone, a real-life board game moving at the bristling speed of Atari. Thick, developed, high-socked legs slid and skidded from one white line to another. What did the lines signify? Why were there three men standing on one court—two on one side of the net—and four on another? Why were those players fighting? What did it matter if "the hour was up"?

It costs money to play here, my father told me; you have to reserve a time. But some people go over their time limit, and that's bad manners, or "etiquette." Another etiquette lesson: "Don't run over onto another man's court if you hit your ball over there. Just wait for the man to finish his point, look at him firmly but respectfully, and say 'thank you.' A lot of these guys can afford to play at fancy clubs. They play here at the park because they're regular guys. That means respect. You have to respect your opponents."

More practically, saying "thank you" on the tennis court meant you knew it wasn't good form to interrupt a game; it also implied your appreciation for another player getting your numbered ball back to you as soon as possible to avoid that ball getting confused with another. "Penn 1," my father announced to our neighbor. "Ah," he replied, "we're Penn 6." "But what happens if everyone buys Penn 1," I asked? "You hope they don't," Dad said. "And then if you hit a ball into their court, and they return the wrong one, you do your best to figure out which one looks newer, and then keep quiet if you get the better one. Shhh."

It was at these squiggly-cracked public courts, perfumed with a mix of salty Long Island Sound air and the musky, overpriced cologne of Manhattan *machas* (Yiddish for "arrogant big cheese-types"), that I learned how to play tennis as well. That is, to hit. My father, a self-taught player, who, after years of watching and playing, had somehow sculpted his strokes into elegant, Björn Borg–ish spins and slices, started me off the same way he—and Sid, and Artie—lived: practically and efficiently. "Keep two hands on the racquet," he'd say. "Bounce. Hit. Bounce. Hit. Always wait for the ball to drop, Ad, and then hit through it like a gate when it's as high as it's gonna get. Hit firm and flat. Don't try to spin it. Don't do anything fancy. And make sure your feet are set before you swing. This is your court, Ad. Your blank slate. Do something unexpected and powerful with it. Be bold."

And yet no matter how privileged I felt to be where I was—to be peacefully away from the Queens traffic, the elevator and sandlot, sequestered for one whole hour in this pristinely green tree-lined diorama, on special green floors, with all these sweaty athletes and tycoons dressed in white, grunting, hissing, and swearing at each other—I didn't want to comply. "Why can't I hit with one hand like the other guys," I whined, between alternating series of solid shots and mishits.

"Not now," Dad said. "Once you get a rhythm."

A rhythm? I wondered. "But how come you can swat at everything when you play Sid? Why can't you just treat me like one of the guys?"

My pattern of entitlement and impatience would continue for the length of that summer and the one following. Standing on that hallowed ground, I'd watch my tiny, mop-topped shadow do battle with the taller, stronger ones downcourt, the New York summer humidity causing the tar-black, wiry nets to loosen as I smacked two-fisted shot after two-fisted shot right into them. Trying to jump up at the ball like that blonde guy in the watch commercial. To loop my forehand around like a lasso as I had seen the big kid do on the court next me. Defying my father's orders at every step and never receiving the okay to take off that crutch, that second hand, and swing away like a man.

Red Jacket Inn, Hyannis, Massachusetts, 1987

It was clear to me—even at this young age—that a tennis court was a discrete space governed by specific laws. But I was also perhaps a little too aware that the space was a manufactured interpretation—a repurposing—of nature. Inside those chain-link walls, players could act more naturally than they could in the unfenced quadrants of the world they moved through daily.

As a kid, I also played Police Athletic League soccer. I knew that, as soon as I slipped my orange-and-blue reversible soccer shirt on, I could run onto a giant rectangle of grass painted with white lines and essentially act like an animal, chasing a ball in packs with my young bowl-cut friends, all kicking at the object of desire, and each other. But tennis was different. Unlike the soccer fields with their weedy strings of flora, the courts at Crocheron were concrete renderings of grass, and the grass on TV at Wimbledon was finely manicured. More jarring, while men on tennis courts were aggressive—wild, even—they seemed to follow a behavioral code: they performed variations of the same series of actions, never deviating too far from an agreed-upon norm.

The rules on the court let adults act differently than they could at work or at home. Maybe there would be a time in the future, an age I would hit, when there would be no more true opportunities to act so improvisationally. While I desperately wanted to engage in this regimented nature play as much as possible—to perform this tennis show with my dad and eventually get good enough to spar with his friends—the idea worried me. And only as I aged did I realize the comfort I could find in limits, limits imposed on nature, formal organizations of dirt and concrete and metal. In the modernist way of building outdoor structures in reaction to history's most elaborate land developers in order to dialogue with the natural world—to breathe with it.

It's still a matter of argument, of course, whether or not tennis, and hence tennis courts, sprung from the minds of the ancient Greeks and Romans, or the monks of medieval France, where men played a form of handball called *jeu de paume* (game of the hand) across cords tied over a dirt courtyard floor. Nevertheless, players soon decided to wear gloves on their red, callused paws, and then to swing webbed racquets they had fashioned by hand. The game has always evoked images of outdoor mano a mano combat, and this hasn't changed: to wit, the existence of the French word *tenez,* which can be taken to mean "take this."

By the Middle Ages, however, indoor courts were built for European nobility and royalty, a fact that has persuaded many contemporary players to believe the game stems from an indoor activity. Curiously, what they mistakenly consider to be the predecessor of lawn tennis—which is the predecessor of what we play on grass, clay, concrete, gravel, carpet, and sand today—is a game called "real tennis," the most prominent site of which, Hampton Court, still gets play in England. "Real tennis" involves hitting a ball against walls as well, and is played on smaller courts with droopy, as opposed to level, nets with a slight drop in the middle. The invention in the 1850s of rubber tennis balls, which could instantly bounce on manicured lawns, was what really sparked the outdoor game's appeal. Soon players took to empty croquet fields. And by 1866, London's All England Club, where Wimbledon is still held, developed a version of—and a series of court measurements for—what we play today.

For my dad and me, tennis was always a give-and-take, rite-of-passage dialogue, and it was distinctly about being outdoors. Only rarely did we play at indoor court clubs, and we didn't much enjoy it there. Tennis was a chance to get out and away. From work, the piano, the screaming of babies, the nagging of spouses, the stressors of the everyday. To displace ourselves from the internal, and to feel the air on our bodies as we sliced through it in service of running down a ball. It just didn't work as well with a roof over our heads, the sounds of players' grunts amplified by the same metallic walls employed for airplane hangers.

I never mentioned this to anyone when I was a kid, but outdoor tennis didn't seem so different from the limbic outdoor dancing we had seen at Tanglewood, that lush green music-concert place in Massachusetts where my mother and father had studied the piano as college students. The performers' bodies seemed to jerk and convulse and extend in random movements, but they all seemed to be working with and against each other on that tree-lined stage. The only discernible difference between us that I could perceive was that, on a tennis court, I was a soloist—or at least, performing one half of a duet—who had a get-out-of-life-free card for an hour. A chance to work out my tension with an increasingly redemptive blend of artistic expression and exercise.

Of course, at ten years of age, I didn't have the same real-life pressures as my dad. But tennis was as much an escape for me as it was for him. I was running from my whiny brother, bratty neighbors, increasingly frequent parental arguments, and the closing in of the apartment walls. I was running from childhood, trying to grow up in an animal's cage where I didn't have to be (too) polite if a meatball hanging in the air and just begging to be pounded came my way. I was finding a way to deal with anger, whether it had nothing, or everything, to do with my father. (Why did he scream at my mom sometimes? How come we couldn't afford the Air Jordans I wanted? Why did we have to leave Queens for fish-stinky Long Island?)

My dad, for his part, learned to be Dad on the court, learned to teach me how to behave myself in an adversarial but social situation that could reappear at school, a first job, a party, or the street. When to strike with power and when to toss things off with finesse; where personal boundaries of stress, fear, exertion, joy, and physicality lay; just how aggressive two loving family members—one a young family man with new financial responsibilities, one the eldest kid in a family trying to grow up as fast as possible—could be with each other and not seem tragically mad or resentful. Crosscourt forehands. Topspin backhands. Keep your second hand on, Ad. Hit on the rise.

Use me as your model for a real-life enemy, the increasingly challenging, but always returnable, shots my father launched at me seemed to say. Practice on me, so when I can't be there for you, I'll know you know how to handle yourself. You are safe in this box with me, but when we leave and the gate swings closed, you may have to be on your own. You will have to know when to spin something and when to slice it. When to run fast after something you need to save, or to know when it's best just to let it go. When to smash a winner, and when to let someone else think he's got your number.

Tennis was, and remains, a mostly physical conversation held in a controlled environment built explicitly for that purpose. And heading down to the courts became a private, special, nearly impermeable block of time for me and my father. This was before cell phones. No one could contact us on a tennis court, though I suspect that, even if they could have, my dad wouldn't have let them. Which made Vacation Tennis—the game we would enjoy on those rare few days a year when Dad was completely disconnected from his daily life—an even more special activity. My dad almost always made sure that, wherever we were to take our annual summer holiday, we would have tennis courts at our disposal. It was a vacation within a vacation, he said. From a vacation. It was bliss.

As it happened, we spent summers in one of the American locales most akin to Hampton Court. Camelot, or rather the Kennedy Compound and its bevy of tennis courts, was just a stone's throw from the Hyannis, Massachusetts, setting of the Red Jacket, an oceanfront family resort on the calm, level shoreline of western Cape Cod, where sea grass and sand made its way onto the cranberry composite courts, and where we as a family could stay in a gray-shingled bungalow with a stove on which my mother could boil lobsters. Why were two of our most favorite outdoor tennis courts so deeply connected to the historical trade of social and economic power, the colonizer's concept of government, and political structures?

It's less curious when you examine the history of the tennis court, and the role it served in Europe, which paralyzed the sport for decades with stigmas related to class, race, and gender. More interesting to me, however, is how family dramas could play themselves out in these green, white-lined boxes. For all their civility, tennis courts are revelatory, confessional spaces that, in their uncommonly organized nature, expose contradictory elements, forcing powers to struggle with one another or vibrate in rhythm, or both. Tennis courts are like music staffs. Systematic but open to invention, they're breeding grounds for anomie and communion altars at once—natural imaging centers where you can't help but submit to a CAT scan of your spirit.

"A person's tennis game begins with his nature and background and comes out through his motor mechanisms into shot patterns and characteristics of play." The *New Yorker* magazine writer John McPhee offered this maxim in a 1969 article, "Levels of the Game." "If he is deliberate," McPhee went on to say, "he is a deliberate tennis player; and if he is flamboyant, his game probably is, too. A tight, close match unmarred by error and representative of each player's game at its highest level will be primarily a psychological struggle, particularly when the players are so familiar with each other that there can be no technical surprises."

Grasping that concept like a Brahms concerto or the New York State incorporation tax—both of which he'd mastered—my father never used his patriarchal authority to make me feel small on the tennis court. Quite the contrary. He had an innate gift for imparting to me the physical tools and semiotic postures I needed to compete while pitting me against a powerful but not too aggressive character to keep me challenged. You improve at tennis, like most things in life, when you play someone who is better than you. You improve more quickly at tennis, however, when you play someone who is better than you but has your best interests at heart. Nowhere was this grooming technique more present in my father's behavior than on the seaside Red Jacket courts when, one day in 1984, he demonstrated my value to him, as a true man-in-training.

He had been fighting with my mother about something for the past couple of days as my brother and I bodysurfed, played ping-pong, and socialized with some of the other vacationing kids. It might have had to do with a mortgage, or in-laws, or the in-laws' mortgage. All I remember was tension on vacation—a catastrophe that should never happen, according to my father's dictum about what the word *vacation* meant, and something I dreaded as I grew increasingly aware of how hard it was to keep a marriage alive.

The walls of our cottage weren't terribly thick, and it was evident to me that the neighboring families probably heard the spats. My father's voice, as consoling as it could be, also carried better than most operatic bassos, and he never exactly felt embarrassed about others hearing it. "Let's hit, Ad," he barked at me, marching from the room he and my mother shared. (Hit?!) "We signed up for three; this is our hour." Court time was at a premium at resorts like the Red Jacket. If you weren't in the mood for tennis when you had scheduled your time, I was quickly learning, it was time to get in the mood.

By this point in my childhood, I had observed my parents' argument styles. My mother withheld at first, said a few smart, simple comments that dug deep, and then internalized her anger, pulling away. My father let his anger out, often speaking sharply and loudly, with consonants so pointed they could slice you in half. It was rather similar, I noticed, to how, say, Björn Borg, the calm Swede, might fare against John McEnroe, the brash New Yorker, or Jimmy Connors, the testosterone-fueled heartland slugger. The only problem was that my father rarely diffused his anger at the end of an argument. Like I had begun to do, he let it follow him into his next activity.

I was scared to face this fury on the tennis court, even though I knew my dad didn't have it in for me. As we walked from the shady campus to one empty, seagull-shit-stained court, I felt, in some way, that I might be in for quite a lesson. I was right.

Surprisingly, my dad didn't say much as we entered the protected, foreign—but strangely familiar—field. The silence was unusual, jarring. But soon we were rallying back and forth, my father grunting to himself about an old elbow injury as I waited for the tension to break. On the next rally, I realized how angry I was. Why was I the older brother? Why did I need to be thinking about this? Why was I afflicted with this responsibility? I wasn't just angry at my father and my mother, I was angry at the world.

It came out in my hitting. Every even-paced center shot my father fed me I pounded crosscourt, my two-fisted forehand still my game's most distinguishing feature and quickly becoming a unique weapon I'd choose to keep in my arsenal. Bounce, hit, bounce, hit. Fuck that, I said to myself the way I had heard my fast-living friends say, as I slapped each shot harder and harder, exploring just how well my newly developing muscles and sense of timing could groove together. See if you can return this one. *Slam.* See if you can catch the next. *Uhhh.* I'm tired of being the go-between here, the mature one. I'm on vacation too. *Wapah.*

Soon, my father picked the balls up and came to the net. "I need some water, Ad," he said. I followed. He proceeded to ask me what was wrong. I said I didn't know. He understood. He was sorry he had fought in front of me. It's just that he and my mother differed on a number of issues. Then he told me, quite candidly, how he often felt in conflict with my mother—secrets I will not even divulge in a confessional essay; secrets, perhaps, a ten-year-old shouldn't have heard. He often felt marginalized, let's say. He said you don't just marry a woman but a whole other family as well, and that that can complicate matters. That there had been a lot of pressure on him this year. The business wasn't doing well. The house was expensive. A doctor had phoned with troubling results. My brother needed new cleats. Grandma and Grandpa were difficult.

It was a lot for a ten-year-old to take. Even one who read Russell Baker's column in the *New York Times Magazine* and bragged about dreams of being a psychiatrist. Still, my parents had treated me like an older kid as long as I could remember, and my father's confessions didn't seem inappropriate. Rather, I welcomed the admissions, the unveiled thoughts, the secrets. Inside this see-through action booth—this sparring cube we had to reserve by the hour—my father was treating me as an equal. I decided to return the favor and give him some advice. You know Mom acts this way, I said, so don't treat her that way. You know you react to certain things with Answer X; next time, try Answer Y. I was precocious but observant. I knew how my parents drove each other crazy, and how they could tweak their actions to help things improve. My father listened. He thanked me. He respected what I had to say. "Pretty soon," he said, "we could play some real matches, and I'll be worried about losing. Your two-hander's coming along." "I still want to take the left hand off," I said. "That's your decision now," he replied. "But I don't know—you sure are making me run the way you're hitting them."

"I love your mother," he told me. "I know," I said.

Kennedy High School, Bellmore, Long Island, New York, 1993

What's vexingly comforting about tennis courts is how different they can look and feel, how many different places they can exist—from the mountains and deserts to office-building roofs and Malibu backyards—but how they always stay the same, at least to a certain degree. We can blame this on math and aristocratic tradition. Tennis courts—unlike baseball fields, surf spots, bike paths, and swimming pools—are always the same size: thirty-seven feet wide by seventy-eight feet long; the service court extending back from the net in both directions for twenty-one feet; the net measuring three feet six inches high (when a court is a maintained well) and forty-two feet long from pole to pole (even when a court is ignored).

A tennis court is a straight-lined grid of decisive quadrants, like that which Picasso used to pioneer Cubism, or on which I drew erroneous sine curves to win me extra help sessions with my attractive high-school math tutor. A tennis court is a planned space, a boxing ring, an improv theater, a panopticist's delight. In the same way that one learns to type, a kid who grows up on a tennis court can learn awfully quickly where on the surface he is standing—from the number of steps separating him from the slightly raised white lines of paint that make up the perimeter of the doubles and singles courts, the latter of which fits inside the former. You're never lost on a tennis court, in other words. It's a map.

Of course, there are numerous types of surface compositions and colors that can distinguish a tennis court. Grass, for instance, is often found in elite tennis clubs, clay is more common in warm environs, and true American-style purists relish the so-called hardcourt composition—a blend of asphalt or concrete covered with acrylic paint into which texturizing sand has been mixed—employed for the new blue courts at the U.S. Tennis Association Tennis Center in Flushing Meadows, Queens, where the U.S. Open takes place. The U.S. Open, of course, used to be played at a grass court club in Forest Hills. Later, at its new campus, it offered green hardcourts. The new blue surface color is, most aficionados agree, a measure intended to improve tennis watching, both from the extreme heights of the center's new giant stadium and for TV viewers, who had complained that the green color, evocative of classic green grass as it may be, didn't contrast enough with the fluorescent yellow fuzz of tennis balls.

What distinguished my crumbly concrete high school courts—located just up the block from my childhood home in Nassau County, on the south shore of Long Island—from these other, prime examples was that they were rather topographically uneven. In short: hilly, bumpy, and unusually sloped. Each one. Differently.

My father explained to me early in life that it had something to do with how the section of the town we called home—atop a finger-shaped peninsula that juts out into the Great South Bay—is, at its core, landfill. At some point in the 1960s, after the national success of the Levittown suburban development located in the belly of Nassau County, between the Atlantic Ocean and Long Island Sound, pioneers started to develop—and build large suburban homes on—marshy areas south of the Long Island Railroad, which travels east to west, with numerous veins extending in all directions, from New York City to Montauk Point.

My town, Bellmore, was one of the areas chosen for development, and soon a separate high school to service the children of the region's nouveau riche was required. But, as my father explained, the school was needed quickly because greedy nature-developers had moved too many people into too many homes at too rapid a pace. The county also didn't have too much money to indulge these developers. So corners were cut, and lumpy tennis courts laid.

Growing up so close to these courts, I began to learn each one's idiosyncrasies, and this tended to help my game—especially when I played against my father, who rarely hung out at his son's high school instead of going to work, and who often preferred to play on more formal and better-maintained park courts when he had the time.

In an essay called "Derivative Sport in Tornado Alley," David Foster Wallace discusses how tennis courts were built in the flatlands of the Midwest, which is, strangely enough, topographically similar to—if slightly more even than—level, landfill-rich Bellmore. "The terrain's strengths are also its weaknesses," he writes. "Because the land seems so even, designers of clubs and parks rarely bother to roll it flat before laying the asphalt for tennis courts. The result is usually a slight list that only a player who spends a lot of time on the courts will notice.... All but the very best maintained courts in the most affluent Illinois districts are their own little rural landscapes, with tufts and cracks and underground-seepage puddles being part of the lay that one plays."

Later in the essay, the writer explains how, as a young math wizard who was especially quick on his feet, he figured out the complicated wind patterns that blew across his land's beloved courts. Soon he could analyze the air vectors and use his natural speed to beat opponents with better shots. And as his opponents grew in size and puberty set in, leaving him relatively small and weak in comparison, he lost his edge and began to lose matches—despite his preternatural understanding of the built landscapes on which his newly burly friends became victors.

Of course, David Foster Wallace didn't publish his tennis thoughts until I was in college. But being slightly overweight, and not the tallest candle on the cake, I realized pretty quickly as a kid that I, too, could beat my fast, professionally taught friends if I simply thought about the unique topography of the court on which we happened to be playing. I observed how the south side of Court 3, for instance, tended to slope up, and how there existed a barely visible divot that collected an inch of rain or dust just right of center on the north side of Court 6. I spent lots of time on these courts, playing on the tennis team, after school, and well into dusk on each weekend day, to be sure.

So when my father and I ended up there on a Saturday or Sunday morning, I knew what I was doing. Somewhat evilly, I admit, I realized that I could seem even better if I simply used the land's slope to my advantage. I could hit into the deep ad-court pocket of Court 4's north side, for example, since my father didn't hit running forehands as well as he hit running backhands; I could slice short drop shots into the shallow service box of its deuce court, because I knew it hurt my dad's back to bend down to reach such a ball (if he could even trudge uphill to get to it in time, that is). After all, this was a teenage opponent he faced. I was not, as a rule, above doing everything I could to defeat the hero who gave me the tools to fight. My dad had recently stopped letting me win. But I wasn't exactly in that generous, truly mature mental space that one who believes in karma tries to stay in as a mindful, humanistic adult. I was in tenth grade, for God's sake. It was in vogue to be a schmuck.

That changed pretty quickly, though, on a day when my father and I were slugging it out in the August heat. Giant mosquitoes and swarms of gnats buzzed in from the high-rent, canal-side homes, where they had presumably eaten a gourmet breakfast, and the courts were as busy as ever with pods of alpha male college kids, pumped with Starbucks and Gold's Gym braggadocio, pounding forehands back and forth. I was hitting winner after winner as the sweat poured down my father's face, and I didn't feel particularly sympathetic when one of my smashes bounced onto a neighboring court, on which two considerably strong-looking guys in their twenties were attacking each other while speaking awfully loudly about their experiences with some girl at a bar. "Thank you," my dad said in his formal, raised-in-the-elegant-New-York-City-Park-scene way. The duo finished their point and ignored my dad, and we both stood in silence. Then one of them looked at our ball, and the other smiled, returning to a discussion about his sexual exploits as they rallied again, fireball after fireball blazing over the net. "Thank you," my dad said again. Still nothing. Then: "Guys, think you could return our ball to us?"

The duo stopped rallying and looked at my dad, apparently annoyed that he had interrupted their game, their conversation, their bonding. I began to feel guilty. This had been my fault. If I hadn't hit so aggressively, the ball wouldn't have traveled off our court. If I hadn't been so intent on proving myself to my father, I would have played more responsibly. If only I had—

"What, this?" one of the guys asked my dad as he raised our ball in his hand.

"Yeah," my father barked back, getting angrier, and assuming the pose and aggressive behavioral mode I'd feared as a kid. "Penn 1. *Thank you.*"

"Thank you, fat ass!" the young guy said, smacking our ball over the fence deep into the high school's football field, a hundred yards away. "Now go fuck yourself! Or you want me to come over and show you what I mean, motherfucker?!"

Silence. Then, worry.

I looked at my father. He was still huffing a bit from the boot camp I'd been giving him. He wasn't particularly well muscled, after years of working himself silly at a family business, developing insomnia, scrimping to pay for lavish Bar Mitzvahs, summer camps, and violin lessons. And then I looked at this young man—this Doberman of a twenty-something. Stupid, strong, and bursting with adrenaline. Ready to do something moronic, explosive, and dangerous.

"Let's hit, Ad," my dad said to me, turning away from the barking aggressor.

"You don't want some of this, old man?" the guy continued. "'Cause you know I'll kick your ass, hahah. You piece of garbage." Then he and his friend laughed louder, imitating my dad's posture and voice.

"Bounce, hit. Bounce, hit, Ad. That's it. Now down the line. I'm coming to net. Hit to me. Good. Now your backhand." We continued to hit for the next twenty minutes, and eventually the hotheads on Court 3 returned to their sparring match, speaking even louder and occasionally laughing in our direction. But I couldn't forget what had just happened. Inasmuch as I felt good about the fact that my father had stood up for me and not succumbed to the bullies, I knew then, for the first time, that we were equivalently vulnerable in the world. My father wasn't an all-powerful symbol of strength. I wasn't yet a well-muscled twenty-something. Would I ever become one? Or did my father's fate await me? Would I grow up to be a respectful, honorable guy who would never ascend to true alpha male–dom? Maybe that was the trick: Be strong when you need to be, but it's not necessary to be a physical threat. Use that energy to do something more interesting with yourself. Think.

My dad had showed reason in the situation. He hadn't egged the guys on, hadn't pressed them further than he needed to. He accepted their bullshit and stood on higher ground, teaching me how not to trip into the trap in which so many bullish young men fall. But at the time, all I could think about was how, if the guys had wanted to fight, I might have had to protect my dad. Or at least help him fight and eventually lose. I wasn't tagging along to the courts anymore. I had as much right to be there as my father did. Both of us could easily feel the wrath of this more obnoxious generation. Tennis court etiquette had clearly changed.

This time, my father and I didn't speak about what had happened on the car ride home; there was no postgame catharsis, no admissions. We both just drank our water, cooled down, and entered the house to find my mother and brother sitting at the table ready to eat lunch with us. We had had one of many private moments on the tennis court that would never see the light of day again (except perhaps in essay form). It was time to move on and reenter our day-to-day roles. The fence, nets, cracks, volleys, and concrete adventures were behind us, for now.

Le Parc Suites Hotel Rooftop, West Hollywood, 2005

I'm hitting easy now, the rugged outline of the Hollywood Hills and their white, modernist, stacked-box homes in high smoggy relief, as my father and I enjoy a relaxed rally on his first trip to California, where I've been living happily for a year now since leaving New York and a turbulent, early-twenty-something life. West Hollywood, and my parents' hotel, sits in a somewhat flat swath of Los Angeles, with the hills to the north, downtown's handful of skyscrapers to the southeast, the crime-ridden cities of Inglewood and Compton farther down the line, and lots of cars in sight at every turn. Like Los Angeles in general, it's spacey playing tennis up here. For one thing, the ball bounces higher and quicker than normal—something, the hotel manager tells me, about building a court on a rooftop capping numerous floors of midrise suites. For another, we can't exactly run through the fence locking us in if the mood should strike is. If we did, we'd fall off the building and onto someone's Maserati. It's not a tennis-friendly scene for me, being on a rooftop court just a few yards away from Paris Hilton look-alikes sunning themselves by a hotel pool with little dogs yapping at their fashion magazines, the cheap aluminum of their Smartphones glimmering in the white light known only as the L.A. midafternoon shine. But it is a truthful, if embarrassing, reality of where I live now, and I want to share that with my parents. I want them to see my current world.

I left a New York City home for Los Angeles, strangely enough, to experience the outdoors more. I didn't breathe enough air in Manhattan; didn't get outside enough; didn't have mountains to climb, oceans to swim in, coyotes to dodge on my way out for coffee. I could have asked my dad to play with me on the courts of Griffith Park, the gigantic mountainous preserve just north of my apartment in the Los Feliz Hills, where Charlie Chaplin and Cecil B. DeMille once lived. I could have asked him to play paddle tennis—a faster, more casual derivation of the sport—with me on the street-vendor freak show known as the Venice Beach boardwalk, replete with scents of cheap swag, body odor, Castrol, and, of course, the ocean. But I'm older now, and my parents are older, and it is easy to simply hit with my dad at the hotel, since a court is just an elevator ride up from the room where he takes his afternoon nap.

L.A. is new to my family of traditional New Yorkers. The city's peculiar blend of urbanity and nature—being, say, five minutes south of rustic Mulholland Drive horse farms while also being five minutes from an Orthodox Jewish neighborhood and minutes east of glitzed-up Rodeo Drive, where the pool girls likely purchased the merchandise resting comfortably in their shopping bags—is a novel experience. How better to introduce my father to my new life, my new reality, in all its positives and negatives, than with an elevated tennis conversation? Except that, just like at our other court sessions, we don't exactly converse. Tennis doesn't make it easy to speak while playing; there's a lot of ground for voices to cover. Rather, we just smile, say, "Good shot, *nice!* And sneaky . . ." and make sure to coat our shots with topspin to stay within the lines and avoid scampering into the invisible wall keeping us up in this skybox. Bounce, hit. Bounce, hit. "You hit forehands with two hands?" Dad asks. "You don't remember?" I say. "You taught me that." "I know," my dad says. "I just thought you took the second hand off at some point. Anyway, you're stroking them. What's the difference?"

Thirty minutes or so pass. The pace and consistency of our rallies start to decrease, something that used to happen at the hour mark. As I embarked on an independent later-twenties life over the last few years, playing less and less tennis with everyone, my father's back has gotten worse, resulting in his having even less ability to chase down balls. "Let's get a drink," I say. "See what Mom's up to." We make our way down to the pool, where my mother is sitting with a hat and sunglasses, the quintessential New Yorker with sensitive skin and a look of unadulterated joy as she sees how happy both her men are to have spent some time together, their lactic acid flowing.

"I'm starting to play more tennis," I say to my dad, as he opens his copy of the *Los Angeles Times*—as luck would have it, an issue with a big article written by his son. "That's great, Ad," he says. "How are you finding partners?" I downshift into a funny discussion about how I use my younger brother's Princeton alumni network to meet new tennis dates; my college doesn't offer the same social opportunities. I tell my parents how lots of courts here are free—it's just that you have to drive to them and then stake them out so a juggler, panhandler, or movie producer doesn't commandeer them for his or her oh-so-specific purposes. It's vacation conversation—a visitation update—but it's also restorative. It's a way for me to let them know that I'm making a home in my new part of the world. There are tennis courts here, and I've used my own specific brand of ingenuity not just to find them but also to find new people with whom to play—to enact the social-magic-tennis-court-stage for me and perhaps follow in my father's young-adult steps, meeting new colleagues and friends, learning new things about the world (but substitute leads on new digital music compression techniques for tax advice). That I can always walk into a green, fence-lined box here and feel something familiar is something I need my parents to know. They will worry less.

It's curious how humans sometimes have to build designated spaces that look like nature—set in nature, with a view of nature—in order to have a place where we're allowed to be natural, primitive, unhinged. For me, it was always easier to connect with my father on a tennis court than almost anywhere else, and for that reason it's also one of the most familiar constructions I can think of: it's where I socialize well with anyone, where I feel most relaxed, where I can be alone without feeling lonely. I often, for instance, have to write stories that take me into foreign neighborhoods and places. When I see that a giant house or hotel has a tennis court, I get excited. I have always lived near tennis courts. Knowing they exist, just a block or two or seven from my house, makes a new residence feel like home. I sign leases based on this knowledge. Sometimes, to my father's dismay, these leases are for spaces with poor door locks, bad parking, or shoddy craftsmanship. Location, I tell him. When I need to, I say, I can head down to the courts and serve a few. I can always park on the street.

The more I play tennis, and the more tennis courts I visit, the less I begin to miss my dad, my childhood, my family home in New York. And that's not a sad thing, exactly. When I visited my college courts, as a younger man, I felt anxious; what was I supposed to do there alone?

Now that I've been on my own a while, I feel my father with me. In me. As I meet new partners, mixing matches with shoptalk or friendly social repartees, I incorporate the conviviality, joy, and elegance that a trip to the tennis courts always brought out in my father. I incorporate him into my person—finally in a conscious way. I dialogue with him, with his traditions, and, hopefully, impart some of that green-boxed glee to whoever happens to have met me at the park, rooftop, boardwalk, hotel, or school in that seemingly routine but unfailingly memorable chapter of my perpetual tennis court romance.

Eden and the Underworld

TRACI JOAN MACNAMARA

The ad that Britain's Sir Ernest Shackleton placed in a London newspaper seeking recruits for his infamous 1914 transantarctic expedition read: "Men wanted: For hazardous journey. Small wages, bitter cold, long months of complete darkness, constant danger, safe return doubtful. Honour and recognition in case of success. Sir Ernest Shackleton." Unfortunately, the foreboding ad was an accurate predictor of the trials that Shackleton and his twenty-eight men faced while in the Antarctic. When their ship, *Endurance,* sank after being crushed by the pressure of the ice pack that surrounded it, the crew survived the long dark winter by clubbing seals for food and even eating their own dogs. Many months later, they rowed through frigid waters to safety in three small boats, several of the men suffering from severe frostbite and near-starvation. Shackleton failed to meet the expedition's objective but, miraculously, all his crew made it home alive.

This type of adventure wasn't exactly what I was looking for when I first went to Antarctica, but I recognized in myself a spirit of adventure, of earnest seeking-out, similar to what Shackleton and his men must have felt before setting out. Nearly a year before I quit my job and boarded a plane to Antarctica, I had been sitting in Wooglin's coffee shop on Tejon

Street in downtown Colorado Springs. Hour after hour, I refilled my mug at twenty-five cents a pop. I could have stayed all day in that booth and just watched people pass by the big windows in the front room, but I had sixty-six essays to grade, and they were sitting in a big pile in front of me.

I was emotionally spent, having gone through the breakup of a difficult relationship that had slowly and painfully come to an end. In that relationship, I had lived with the hope and promise that things would one day turn into something more than they were, but the lonely and disappointing reality I finally faced was that the relationship wasn't working and this fact would not suddenly, or even gradually, change. When it was all over, I found myself living a life sorely lacking in adventure and love. It was January, and it was cold.

I was cold.

While I sat there, a friend I hadn't seen in more than a year and a half walked in, and I felt happy to see him. But I was also struck with the realization that my life had not grown better—or even different—during the time that he had been gone. He had just finished fourteen months as a mechanic at McMurdo Station, Antarctica's largest base for scientific research and exploration, and I laughed out loud at the wild stories he told about the station and the months he'd spent traveling in Europe before returning to Colorado. What I remember most about that afternoon, though, was his collection of photographs. On his laptop computer, my friend scrolled through photo after photo of snow and ice, revealing to me open spaces so vast and white that I wanted to shout out at the sight of them. Antarctica was Eden, I thought—a landscape more pristine and beautiful than anything I'd ever seen. It was untouched, divine.

The images left a strong impression on me, and during the weeks that followed, thoughts of the antarctic landscape kept coming back to me. In the literature of the medieval courtly love tradition, a person falls for his beloved at first sight: Cupid shoots an arrow straight into the lover's eyes. The arrow is barbed, and it takes the shortest path through the lover's eyes to his heart, where it becomes lodged. Fixed, the arrow can't be removed, and the lover is tormented by the sight of his beloved. That was how it was for me when I saw Antarctica.

In the absence of any real love in my life, this new love for a place began to grow in me. A vast and frozen landscape was lodged in my heart, and I couldn't stop thinking about it. In love with the idea of the place, I wanted to go there to work, to see it for myself.

Unlike Shackleton's men, I was not recruited to work in Antarctica. I actively applied for several different jobs at the Raytheon Polar Services Company's annual job fair in Denver—shuttle driver, administrative assistant, and power plant operator among them. With no trade skills or specific experience that would qualify me to drive a van, organize recreational activities, or even wash dishes, I wasn't offered a job. But I was granted a phone interview for an alternate position as a general assistant. After being told I was interviewing for a job that would require me to do physical labor outdoors in Antarctica—and that I could be called to work at McMurdo with as much as two months' or as little as two weeks' notice—I was asked the following questions:

"Do you have any experience operating snow-tracked vehicles?"

"Do you have any areas of mechanical expertise?"

"Do you have any extreme cold weather experience?"

"Would you be able to cook for scientists at remote field camps?"

Since the latter question was the only one I answered with an even slightly affirmative response, I'm not sure why I was offered the position, which had the potential to turn into a job for the austral summer's science season—October through February—when the sun would shine all day and the temperature would climb to a relatively balmy thirty degrees Fahrenheit. But I accepted the alternate position, hoping that a deploying position would open up and my alternate status would change.

Five months later, I got a phone call from Raytheon Polar's corporate offices in Denver offering me the position at McMurdo Station and giving me two weeks to pack the things I'd need for the next four months in Antarctica. Without having ever been paid to do physical labor in my life, I quit my job teaching writing at a university in favor of suiting up each day at McMurdo in work boots and insulated Carhartts. Along with seven other general assistants, I'd be assigned some type of grunt work every morning—perhaps chipping ice with a pickax, painting frozen metal storage units, or delivering fuel to scientists at remote field camps.

I'd never been asked to assist anyone in such a manner before, and I had certainly never worn Carhartts and work boots on the job. But somehow, at McMurdo, I got to join a population of twelve hundred scientists and support staff where these things were just as common as suits in New York or flip-flops in Long Beach, California.

On the day I flew more than twenty-four hundred miles south from Christchurch, New Zealand, to Antarctica in a LC-130 Kiwi military cargo plane, I got my first real look at Antarctica. I had never seen ice on water like that before. Big chunks of it, jagged like broken glass, floated on the surface of a sea the color of sapphires, all of it glittering in the sun. Even more impressive than the water I saw below was the icy land I saw ahead.

There Antarctica crouched, a series of ominous glacial peaks on the horizon, a lonely mass made almost entirely of ice and hard-packed snow. I anticipated that I would experience, among other things, a sketchy landing on an ice runway, frostbite, crevasses, killer whales, whipping winds, and lots of quiet time for the next four months. My expectations got upended rather soon. After a quick jolt no greater than that of a Delta 747 touching down at Dallas–Fort Worth, I was birthed, pushed out of the plane and onto an immense blanket of snow and ice, a landscape where I knew I wasn't fit to survive in the wild for more than a few hours.

As I was shuttled by van into McMurdo Station proper, the image of Antarctica I'd had in my mind confronted the reality of the place. I'd been plopped down on the ice shelf between continental Antarctica and Ross Island, whose rocky coast was visible across the great white web of ice that entangled it as if it were a tiny black fly, connecting it to the continent. Behind me were some of the most impressive mountains I had ever seen: the Royal Society Range. Part of the Transantarctic Mountains, which rippled three thousand miles across Antarctica from one ice edge to the other, the Royal Societies rose abruptly from the ice shelf. Standing shoulder to shoulder, their scoured glacial peaks shone golden in the afternoon sun while dark shadows danced across their wrinkled faces. Ahead of us, McMurdo Station, cradled on Ross Island between scree-covered hills, grew larger as we drove up from the pancake-flat sea ice.

I don't know if I had ever envisioned vehicles or buildings in Antarctica, but as we drove on the only road through the station and approached a three-way stop—McMurdo's dusty hub—we were surrounded on all sides by wind-battered buildings covered in brown and aquamarine sheet metal faded by the summer's twenty-four-hour sun. Rows of cargo-filled lots ran up the hill, and Caterpillar bulldozers were the only other traffic on the road. Stray pedestrians in Carhartt jackets or oversized red parkas walked between the buildings, and I was struck by the realization that the scene could have been some cargo stash visible from the parking lot of any suburban Home Depot. The initial excitement I felt about being in such a novel place gave way to disappointment in finding that McMurdo Station, the center of the United States' scientific activity in Antarctica, looked like a strip mine crossed with a Detroit dump—not the immaculate image that my mind had entertained.

Emotionally, I was feeling pretty raw when I arrived in Antarctica, and I hoped that I would leave a stronger person, mentally and physically. I thought that the simple life I would find in the Antarctic would work as an antidote to the pain of my life's recent disappointments. In Antarctica I hoped to confront real loneliness and isolation in order to inoculate myself somehow against the kinds of things that had plagued me in my relationships with others.

I'd also prepared myself physically for several months of extreme cold in one of the most geographically remote places on the planet. Having carefully packed my seventy-five pounds of allotted baggage, I thought I was ready to live a life without shopping malls, grocery stores, restaurants, and movie theatres. I figured that, at McMurdo, fresh fruit and vegetables would be luxury items flown in only on special occasions. And while images of Shackleton and his men burrowing at night into sleeping bags made of damp and rotting reindeer hair filled my mind, I had been told I would be living in a dorm room with a community bathroom down the hall. That I could deal with just fine.

So I was fairly optimistic about the living arrangements, but when I showed up at my assigned room with my bags, I met Karl—the boyfriend of one of my roommates—sitting on the couch by himself, watching TV. My two female roommates were taking showers, he said, and he directed me to my portion of the room, which contained a twin-size mattress on the bottom bunk of a bed pushed into the corner, sandwiched between a wardrobe and a nightstand. The room was also stocked with a VCR and a minifridge, and it had its own telephone for making calls to the United States, charged at normal U.S. long-distance rates.

My roommates had partitioned off their corners by hanging sheets to divide the room into sections, which I eventually did to my corner of the room as well, but the attempt to secure a personal space eventually proved useless at night, when I could hear them in bed with their boyfriends, giggling and rustling around. All five of us regularly stayed the night in the 280-square-foot room, even though there was barely enough space for three. I would lie awake at night in my standard-issue bed linens and try to sleep, thinking of anything besides the noise of the squeaking bed frame one corner away.

It didn't take long for me to realize that my dorm room wasn't the only place on the station charged with a primal vibe. During one of my first Saturday nights at McMurdo, I attended a large organized party—a rave—in the Science Support Center, an office space for field support staff and snowmobile mechanics. The center had been transformed into a psychedelic nightclub, complete with a six-by-eight-foot cage within which women and men wearing leather took turns playing with whips and chains. Yellow and pink highlighters had been passed around, their traces brilliantly illuminated under the black light: flowers, spirals, and bar codes on the arms of women wearing tank tops and on the backs of men without shirts. Glow sticks somehow showed up in Antarctica for the occasion, the radiant blue and violet rings wrapped around the bare wrists and necks of people whom I normally saw wearing insulated overalls and polypropylene turtlenecks during the day. Never mind the howling winds or the frozen tide, I thought—this population knows how to party.

I'd prepared myself for the Antarctic climate and the lack of certain luxuries, but I hadn't expected McMurdo's vibrant social life. I had enough trouble completing the regular Monday through Saturday work schedule—7:30 A.M. to 5:30 P.M. each day—but had I wanted to, I could have chosen from a menu of nonstop community activities to fill my limited free time. Maybe participation in these activities was just displaced desire—when one can't do the things one really wants to do (go to a baseball game, the mall, or a restaurant), other things must take their place.

Instead of experiencing a landscape in Antarctica that fostered serenity and a sense of connectedness with the natural world, I found the opposite. The availability of the Internet at a twenty-four-hour operational computer cluster allowed those living at McMurdo to maintain websites detailing their adventures in Antarctica and to shop online. When the items for sale at the McMurdo Station Store became tiresome—souvenir sweatshirts, shot glasses, and Cadbury chocolate bars—the regular flights between McMurdo and New Zealand allowed workers to order flat-screen TVs, video games, and other luxuries. Fresh fruit and vegetables arrived regularly during summer, and freshly baked bread and desserts were served with meals three times a day in the station's large dining facility. At lunch and dinner, the Frosty Boy soft-serve ice cream machine was turned on and the requisite toppings of rainbow sprinkles and hot fudge set out.

On days when the wind was calm, I found that running outside alone or hiking up Observation Hill, a steep pyramid-shaped mound on the station's outskirts, provided the distance I needed to deal with the disillusionment that seemed to define my life. My disappointment about life in the Antarctic mirrored other disappointments—my failure to achieve things I had wanted to accomplish professionally, be part of a healthy and loving relationship, communicate openly with my family members and closest friends, and feel settled in any particular geographic location. It seemed that my life so far had been nothing but a string of high expectations followed by grave disappointments, and at McMurdo I was again experiencing this same old pattern.

From atop Observation Hill, I could look down on McMurdo, its usual grating clatter of heavy equipment and buzzing generators muffled down to a low hum. Mount Erebus was visible to my right, off in the distance. An active volcano with a cloud of steam hovering just over its head, it looked like an old man reclining in a rocking chair and puffing on a cigar. Behind me and to my left was the McMurdo Ice Shelf, the vast white sheet connecting Ross Island to the continent; across McMurdo Sound, my eyes followed the hollow expanse until it hit the Royal Society Mountains, which jutted up sharply. Looking at the imposing peaks, I felt my desire for the different life I wanted but was never able to attain. If having a certain life or relationship or job or place in the United States couldn't satisfy this desire, I didn't know why I thought life in Antarctica would make it go away. From the top of Observation Hill, it seemed so easy to see that the ice shelf was my emptiness and the Royal Societies were just the next best thing looming in the distance, teasing me with an image I hoped would turn into the reality of something better. I should have known by then that life didn't happen this way.

As a general assistant, I was a McMurdo Jack-of-all-trades, assigned daily to assist at work centers where extra hands were needed, or added to the general labor pool to help with weekly tasks. Some of the jobs were more exciting, like being dispatched on missions to offload fuel at research huts on the ice shelf or plant flags by snowmobile to mark travel routes. When my boss assigned two of us the job of removing ice from inside a metal culvert with pickaxes and then hauling it out on a sledge, a general hissing and murmuring arose from the rest of the crew awaiting work assignments. This daylong job in the culvert sounded cruel and unusual.

It was.

When Deb, one of the other general assistants, and I arrived on the scene, we had no idea why the culvert—a water channel about four and a half feet in diameter and as long as a semi—had been moved out in the middle of a snow slope at a site where environmental research was being conducted; it wasn't clear why we were being asked to gut the culvert, whose origin was unknown. An equipment operator might have dug it up somewhere and pushed it out into the open for easier access. Upon approaching it, we found the sledge, with a rope attached to one end, leaning up against its side. It took only one depressing glance to see that the dark metal tunnel was occluded like a cholesterol-clogged artery, with several feet of thick ice and hard-packed snow.

With our axes and an assortment of other tools designed to destroy (shovels, skinny and wide, short- and long-handled; heavy metal bars shaped like spears), we started hacking away. After a few minutes, we abandoned all but the axes, because we were unable to stand upright in the culvert and wield such weapons without hurting each other. Speaking little and quickly gaining precision with our axes, we sunk them into the ice with solid whacks, following up with secondary blows close to the original point of contact. After a few more hefty whacks, the ice would cleave and big chunks would come crashing down. We loaded the pieces—sometimes so heavy that the two of us could barely lift them—onto the sledge and together pulled it out of the culvert, heaving like workhorses, one behind the other, with the rope cutting into our shoulders.

Deb worked powerfully and quickly, muscling away one large section at a time. She had been a climbing guide in Yosemite and Alaska, and as the day in the culvert wore on, she never seemed to fatigue. I wondered if the things driving me to attack the job were the same things that drove her.

At the end of the day, we had removed ice from only about a quarter of its length, and we sat inside to take a break. Catching our breaths and drinking water while we rested on chunks of ice, we surveyed our meager progress. That day in particular had a strangely Sisyphean quality: our efforts in the culvert seemed to have no real impact at all on the life of the United States Antarctic Program, or on anything either more or less important. But though chopping ice itself was absolutely devoid of meaning, it left me with a certain clarity I had never experienced before. The repetition was a meditation. I had a sense that there was no other place in the world I'd rather be, and no other thing that I'd rather be doing. I didn't care how painful or tiring it was—the work was simple and, maybe for the first time, my life was too.

The shoveling, chopping, and loading became ways for me to express the anger I had been allowing to accumulate in my life for as long as I could remember, mostly anger at myself for feeling like I never measured up to my own or others' expectations. Sometimes my rage would be general, but other times it would stem from a more specific sense of how I thought my life fell short—like the sense that I should have been a doctor or lawyer instead of the person I turned out to be: a contract laborer in Antarctica with aspirations of living in a van upon returning to the United States.

As I hacked away at the ice, I began to feel as if I were also slicing into the layers of questions that had kept me from thinking clearly. Earlier, questions about life's day-to-day details had nagged me, but now, at McMurdo, some of those worries—over things like traffic and dry cleaning and lines at grocery stores—were simply insignificant. Concerns about the future still seemed valid, but because I had certain quantifiable tasks to complete each day, my focus was on the present. My work in Antarctica ended up being an eclectic mix of raw labor and ridiculousness, but it became a meaningful way to gain some perspective on life. When I labored in the outdoors, present and past disappointments melted away and a purely visceral experience of the environment seemed to be all that remained.

On a day spent outside painting MilVans—large metal storage containers—with blue latex paint, all I felt was the wind against my face, and I knew that I was alive in a way I had never been before. Gnawing and stinging even at thirty degrees Fahrenheit, the wind, finding its way through thick jackets and underneath goggle straps and into one's core, causes a discomfort that nothing can prevent. The paint froze onto the metal as I applied it, and I knew it would likely crack and peel, sloughing off the outside of the MilVan by the next season, contaminating the surrounding snow along the way. The wind made that day's work bitter, seeming to howl at the absurdity of the task while it whipped in streams around the container's corners. But it also gave me a sense of my place inhabiting and working on a continent normally hostile to human life. The wind made me feel strong for simply being there. Life in the Antarctic was an anomaly, it reminded me. And at night, I slid into a sound sleep, warmed by the idea that it was good just to be alive.

I had hoped to find life in the Antarctic otherworldly, but instead I found that, at McMurdo, located on the cusp of the divide between heaven and earth, both sides were so palpable that I could touch them simultaneously. Antarctica—the idea—was to me still the dream of something better, a heaven of sorts. McMurdo was paradise lost. While I had hoped that McMurdo would be the Antarctica I had imagined, it just wasn't, and in order to live there, I had to take the good with the bad, something that I hadn't always been comfortable doing. Forced to face the frustrating reality of things, I was stronger for it. I left McMurdo feeling not so crushed by personal failures or plagued by anger, disappointment, and loss, because there I had daily encountered an environment in which these things were the defining features of my life.

Late one afternoon, I skied back into town after a morning spent inspecting fuel tanks at the ice runway. That day, every time I planted a pole and pushed off my skis on the way back to McMurdo, I felt a corresponding lightening of spirit. Smooth and coordinated, each push-*glide,* push-*glide* moved me back toward what had become a home, and all was quiet except the sound of my skis sliding across the snow. As if it had been dusted with silver glitter, the ice shelf dazzled me as I looked across its great expanse. My gaze would have extended to the very edge of the earth if the Royal Society Range had not been there, massive glacial reminders of the ways in which the world is shaped and changed over time. Their pyramid summits punctuated the sky, their long faces scoured by churning ice that slid down frozen slopes and calved off in cliffs, crashing to the ground so that a glacier could continue to move forward. Glacial movement and mountain formation are slow and painstaking natural processes, but the result was a scene more beautiful than I could comprehend. In it, I saw hope for the outcome of my own life's chaotic process.

Midway during my trip back to McMurdo, there was a moment in which the air was clean and dry; I couldn't smell or hear a thing. Turning my back on McMurdo and looking away from the airstrip, I found that the landscape fit my vision of Eden—pure, white, and frozen in time. I went to Antarctica with the hope that Eden still existed, somewhere, and even though the reality of it didn't exist in my life at McMurdo, the vision of it was still enchanting. Pointing my skis back toward McMurdo and pushing away from that landscape—a landscape that was the dream of everything that never came to be—I longed for reality. With its imperfections, disturbing and sometimes even shocking, McMurdo was real, and I accepted it, simply, for everything it was, instead of being disappointed by everything it was not.

Immersion

GREGORY MONE

or most of my life, I thought camping meant sleeping with my bedroom window open or my air cleaner turned off. As an asthmatic with allergies to grass, pollen, and various other kinds of nature's dust, I regarded the great outdoors as a dangerous place. Even the small backyard of our family home posed significant risks. Lying in the grass and staring up at the bright blue sky may be ideal to some; to me it meant a sneezing fit and a vague, accordion-like wheeze.

Because of my allergies, my family's excursions into the outdoors were primarily aquatic. We swam, surfed, kayaked, fished, sailed, and snorkeled; scuba diving, unfortunately, is off-limits to asthmatics. But the water wasn't just for recreation. The Atlantic Ocean and the Long Island Sound, our favored destinations, were also places of healing. According to my parents, salt water could clear sinuses, cure scabs, and clean up teenage skin. There was nothing there to slow me down—no pollen, no grasses to kick-start a head cold.

As a result of all this, I'm addicted to large bodies of water. I can stand for hours watching waves roll in from the horizon, rise taller as they approach the shore, peak in the shallows, and crumble from top to bottom as their whitewashed remnants rush forward onto the sand. It's not the immensity or power of the scene that affects me, but the beauty. A clean, clear three-inch-tall wave breaking smoothly from right to left in the Long Island Sound can be as beautiful as a bright blue, head-height barrel curling off the California coast.

High tide gets me seriously, strangely excited. When I see an overflowing body of water, I react like I've just seen a whale wave its fin toward me in greeting. I'll shout and point. I'll gesticulate wildly. If we're driving, I'll force my wife to pull over to the side of the road and look for herself. Though I know it's a regular occurrence, a good high tide never fails to start me hoping that this time the water's not going to stop flooding. That the world is going to overflow. That all the cities in the world will transform into canal-lined places filled with water. Then I'd be able to swim to the office in the summer instead of stomping down sidewalks through heavy, humid air. In this fantasy world, there would be no pollen.

I've hiked. I've tried camping. During a brief surf trip with friends, I once slept on the deck of an unoccupied house. A deck isn't nature's bare floor, but this certainly felt like roughing it. The night sky was our ceiling, the trees in the yard were our walls. There was a chill in the air. We wore hats. I had my inhaler in my pocket in case I started to wheeze, and I was slightly worried about being attacked by coyotes. Did I mention that we each pulled a mattress out of the house and onto the deck and spread our sleeping bags on top for a little extra cushion? Does this still count as camping? I have another example.

A few months after the surf trip, I visited my parents in Florida, flying down from New York for a dose of ocean air and blue sky after too much time spent cleaning soot off my windowsill and puffing on my inhaler while waiting on subway platforms. There, the Atlantic was only a few steps from the elevator banks on the ground floor of their building. Both the Loxahatchee River and the intracoastal waterway—which runs parallel to the coast, allowing boaters to travel in heavy seas—emptied into the ocean a mile to the south. At this point, the three bodies of water formed a wildly active three-way intersection. The water was typically a bright greenish blue, whitecapped in windy weather. The ocean rushed in through the channel when the tide changed from high to low, then flooded back out like water through a burst dam when the process reversed.

It being Florida, the area was flush with anglers, Jet Skiers, and beer-swilling day-trippers, but the seemingly crowded surface was in fact sparsely populated when compared to the undersea world. Slow-paddling turtles, gliding manta rays, chunky manatees, sharks, and porpoises, as well as yellow-and-black-striped sergeant majors, alien-looking needle-fish, and all other kinds and colors and sizes of fish lolled in the shallows or kicked about in the currents. Schools of jacks swam in tight formation, haphazardly shifting dark spots on the water's blue surface. The rays and sea cows moved in and out of the intersection with the tides, drifting lazily along in the tidal current that rushed up and down the beach.

On my first day there, I decided that my campsite would be on the beach at the edge of this aquatic highway, above the high-tide line. I spent most of that day in the ocean, but it wasn't enough. I needed to bond with the stars and the breaking waves and the breeze blowing through the palms. I needed to wash New York off me, to get it out of my lungs and hair. I needed to sleep outside.

People had done this before in the history of the world, I thought. Plenty of them. Pirates and sailors probably did it often, and I knew some surfers who used to do it in Santa Cruz—hiding behind bushes if a park ranger drove by on a quad bike checking for exactly their sort. This was not insane or risky, but a perfectly regular, normal thing to do. Maybe not in a retirement community, but anywhere else? Definitely.

After dinner, I ventured down to my camp. The moon and stars were bright. The beach was empty and it was past eight o'clock, so all the locals had been in bed for hours. The conditions were ideal, but I didn't get much farther than the gate at the edge of the faux marble patio before I started worrying about the turtles. It was not that I was scared of the turtles. I'm slow on my feet, but even I could outrun one if it turned ornery. No. I was scared of turtle mating season.

There were tracks leading from the high-tide line to dry spots in the sand where the turtle ladies could lay their eggs. These were left over from the night before, but they got me wondering. Would the turtles be back again tonight? Would one of them crawl into my sleeping bag? I'd seen *Alien*. I knew what could happen if I wasn't careful. Tiny turtles crawling out of my belly in a few months' time? Sleeping out didn't seem like it would be worth the trouble. And even though this was a little extreme—a possibility that was a little too ridiculous to prevent the execution of my plan to sleep on the beach, a sad excuse that would let me bed down inside on a comfortable mattress—then at the very least the idea of sleeping amid turtles storming the beach in the middle of the night would lead to unsettling dreams. Before even opening the gate, I bailed.

The problem was that I'd announced my intention to camp. I had to save face; this was part of a lifelong effort to prove that I was different, that I could overcome the family allergies and be an outdoorsman. That I was a new, improved, more evolved form of Mone. One way or another, I was going to sleep outdoors. The patio it would be. Triumphantly, I returned to my parents' eighth-floor apartment. The stars were still visible. The ocean was loud, the air fresh. And the turtles, even if they were the mutant karate-chopping kind, wouldn't be able to get in through the building's high security. The only obstacle left: the deck was on the eighth floor.

I've been told that I'm a sleepwalker, and here only a four-foot-high railing would prevent me from tumbling over the edge. As a precaution, I took the belt from a bathrobe my mom had borrowed from the Four Seasons and tied one end around my ankle and the other around the railing. I pulled it tight, checking the knot like people do in movies. It might not hold me if I went head over heels off the ledge, but the tug on my ankle might wake me up if I started sleepwalking and prevent that fatal accident from happening.

In the end, I slept soundly, waking up now and then to stare up at the stars and allow the crashing water to lull me back into dreamland. Purists might argue that, had I wanted to be a true camper, I would have had to sleep on the ground, defecate in the woods, and use leaves as toilet paper. I would counter that my little perch above the ocean was actually a more primal abode than a tent pitched miles from a working toilet. More real than a campsite in Patagonia. And why? Because one of the closest living relatives of *Homo sapiens,* the orangutan, makes similar sleeping arrangements every night.

The Sumatran brand of this long-limbed great ape, which lives entirely above the forest floor, builds a different bed every night by pulling and tying together nearby branches, working in broken-off limbs, and then padding all this with soft leaves. Similarly, I moved my parents' deck furniture away, gathered pillows, linens, and blankets, and then pulled an air mattress outside and, using a foot pump, expended a not insignificant amount of energy inflating it. The orangutan works, gathering certain nearby materials and pushing away others, to form its bed. So did I. We both slept high above the ground. I was safe from egg-laying turtles, the orangutan from prowling tigers. Both of us could urinate off the ledge if needed, though there might be repercussions if I chose this option rather than the bathroom a few steps away, and the condominium board found out. The final, and perhaps most important similarity, aside from the fact that we're both burdened with long chest hair, is the fact that the Sumatran orangutan always sleeps with one hand or foot loosely grasping a strong branch for safety—presumably, in case the bed comes apart or it rolls too far to one side. My use of the Four Seasons bathrobe belt, therefore, was perfectly natural. It was merely an expression of primal behavior. I was tapping into my tree-dwelling past.

Though I was encouraged by the fact that I'd built a nest and, in the process, developed my own brand of luxury camping, my trips to Florida were rare. What I needed was a simpler, more accessible means of communing with nature. An easier way of rinsing off the city. The solution revealed itself in a backhanded sort of way a few months later. I was living in San Francisco, working from home in a shared apartment with a magnificent view of the bay. Several large windows at the back looked north over the water, and I spent a good part of each day watching it change. The water was calm and gray in the morning, deep blue and whitecapped in the afternoon. Alcatraz rose up like a half-submerged boulder a mile out from shore, and Angel Island, a green-and-brown sun-baked mound, loomed behind. This bay, though beautiful, was seriously forbidding. The water was take-your-breath-away, ice-cream-headache cold. Not to mention there were all sorts of rumors about sharks.

Still, I was raised in the ocean. How could I not run down there and swim? Loads of people waded in that water. There was even a club. Every year there were several races from Alcatraz to shore in which hundreds of competitors braved the icy bay. I could safely excuse myself from most of them, as they were triathlons and I cannot run for more than a mile. But there was one race, the Escape from Alcatraz, that was strictly for swimmers. A simple one-and-a-half-mile dash through fifty-something-degree water from the old prison to shore. Before long, the water, the rock, the race started taunting me. I had to enter, if only to be able to stare out that window in the morning and think to myself how I'd been in that water, all the way out by that rock. If nothing else, it would improve my view.

◎   ◎   ◎

Since this was the sort of thing that people trained for, I started swimming in the bay a few months after signing up, in a small, enclosed marina near Fisherman's Wharf. Not for very long. The first time I dove in, I was afraid my face had been paralyzed from the shock. Immediately, I lifted my head out of the water and treaded in place. No one in the history of the world has ever swum in water this cold, I thought. I wondered if that day was an anomaly. If some sort of strange current was flowing through. Something from Iceland. There was a lot of talk about global warming at the time; maybe a glacier had melted nearby.

Two old ladies waded into the water in their sagging suits and large rubber caps. Was there a warm spot there? Surely they weren't moving so casually through the same water as I? They dove forward and started to swim out and away from the shore. The chill was spreading, the cold moving past the skin and into my muscles. It was swim now or turn back in. The old women stroked forward. I pressed my face down into the water and started swinging, swimming nearly as fast as I could and thinking warm thoughts. Sun. Hot chocolate. A shower. Certainly I wasn't thinking about my face, which felt like it was planted in snow.

That first day I lasted maybe five minutes; the race would take a little more than a half hour. I swam a few times a week, getting up to ten or fifteen minutes at most. My girlfriend—now wife—expressed concern that I wasn't in shape. I proudly reminded her that I swam competitively for eight years. She reminded me that I'd been retired for five. Well, I answered, the hardest part would be the cold and I was working hard at preparing myself for that portion of the race. For weeks I'd been driving at night or early in the morning with the window in my car open and generally refusing to wear more than a T-shirt when the air temperature dropped below sixty degrees.

On race day, the competitors gathered down at Fisherman's Wharf around eight in the morning. Seven-hundred-plus swimmers changing into their wetsuits and swimsuits, spitting into their goggles, pulling latex bathing caps on over their hair. We all walked down the street in flip flops and swimsuits and black rubber wetsuits, looking like lost oversized penguins, moving in a crowd toward the ferries that would carry us out to Alcatraz, to the floating starting line on the far side of the island.

Though the island's prison hadn't functioned as such for almost forty years, the high rock walls and rusted fences made the place seem intensely forbidding. We cruised around to the north side and came to a stop, and people started jumping off, true to form, like penguins off an iceberg. There wasn't any order to it. No one was telling us to be careful. It was just a bunch of maniacs aged twelve to seventy diving into ice-cold water for a muscle-burning swim to shore. My so-called training proved insufficient the second I hit the water. My chest seized up, I treaded as high as I could above the chop and considered escaping to Alcatraz, not from it. People splashed and flailed around me, swimming with their heads above water, moving toward the starting line: a row of kayaks lined up front to back, along with two large buoys on either end.

As we got ready for the start—all seven hundred people trying to get up toward the front of the crowd for whatever advantage they could muster, hoping someone would blow a whistle or fire a pistol or just yell "Go" so we wouldn't have to stay in place getting ever colder—I looked back toward the city in the general direction of my apartment. I'd finally gotten myself out there, at the far end of the kitchen view. And yet it didn't feel like a chest-thumping accomplishment. The scene didn't feel real or entirely natural. There were too many people around for it to be nature; it felt more like we were in a really big, murky community pool.

Thankfully, that feeling disappeared ten minutes into the race, when my friend Root and I raced out toward the front after the kayaks paddled away from each other, breaking up the floating starting line and freeing everyone to head for shore. We sprinted side by side in the crowd, moving through all the flailing arms and kicking feet, grabbing ankles to pull ourselves forward, periodically stroking ahead with our heads high out of the water to ensure that we were going the right way. Before long, we were out in the middle of a watery no-man's-land between Alcatraz and the shore. Hundreds of people chopped through the water behind us. The surface looked like it was boiling, splashes of white water everywhere. But where we were swimming, it was empty. We settled into the race, adjusted to the cold, and pulled up every few minutes to get our bearings. We had a few brief directional disagreements—at one point Root correctly informed me that I was heading toward Oakland, not San Francisco. Eventually he got tired of chasing me down to tell me I was off course. We silently agreed to part ways and head for shore independently.

The water wasn't too clear out in the bay, a kind of bright green at the surface, where the sun was hitting, and a foreboding darkness only a few feet down. A deep, dark green that led down to the bottom some eighty feet below and out into the wide-open Pacific Ocean to my right. It didn't take long for me to start thinking about sharks. Murky water inevitably kick-starts my imagination. Because I couldn't see more than three or four feet down, I began populating the surrounding water with dangerous creatures. I became convinced that a school of sharks might be keeping pace with me, just ten feet below the surface. Maybe a pair of sea monsters lamenting the lack of good food in the open ocean had just kicked into the bay in search of a different kind of meal. Adjusting my stroke, I switched to a more shallow pull so that my hand wouldn't brush up against any of these unseen predators. I tried to reassure myself by recalling the words of an Alcatraz tour guide I'd heard a few years earlier—something about how the shark tales were really myths designed to discourage the prisoners from trying to break free. But as anyone in the area knows, there are also quite a few great-white breeding grounds not too far to the north and, well, sharks can travel far. The effect of these little daydreams about being eaten alive was, in the end, positive, as they distracted me from the tremendous and growing fatigue in my arms, and the tightening cramps in my back and legs. Really, my fear of sharks just made me swim faster.

I began to realize that my fear of predators was a side symptom of something deeper. Behind me, Angel Island, Alcatraz, and Berkeley sat in the distance. The Golden Gate Bridge was off to my right, the sailboats and piers of Fisherman's Wharf straight ahead. There were boats and kayakers nearby. People were everywhere, man-made structures were in view, and Root wasn't too far away. But with my face down in that water, staring into the dark green depths, I felt as if I were alone in the middle of the ocean. And that's when it became clear that I'd found my cure.

What I'd been looking for in nature was a way of slipping out of time: a means of getting away from the endless highways and towering buildings, the blaring car horns and screeching subways, all the sights and sounds that ground me constantly in the here and now. The brook in my neighbors' backyards, the deck, my parents' patio—these were all connected too specifically to the present. I wanted to feel like I was living on planet Earth, the 4.5-billion-year-old oasis in the middle of a mostly empty universe. Not in a particular city in a certain country on a specific date. I've never gotten this feeling from hiking, because my experience has been limited to well-worn dirt paths. But out there in the water off San Francisco, staring down into the deep green darkness, it might have been any moment in the last thousand years. I could have picked my head up at any time and seen the tall, skinny pyramid that is the Transamerica Building, but when I didn't, I felt more a part of the natural world out there than I did hiking in a redwood forest. Maybe it's the asthma and allergies that pushed me away from the woods and into the water, but what struck me then as I gazed into the bay's watery depths was that, for me, these immersions were an absolute necessity.

That bit about being able to stand and watch waves break for hours? Not exactly true. I can conceivably remain transfixed for five, maybe ten minutes. But eventually, as long as the temperature's decent, I have to ditch my shoes and shirt and wallet, sprint to the shore, and dive in. I can't just watch. I have to join myself to that immense seascape, because it's the only way I have to feel a part of Mother Nature—who, in my case, is open water in all its big blue glory.

Outside in Africa

ALEX P. KELLOGG

The first time I was called *mzungu,* I was trekking along a muddy trail in the plush green of the Taita Hills, a region of foothill forests in southeast Kenya on the border with Tanzania. The sun was bright in the sky, and one of my hiking boots was soaking wet and grimy because I'd slipped while jumping between rocks to cross a shallow river. The mud and the small, polished stones gathered in my boot didn't bother me, though. I was enjoying the sensory overload of the dense vegetation all around—the countless bamboo and banana trees—and the company of several fellow study-abroad students and those who were acting as host siblings for the week we were to spend there. We wound along worn dirt paths barely wide enough for two people to walk side by side. As we traced the soft curve of a hill, our narrow path merged with a main artery, and we were greeted by dozens of children just being let out of a one-room concrete schoolhouse nestled in the trees, miles from the closest major town.

Seeing the novelty of us—our light-colored skin, our exotic, bohemian clothing—the children spilled forth from the school and ran in our direction. They were dressed in uniforms—the boys in blue pants and white shirts, the girls in blue skirts and white blouses—which stood out vividly against the green backdrop of the hills. They all pointed at us, shouting in excitement and awe at the top of their lungs: *"Mzungu! Wazungu!"* Whitey! Whites!

Mzungu, a Kiswahili word, literally translates as "one who walks around." A word first uttered by black East Africans trying to describe the earliest white explorers who came to the region, *mzungu* is today the closest word in Kiswahili to *whitey* that there is. So once you learn enough Kiswahili to understand what people are saying, being called "whitey" countless times a day just isn't cool no matter which way you cut it. And wherever you are in Kenya, if you're white, you get called it quite a lot. Even if I'd wanted to believe that the children we encountered were only talking about my classmates, it was clear that they were pointing indiscriminately at all of us. I, a self-identified African American of mixed black-and-white heritage, was not black enough to be distinguished from the rest. If nothing else, their pointing and yelling made me understand that.

It was then that my thoughts turned from nature to race. My gaze shifted from the miles of rolling hills before us to the beautiful children running toward us. It was a singular moment. Never in my life had I been called white. Never in my life had I been lumped in the same racial category as someone who was white, as the twenty-two other students in my program were. For years, I had struggled to accept my own white heritage. As a youth, I had embraced Afro-centricity at the expense of acknowledging my white background. I'd come to Africa to gain some exposure to the continent from which my black Eritrean father came. And here I was, basking in nature, secure in my own self-image, being confronted by my worst nightmare: I might be half African, but first and foremost, I was white and thus, by definition, an outsider.

"Mzungu!" the children shouted as they ran past us toward their homes, which lined the winding paths that snaked in every direction from the main artery like tributaries to a massive river. *"Mzungu, wazungu!"*

I hadn't come to Africa to experience or enjoy its natural wonders. I'd come to connect with my ancestry. Still, a large portion of the program in which I'd enrolled involved outdoor activities—camping, hiking, animal spotting. Thus, after just a few weeks in Kenya, I knew that its natural environment was stunning. The grasslands, savannahs, and semiarid plains were particularly striking when I arrived in January 1998 for a four-month study-abroad program. East Africa had been hit by El Niño in the weeks and months before. A warming of the equatorial waters in the Pacific Ocean that causes unusual weather patterns—including heavy rains in some regions of the world—El Niño comes around every three to seven years and can last for weeks or months. This one caused massive rains and made the tangled green of Kenya and Tanzania's tropical pockets spill into every corner of the country. The brown of the savannah, the grasslands, and the plains was gone. The animals had ballooned; predators fed off prey fattened by the abundant vegetation. Everything in nature was robust.

Yet most East African people weren't doing nearly as well. Kenya was wracked by ethnic violence following a contentious presidential election in December 1997 that was marred by vote rigging and ethnic clashes. What's more, the excessive rains of El Niño had ruined many crops throughout the region. And though Kenya and Tanzania were relatively stable compared to their neighbors, Kenya, the once-prosperous hub of the region, had seen foreign aid and study-abroad programs like the one I was in dry up due to rampant corruption and governmental mismanagement.

Regardless of the political strife, many Westerners still came to visit Kenya and its southern neighbor—most not to help out but to go on safari. Kenya, because of its relative stability, pulls in millions of dollars annually from tourism revenues; Tanzania also earns money from tourism, although less than Kenya does. Just like most of the nation's visitors, many of my fellow students had come to Kenya to study the natural environment. They were avid hikers, seasoned campers, budding botanists. They aspired to work in jobs that involved, among other things, wildlife protection and environmental conservation. My interest, by contrast, was primarily in the people—their cultures, traditions, and ways of life. I resisted the allure of traveling to Kenya—or to any country, for that matter—just to see its natural environment, and I was particularly sensitive because Kenya was a recognized magnet for visitors interested in landscapes and wildlife.

What's more, I didn't like the fact that most of the natural environment in Kenya appeared to be racialized—if you were on safari, for example, you were most likely wealthy and white, and if you were serving travelers or hawking goods, you were unquestionably black. And that, the nation's colonial history taught, was the way it was supposed to be. Not for me. I initially held Kenya's natural environment at bay. I resisted going on safari, an almost daily pastime for many foreigners living in Kenya. I wanted to get to know our teachers, our African peers, and our support staff, without the troubling ghosts of the nation's white conquerors and black supplicants rearing their heads.

Yet my desire to keep Kenya's natural environment separate from its people proved futile. The strength of its beauty compelled me to acknowledge it, and I came to realize that the natural environment was an important aspect of everyday life for many, many Kenyans. Though I'd come to the region for its people, and thought little about the natural environment, what I did not anticipate was that the two and a half years I would spend living in Africa—roughly twenty months in Kenya and nine in Eritrea, my father's homeland—would change my perceptions of both nature and race. Connecting with Africans, as I would learn, didn't require being black, and enjoying the continent's natural environment didn't require being white.

On the way to Taita, our first trip out of the Kenyan capital city of Nairobi, we drove through the nation's vast flat expanses for the first time. The outskirts bled into plush but normally dry plains, and we were all immediately struck by the large number of wild animals, more than any of us had ever seen in one place. There were small herds of gazelles and zebras and troops of baboons chasing after our truck, hoping that we'd throw scraps of food. There was even the occasional giraffe meandering around. Later, many of the students, myself included, complained that we'd taken too many photos of animal backsides, so bemused were we by the idea of real-life animals running around in packs (and away from our noisy vehicle).

Here, in Kenya's sparsely populated flatlands, I learned that there were few of the things that I felt conflicted about in Africa's natural environments. There were no subservient Kenyan support staff, no wide-eyed hawkers, no packs of tourist vans congregating to see the same pair of lions mate. We would often find ourselves alone in the environment. I'd never seen anything in the States like what I saw in Kenya: I'd never seen a pack of deer running free, for example, or a family of moose walking around. I'd gone hiking only a handful of times in my entire life, and I knew little, to be honest, about natural environments that remained so pristine.

Two weeks later, we packed our gear and ourselves into the back of the old blue truck our program used to cart us around (an open-air human fishbowl if ever there was one). We headed roughly 160 miles south from our main campus in Nairobi to Arusha, Tanzania, a quaint, scenic town that, like Nairobi, lies along East Africa's famous Rift Valley. It's the nation's jumping-off point for most travelers on safari. After stopping there to meet our guides, we were to spend two mandatory weeks on safari in northern Tanzania, seeing the valley—a tectonic rift that stretches from northern Syria to central Mozambique—and the Serengeti Plain. I couldn't admit it fully, but I was excited. I figured if nothing else, given my hostility to the idea of going on safari in general, this might be the first and last safari of my life.

Before arriving in Arusha, we hit the dusty, nondescript village that housed the tiny immigration offices located on the border between Kenya and Tanzania. As soon as our truck came to a stop, we were bombarded by hawkers, mostly Maasai of all ages: old men, children, mothers. They greeted us with calls of "Wewe, mzungu, kuja hapa ta-fadhali" (You, whitey, come here please) or "Mzungu, kuja kuonyesha kitu" (White man, come, I show you something). The Maasai, a semi-nomadic tribe of pastoralists who are also polygamists, live throughout much of Kenya and Tanzania. In Kenya, they are known for bringing their livestock to graze right in the capital's main streets when water and vegetation are sparse in rural areas. A handful of them are savvy hawkers of goods of all kinds, from traditional Maasai wedding garb to the jewelry worn by the young warrior class.

Outsider. Foreigner. *Mzungu.* These words are synonymous, and in my three weeks in Kenya I had quickly become familiar with the concepts behind them. After all, I couldn't go a few minutes in Nairobi without being reminded of my white heritage. But when I left the capital, I came to learn that, though the natural landscape was not a perfect escape from labels, in either Kenya and Tanzania, it was a partial one. Though I'd still have to walk Kenya's jagged racial line in its rural areas, encounters were so much less frequent, and so much more benign, there. In fact, simply by seeing fewer people, I could worry about race—and humanity—a little less. In Nairobi, where we spent three of our first four weeks, glances heaped upon us. Never were we unaware of the implications of our skin tone. *Mzungu* was a double entendre. In Tanzania, where I camped out for the second time in my life, and where I hiked as an adult for the first time, I began to appreciate the fact that, outdoors, far from the dense pockets of people, one could imagine oneself as an individual for a moment—free from racial categorization—and even learn, despite one's politics, that more than anything an individual is all one hoped to be.

"There goes a tire," I thought, as the Land Rover we were riding in jerked right, in the direction opposite from our left rear wheel, which was playfully bouncing off to our left, as if in a cartoon. We'd have to stop. The rear axle was bent badly out of shape. No matter. Several of our guides simply sledgehammered it straight. Within minutes, we were speeding through the Serengeti plains once again. They were flat and green in all directions. And though all three of the students riding with me had their jaws agape as we settled back atop our vehicle, we were quickly becoming accustomed to the unexpected.

And then there was the unparalleled: seeing African wildlife gallop about freely. I remember, for example, the panoramic. That's what I call it. The moment I saw a giraffe loping along—well, it was actually sprinting, but its legs were so long and its movements so graceful that it looked like it was barely breaking a sweat. We were driving up the crest of the Ngorongoro Crater, an extinct volcano near the northern border of Tanzania that houses one of the largest and most diverse collections of wildlife in the entire world. I clicked a picture of the giraffe, but it couldn't capture the moment. That I had to keep in my heart.

Once we were inside the crater, the first thing to capture our attention was a pair of old male water buffaloes lying beside each other along the soft decline of a hill within the crater. When they get old, male water buffaloes pair off for protection and, presumably, companionship. These two looked at us with surprisingly inquisitive eyes, given the millions of tourists they'd likely seen in their lives. Old age would almost certainly lead to their death in the jaws of a pride of lions or a pack of hyenas, if no gentler ending greeted them sooner.

I had to admit that my fellow students, most of whom had interests in Africa much different than mine, were right about at least one thing: the natural environment of the region was hard to ignore. On my fourth day in Tanzania, I wrote in my journal: "At sunset, I cried out of happiness for being here." The divide I'd established in my mind between being interested in the people and being interested in the environment began to seem artificial, but the divide still wasn't easy to resolve. During our time in Ngorongoro, we came upon a pair of lions mating in the middle of a green field of short grass. Anyone who has seen a pair of lions mating knows how bizarre it is to see for the first time: lions literally do it dozens of times, if not more, for minutes at a time, if not less. This goes on over and over again, for hours and eventually days. But despite the lioness's growling as she flipped her tail in her mate's face, the male's golden mane, the crater in the background, and the uniqueness of the moment in my life, the most striking detail was a fleet of tourist vans—all white and virtually identical—forming a crescent around the feline couple. We could have easily slid in line with the rest on the very end of the half circle, but instead, we stopped a hundred feet away. In hindsight, where we stopped was perhaps suggested by our program director, or the lead guide, who may have wanted us to see the entire spectacle framed by the way many people encountered the natural environment in Africa: in air-conditioned vehicles and, often, in packs.

Not that we students were so different from the tourists nearby. There were some key differences: the roofs of our vehicles opened, and there was no air-conditioning, so we experienced the dry, direct heat near the equator. We also camped out. Many tented tourist resorts have running water and electricity, for example, and most of the trappings of a luxury hotel. But even though we were traveling a bit closer to nature, we weren't traveling in an entirely egalitarian fashion. Our African guides cooked our food and cleaned up after us. Sure, we paid them for their services, but there was no way in my mind, given the colonial history of the region and the racial inequality still pervasive in the region, to avoid the appearance of our superiority, however unintentional.

And among foreigners in Kenya and Tanzania, a feeling of superiority to—or complete disinterest in—native Africans isn't unheard of. During our two-week trip to northern Tanzania, we had the opportunity to talk with an elder in one community about local remedies used to treat certain illnesses, and the plant life associated with them. One girl, a short brunette named Maura, made a special request to be excused from listening to the lecture. An aspiring botanist, she was more interested in collecting plant specimens. It seemed to me that there had to be a way to mesh her interests with the old man's presentation. But Maura's choice was a minor example of a bigger problem: like many foreigners, many of my fellow study-abroad students seemed not to appreciate the people in Africa as much as they did the nature. To me, it was as if they saw the entire study-abroad experience as one big safari, with Kenyans and Tanzanians at best a complement to—and at worst a distraction from—the natural environment.

For my part, I finally felt compelled to seek out a balance between enjoying the natural terrain, like what I'd seen in Tanzania, and interacting with the people who lived in it. I found that balance with the Samburu.

"They make red look regal." That was my first thought when I saw Samburu men dressed in their traditional red waist wraps and red shawls wrapped around their shoulders and upper torsos. Most carry long wood-and-metal spears as well as a *rungu,* a traditional club. They spend considerably time grazing their livestock, and they live in an arid environment where few other tribes venture. Genetic cousins to the Maasai, the Samburu live just above the equator where the foothills of Mount Kenya merge into the northern desert. They speak Kimaa, the same language as their Maasai brethren, and they too are polygamist, pastoralist, and seminomadic.

After spending several more weeks back in Nairobi taking classes and improving our Kiswahili, we once again headed out of the capital in our old blue truck, this time to Samburu land. Already, I'd had a change of heart about being in nature. Three days after arriving in Samburu, I noted in my journal: "Surprisingly, I'm superpsyched to be out in the field, camping again." It was a Tuesday in early March, and we'd just met the dozen or so Samburu elders with whom we would be camping, traveling, and living for the next two weeks.

Several days later, we set up camp in a rocky patch near the *bomas,* or enclosed-camp homesteads, of several of our elders. Lesita, the elder responsible for my group of students, took the three men in our group to bathe in a nearby river. We arrived there, a half-mile walk from our campsite, to find two bathing areas: the riverbank on the west for men, and the one on the east for women. We proceeded to wade through the water to the western bank, where men of all ages were gathered. One young man who'd decorated his face with red clay was washing it off to replace it with new clay. Other men washed their garb or simply stood talking on the side of the river.

I undressed and washed as best I could, never having bathed in this fashion before. The other two students joined me, as did Lesita. Normally, I might have been uncomfortable stripping down naked and bathing in a river surrounded by strangers. But for Lesita and the other Samburu men, it was so natural as to be insignificant. Somehow, the communal quality of the experience helped me and the other students feel at ease. Men were chatting, sharing small mirrors, relaxing. For the first time, I enjoyed bathing outdoors, in the presence of others, as I never would have thought possible before.

The real connection between the Samburu and their natural environment hit me while spending three days living in their *shambas,* or homes. Samburu live in wood, mud, and dung structures built by the women and surrounded by fences made of shrubbery to keep cows and goats in. There is a separate home for each additional wife, and, if there are multiple homes, a larger fence of shrubbery encapsulates the entire compound. Lesita had two wives, the second of which lived in a separate *boma*. We traveled to the closest *boma,* roughly a six-hour walk from our campsite. It was a Saturday. The sun was high in the sky. The foothills were green from El Niño rains. Flies attracted by the livestock crawled all over us. Zebras meandered about in small groups, content that humans were not a danger.

We arrived at Lesita's *boma* about two and a half hours later. It included sixty to one hundred cows and goats. I know that both my travel companion—a buzz-cut guy named Mike—and I were struck by how small the *shamba* was when we actually stepped inside. I couldn't stand up straight in the thing, it had no running water, and the bathroom was synonymous with the outdoors. But I was struck by how happy Lesita was to arrive there, and how happy his wife and three children appeared to be to see him. On the first evening, we leaned against his home and talked in broken Swahili for several hours. Lesita asked why I didn't quite look like other *wazungu,* and I explained that my father was African and my mother white, which seemed to clear up a deep mystery for him.

That night, it rained like hell. I shared a pile of cow hides with Lesita, his son, and another student while water trickled through the roof cracks and onto our faces, legs, and arms. At one point, Lesita's wife climbed the roof to try to patch up some larger holes. Half asleep, I briefly thought an elephant was attacking the house.

By the third day with Lesita, though I was growing more comfortable with this lifestyle, I was ready to return to the relative comfort of the tents we were used to. But I had learned one thing: that I could be in nature and with Africans and enjoy both, together. There need not be a separation. Lesita lived in a largely traditional natural environment, and he was happier there than he was camping out with students while eating Western food and imparting his knowledge. I could respect his fortitude and appreciate his love of nature. Mine had already grown tremendously.

Passeggiata is a popular pastime in the Eritrean capital, Asmara, where I arrived, almost three years to the day after I left Kenya, to finally visit my father's homeland. Inherited from the Italians, *passeggiata* refers to the constant back-and-forth movement the outdoor pedestrian traffic creates on a city's main strip, particularly on Sunday afternoons.

Thousands walk up and down Godena Harnet, or Liberty Avenue, Asmara's main strip, on the weekend for hours on end, taking in the air, watching the people. For me, walking around the city was a mixed experience. I enjoyed walking, but as always, I didn't enjoy being stared at for looking so distinctive. Always a relief, though, was running into a friend who was, like me, engaged in the endless back-and-forth. He or she would pluck me from the crowd and insist that I sit and have coffee and cake with him or her, as was the tradition.

And for a moment, caught up in the simple joy of a culture at once mine and not mine, I would forget that I had always been caught somewhere in between. It wasn't exactly the wilderness, but it was outside. And because of the lessons I'd learned in both the region's rural and its urban landscapes, I found a place that was my own.

Rifts

ANNA BAHNEY

We are to meet by the yellow caboose at Bosselman's truck stop, off Interstate 80 just outside Grand Island, Nebraska. I park at the far side of the parking lot, near the stationary Union Pacific rail car, and run against the wind to get a cup of coffee. Inside, truckers are playing video games and eating hot open-faced roast beef sandwiches. Beneath fluorescent lights that make night and day comfortably irrelevant, my bleary eyes stop on the stacks of boxed-up cowboy boots.

It is late by my New York clock, a time when I would usually be slinking past the shuttered metal gates of the storefronts along Norman Avenue, ears still ringing from a rock show or bar, toward home. But because I'm crawling out of a truck stop on the other side of too little sleep, it is early—four thirty in the morning, Nebraska time.

I retreat to my car, pulling on a cap and stuffing my hands into gloves to guard against the raw March morning. While I wait for the others, I take inventory: camera, notebook, tape recorder. I'm nominally here on a reporting job, but I'm a bit of an emotional tourist, too, since this is where I grew up. As I nurse my coffee, it occurs to me that this truck stop was the very one at which I was stranded on a much colder night, twenty years earlier.

We were only twelve miles from home, but the two-lane highway to Grand Island was closed by a debilitating blizzard. Dad pulled the white Oldsmobile station wagon to a stop on the side of the road, before we skidded off. He put on his stocking cap and ran over the drifting banks of snow, disappearing into the lights haloing around the hotel. There wasn't any room there, he told us when he got back, but we could go to Bosselman's. My parents trudged across this parking lot toting my brother, then a toddler, and me, just into grade school, against the wind and snow.

In the diner, we were taken into the warm hive of refugees from the road as travelers and truckers cackled together over coffee, all lined up along the lunch counter. There were a lot of other kids there, and we all made forts out of blankets on the banquettes, then spread out to sleep on the tops of tables, never minding the din. People milled around and gave cursory looks out the window. We stayed there all night, with the wall-mounted television giving constant weather updates. In the morning, white sunlight came through the blowing snow, and we were driven home in a snowplow.

I was five when my family landed in Grand Island, the third-largest town in the state at the time. We stayed until I was ten. Grand Island—so improbably named as to be a droll punch line—is landlocked, on the flat, treeless prairie near the wide, shallow water of the Platte River. It remains remote to me, both in terms of land and memory.

And yet, I had my yellow-haired little-girldom here, parenthetically separate from what came before or after. I've found that being here—I've been back only twice since I was ten—pushes around in my mind images from childhood, when my aperture was at its widest. The pictures are large-scale, epic. They fall in a stack, old photos dislodged from behind other, more familiar piles of pictures, and I find that, after all this time, there is still some sorting to do.

When I was a teenager, my friends and I went out on what I liked to think of as adventures; although they invariably culminated at dam sites or railroad trestles or riverbanks, they never began with a destination. Our only need was to experience something that we could consume whole, unlike the vast stillness, the huge emptiness, the massive space around us.

Growing up in the middle of a state in the middle of the country, I climbed the walls of my predictable town. Feeling out of place and trapped, I escaped to the road and what lay on either side of it. By the time I was sixteen, I lived on the suburban cusp of Omaha's west end, where subdivisions of freshly minted five-bedroom neocolonials abutted cornfields. With ten minutes and four wheels, I could be thundering down the maddeningly straight roads of Nebraska nowhere. Passing rotting wooden fence posts bordering long-abandoned farmhouses with skeletons of windmills moaning in the wind, I could become lost. Every gravel road held the same farms, the same fields, the same sky.

There is nothing to say about the land except that it is transparent. Brown grass runs in place, bumping into restless trees whose craggy claws swat at the sky. Spaces are so large that, on all but the few most vivid summer days, color can hardly cling to them with any authority. The landscape is beige, but less the color itself than the feeling of that color: the flat, stark color of truth.

Immutable, it tells a story of flat land and big sky that it sticks to for five hundred miles, unchanging and constant, passionately stoic. If you drive it long enough, it seeps into you, the steady rhythm of the raspy blonde fields interrupted at a crossroads every country mile beneath a washed-out, cornflower blue sky. You don't see the abandoned barn decaying along the highway or the sleepy cattle eyeing you as the car hums through a wave of stench from a feedlot that you can no longer smell.

But the stoicism steadied me during the series of now-forgotten injustices that fueled my anger and frustration at sixteen. My feelings seemed capable of moving earth and sky, but like a knowing parent, the land knew I would wear myself down emoting on a desolate roadside, tiring long before it would.

Such a landscape, because of sheer size and indifference, makes self-consciousness painfully necessary. The most significant movement in the frame may be your anger, and it becomes part of the landscape. This unforgiving land absorbs you, and won't give you any more of the story.

But that did nothing to stop me from trying to pin it down. I would sit crouched in the long, lapping waves of prairie grass, cupping my camera like a mason jar, hoping to capture the elusive sky. If I could affix it to paper, I could keep it. I could focus on it, figure it out. I could lose myself in it.

The sun would set, inevitably yielding a flourish of colors moving around the tonic tone of the sun. I would flutter the shutter. I was determined to capture the racing of my heart and widening of my eyes. The entire breath the view breathed into me. I was determined to capture it all.

Of course, I was disappointed every time. Even enlarged, the photographs seemed preposterous, wrong, like a lithograph or a painted picture postcard. The sun bit the glossy page in circled spots. The horizon I had seen ablaze with color lay flat, invisible, and lifeless.

There is a knock on my window.

A young woman, a naturalist for the county, will be our guide. She beckons with her mittened hand, smiles as she bounces for warmth, and wipes her watering eyes. A dozen or so Gore-Tex-clad crane-seekers who have traveled from a half dozen states gather around her, jackets whipping in the wind. From this caravansary, she says, we will travel to the site of the blind. When we pull into the area, we will turn off our headlights so we don't wake the birds.

There are now several nature sanctuaries, interpretive centers, and wildlife refuges along the Platte River that offer guided sandhill crane viewing. When I was younger, my parents would simply drive us out on country roads in late fall and spring afternoons, and we'd watch the birds on the fields feeding and jumping and tossing corncobs in the air. Then we'd pull around to where there was a view through the brush of the braided riverbed and watch out the rear window of the car as the birds came in to roost.

Nowadays, with a naturalist-led group, bird-watchers and people like me can get onto preserved land and be close to the river by gathering in a blind. I've never seen the morning ascent, which I had been told would be more magical than the arrival of the birds on the water in the evening. I chuckle to myself as I get out of the car, trying to imagine such nonsense as magic going on in Hall County.

The moon beams down on what darkness is left as we arrive, even as a rouge streak warms in the east. We tumble silently across a field of matted prairie grass, moving toward the wetlands, where an ancient cooing seems to be coming from the land, blending with the high sound of trickling water and a deeper rustling of grass in the wind.

When watching the sandhill cranes mill and bob in the middle of the low water of the Platte River in the early dawn, a person could be forgiven for mistaking the optical illusion of the light for something like magic. What looks like moving water, especially in the blue misty light of dawn, is actually birds. Statuesque gray birds with red caps hopping on the sandbars. As the sun rises, the birds in the water look cast in silver. Then, all at once, thousands of them take to the air in a rush of wings and warbles. There are so many that it seems as if the earth is falling away from them.

I tape it, snap photos, scribble notes. I squat in the grass watching their silver bellies speckle the sky. Take more photos. Make a long tape recording. Pull out another notebook.

Every spring, between mid-February and mid-April, more than a half million sandhill cranes stop in this eighty-mile-wide stretch of the Platte River during their seasonal migration from their winter habitat. They come from Arizona, New Mexico, and central Mexico on their way to their summer nesting grounds in Canada, Alaska, and even Siberia.

While there are other migratory events with thousands of cranes in Asia and Europe, this is the only place where the birds are counted in the hundreds of thousands. And that's not including the millions of other migratory birds like geese and ducks that filter through this nipped-in waist of the hourglass-shaped flight pattern called the central flyway.

These ancient birds, *Grus canadensis,* are so easy to love and to anthropomorphize with their familiar-looking mating dances and courtship rituals. Their voices change in adolescence, and they are not above fighting over a mate or turf. They have long life spans and are monogamous, and each pair will bear a couple of young each year.

The narrative, retold each spring, is easily digestible: during the time in Nebraska, the birds roost in the river and forage through the fields and wet meadows. They gobble up corn, earthworms, and snails, packing on 20 percent of their body weight and giving themselves enough strength to finish their journey. They will raise their heads and spread their wings, hop around in the fields performing courtship dances, and leave with a strong pair bond after all that socializing.

But that is the story people give to the migration. The starker truth is that the birds have been stopping in this area for the past 9 million years and are as constant as the plains and as unimpressive to locals as pigeons are to New Yorkers. Land is land and birds are birds until people start telling stories about them.

Home is not that different. The home I think of when I talk about the place I'm from is easy to love because I have told myself so many stories about it. I pass through Nebraska like the cranes, on a twice-yearly rhythm. I feed and roost, I commune and socialize.

My starker truth comes when I arrive to find the story I had told myself is a shoddy melodrama of the wind blowing up over the bluff and into the low riverbed. The picture I had in my mind is a fading facsimile of a sunset over a field. What I experience is always more powerful than what I remember.

I've stared at the sky—watching the watercolor wash of light fuse into the hard straight line of the horizon, or tracking a cloud-head gathering above a parched soybean field—but not so purely that I didn't compare it or pass judgment. Not so continuously that I didn't block the view with a camera, or take notes, or hold up a tape recorder, or beckon friends to come see, come see. The problem is one of digestion more than distraction. I want to remember the story more truly. I want to capture the light more accurately. I want the sound of a million birds sobbing to echo in my ears until I hear them again.

Sitting in the bird blind, my ruddy face poking out through a little grapefruit-size hole in the burlap facing, the sensation of watching and hearing tens of thousands of birds ascending at the same time is, in a word, overwhelming. Like the landscape, I can't consume it all at once and I am at the precipice again, unable to carry what I've collected.

Why do I want to give myself to this place? Why do I want it to love me back?

This land is my home, and I am across a rift trying to get back.

After my morning with the cranes, I drive north on Highway 281 to spend the day in Grand Island.

I turn onto Locust Avenue, a street that became a decimated disaster area after it was wiped bare by a tornado in 1980.

Besides the cranes, the other spring ritual in Grand Island is the tornados.

It was late on a Saturday evening, June 3, 1980, when the worst tornado system ever to set up in Nebraska hovered over Grand Island and ground the town to a pulp, leaving a snarl of debris. There were seven separate funnel systems sighted that night, while my family huddled under a table in our basement and waited out the storm.

When I woke up, my father took me to the front yard of our house, which had seen hardly any damage, to look at those on either side. Huge trees lay on top of cars, and roofs were cleaved off at unnatural angles, with wooden fences and swing sets thrown up alongside. As we moved toward the end of the street, there was less and less that was identifiable—a muddy refrigerator here, a yellow bathroom door there. The back of one house was sheared off from the rest, leaving a cross section of a living room, bedroom, and bathroom, with soap still in the dish. At the end of the block, the houses were gone, with nothing left but foundations.

This irreproachable land does not respond much. But when it shudders with something proportional to its vastness, the world spins dramatically. Nonnegotiable snowstorms immobilize, and deadly tornadoes sit on a town for three hours, leaving devastation. It all makes people spin.

And so does a sky that grows darker in silver-bellied specks as the cranes circle to the river in enormous groups. The ground begins to move as the birds hop and bob over a field that is all but invisible under the carpet of undulating feathers and beaks. Water rises upward from a sandy crevice in a rustle of flight.

I inhale deeply. All I can do is take notes for another story and push the button on the camera to add to my pile of photographic mnemonics.

Some local people have created a sort of seasonal celebrity out of the crane, with their crane-related music, paintings, and photographs. I buy up their pieces as if they were maps to a place I need to go. The stores are stocked heavily with crane-themed note cards, books, mugs, and T-shirts. I hungrily lap it up, stowing away the morsels in my carry-on bag.

The farther away I get, and the more complicated my surroundings become, the more I try to manufacture that feeling of transparency, emptiness, and beige.

I'm looking for anything that will help get me across the divide. I frame photographs of a single lateral line with yellow at the bottom and blue at the top: the Midwestern horizon. I sit with books on Nebraska cloud formations and pioneer history. I give more interest to my coffee-table books, the ones about the ritual arrival of the sandhill cranes every spring, and to calendars with pictures of roadside attractions, like a re-creation of Stonehenge out of American-made cars in Alliance. I look at special editions of *Nebraskaland* magazine with pictures of haystacks and rivers. Gold light falling over a field of geese. Rose embers setting behind Chimney Rock.

Even though the pictures are small and not right, sometimes I can feel my spine lengthen a little. I tell myself that is all I ever hoped for by trying to catch the sunset, the landscape, the ascent of birds on film. But I know I want more.

As I fly home from Nebraska to New York, I can't stop staring. The sun sits in front of us as we soar over the Midwest—it is a finger's width from the horizon, beaming through the clouds in thick, orange shafts that cast shadows on the land below, revealing the liver spots of the hills and age lines of the river.

The land becomes an outstretched palm. I study it like a fortune-teller.

This nearly changeless land will always surprise me. It will always make my story pale and my photos fade. Even though I may never live there again, Nebraska is the only home I will know. I will collect and capture and carry on.

When I get back to Brooklyn, I flip open my laptop and load up the crane cam. The rhythmic sweeping of the robotic camera over the Platte River during roosting time captures the birds in a silver-bluish mist making their distinctive undulating calls in a small frame on my screen.

In a pixelated postcard-size window, I have a portal to the Platte River as I listen to their noises, watch them flutter and coo. It is comforting to watch it, although I know this is exactly the sort of thing that crops my view even as it keeps it open.

It is almost dark on the screen, with a tapering decrescendo of calls, when I hear someone in the blind sigh, followed by the automatic rewind of a 35mm camera.

About the Contributors

Adam Baer lives in Los Angeles, where he writes on culture and composes scripts for films and television. Originally from New York, he is a former concert violinist and producer for National Public Radio; his work has appeared in numerous publications, including the *New Yorker, New York Times Book Review, Los Angeles Times, Men's Health,* and *Travel + Leisure.* Baer also practices sketch comedy, volunteers at the 826LA writing lab, and blogs at glassshallot.com.

Anna Bahney has written for the *New York Times* for the past five years. She grew up in Nebraska, attended Emory University in Atlanta, Georgia, and spent a year after college cofounding a theater company and working as an actress in Moscow, Edinburgh, and London. She now lives in Greenpoint, Brooklyn.

Nicole Davis is a freelance writer and arts editor for two weekly papers in Manhattan, *The Villager* and *Downtown Express.* She has written for *Backpacker, Budget Travel, Plenty,* and *Rolling Stone.* She lives in Brooklyn with her husband.

Christine DeLucia comes from Manchester, New Hampshire, and studied American history and literature at Harvard University, where her research included work on northeastern urban renewal projects. Her thinking has been shaped by the hilltop ruins of Rocchetta al Volturno, Italy, her great-grandmother's birthplace; the cliff dwellings of the Southwest; and the mill yard of downtown Manchester. She is currently studying environmental history in Fife, Scotland.

McKenzie Funk, a former rafting guide and sometime ski bum, was a finalist for a National Magazine Award in 2004. He is a contributing editor for *National Geographic Adventure* and also writes for *Harper's, Audubon, Popular Science, Mother Jones, Men's Journal,* and *Skiing.* Treks and mountaineering expeditions have taken him to Panama, Tajikistan, Corsica, Georgia, Tibet, Bulgaria, and Trinidad. He graduated from Swarthmore College in 1999 and speaks Spanish, German, Italian, Russian, and French. An Oregon native, he now lives in Manhattan. He likes hiking and trees and has abnormally high bowling scores.

Jaime Gross is based in Berkeley, California, and writes about travel, design, and culture for publications including *Travel + Leisure, Interior Design,* and *Surface,* to which she is a contributing editor. When she is not scrambling to meet her deadlines, she is longing for a puppy and taking out more books from the library than she'll ever read before their due date. She is currently at work on a book about great rooftops around the world.

Tim Heffernan was born in Cambridge, England, grew up in Miami, Florida, and spent many of his childhood summers on his grandparents' farm near Moorefield, West Virginia. Appalachia, with its narrow valleys and thick woods, and the Everglades, with its overwhelming expanses, both fostered his practice of looking mostly at what lies at his feet when hiking. He graduated from Swarthmore College in 2000 with a degree in economics. He has written for the *Boston Globe, Village Voice,* and *Atlantic Monthly* and now contributes regularly to *Esquire.*

Nathanael Johnson grew up in Nevada City, California, a gold rush town in the Sierra foothills surrounded by rivers. He attended Pomona College and the U.C. Berkeley Graduate School of Journalism. He now works as a freelance journalist based in a ten-foot-by-twelve-foot room in San Francisco. He has written for *Harper's,* the *New York Times Magazine, Outside,* and *Frontline,* and is a producer for KALW News, a weekly radio show for the National Public Radio member station KALW. He has received awards from the U.C. Berkeley Graduate School of Journalism for science writing and from the Public Radio News Directors Incorporated for a radio feature.

Alex P. Kellogg, a metro reporter for the *Detroit Free Press,* has been a journalist and freelance writer for eight years. He began as an intern at Reuters TV Ltd.'s East Africa bureau, based in the Kenyan capital of Nairobi. During nearly two years with the company, he traveled to more than a half dozen countries, producing stories that aired on CNN, BBC, and other international broadcast networks. He has also worked as a reporter for the Chronicle of Higher Education and the Associated Press, and has written for the *Atlanta Journal Constitution, Boston Globe, Washington Post, American Prospect,* and bet.com.

Jonathan Kiefer is the associate arts editor of the *Sacramento News & Review,* an alternative weekly newspaper in Northern California. His writing has appeared in various periodicals, including *Salon,* the *New Republic, San Francisco Chronicle, Los Angeles Times,* and *San Francisco* magazine, where he was a pop culture columnist. He writes a biweekly film column for *Maisonneuve* magazine and is at work on a book, to be published by City Lights Books in 2007, about the cinema of the San Francisco Bay Area. He likes driving to places, but still doesn't own a car. He likes walking to places, too.

Traci Joan Macnamara has spent two summers and a winter living at McMurdo Station, Antarctica. From 2003 to 2004, Macnamara worked as a station general assistant. She returned to McMurdo during the 2005 to 2006 austral summer to maintain station communications with polar scientists conducting research at remote field camps. Her antarctic writing has appeared in magazines and journals, including *Vegetarian Times, Backpacker,* and *Isotope.*

Gregory Mone is a freelance writer, novelist, and former columnist for *Popular Science* magazine. His first novel, *The Wages of Genius,* follows a young business analyst who believes he is the reincarnation of Albert Einstein, and Mone is currently working on a book about a brand marketer who accidentally falls through a gate to hell. He recently moved with his wife and infant daughter to Canton, Massachusetts, which, in the fall, seems to be a repository for all the leaves within a hundred miles. On certain occasions, he likes to wade into Long Island Sound and pretend he is a whale.

Sam Moulton is forever beholden to Camp Manito-wish—and firmly believes that tramping about the wilderness with others for a while is the equivalent of taking a multivitamin of essential life skills. Sam has been an editor at *Outside* and *Skiing* magazines and has published pieces in *Men's Journal, Backpacker,* and *Hooked on the Outdoors.* He currently lives in Chicago with his wife.

Tim Neville, who discovered the outdoors by ditching his parents' house in favor of a tent in his Maryland backyard, has spent much of his life checking out some of the planet's most beautiful and bizarre places. After living for two years in Europe, he eventually dropped anchor in Bozeman, Montana, and then worked as a mountaineering guide in La Paz, Bolivia. In early 2000, the six-foot-seven Neville packed everything he owned into a two-door Ford Escort and drove from Salisbury, Maryland, to Santa Fe, New Mexico, where he worked for two years on the travel desk for *Outside* magazine. He now freelances full-time and lives under a real roof in Bend, Oregon, contributing regularly to *Outside, Men's Journal,* and the *New York Times.*

Cecily Parks has published poems in the *Antioch Review, Boston Review, New England Review, Virginia Quarterly Review, Yale Review,* and the anthology *Best New Poets 2005.* Her chapbook, *Cold Work,* was selected by Li-Young Lee for the 2005 Poetry Society of America New York Chapbook Fellowship and was published in December 2005. When she is not in New York City, Cecily can be found fly-fishing on a spring creek or fleeing thunderclouds somewhere near Daniel, Wyoming.

James Prosek made his writing debut with *Trout: An Illustrated History* (Knopf, 1996), the first book to document the species, subspecies, and strains of North American trout. *Trout* was followed by *Joe and Me* (William Morrow, 1997); *The Complete Angler: A Connecticut Yankee Follows in the Footsteps of Walton* (HarperCollins, 1999); *Fly-Fishing the 41st* (HarperCollins, 2003); and *Trout of the World* (Stewart, Tabori, and Chang, 2003). His next book will be a young adult novel called *The Day My Mother Left* (Simon and Schuster, 2007), the story of a boy who, in the wake of his parent's divorce, goes into the woods to find solace. Prosek works out of a studio in Easton, Connecticut, a one-room schoolhouse built in 1850, and is writing a natural history of eels for HarperCollins. He is a contributor to the *New York Times* and won a Peabody Award for his documentary about Izaak Walton, the seventeenth-century author of *The Complete Angler.*

Hugh Ryan is a freelance writer who lives in Brooklyn but dreams of the mountains of Tennessee. In his free time, he hopes to join the circus. Or write the great American circus novel. A native of upstate New York, he has written about everything from the finer points of squatting in Berlin to choosing flowers for a wedding. His work can be found in *The Brooklyn Papers,* gawker.com, *Skope* magazine, and the forthcoming anthology on bus travel, *Where Do We Get Off?*

Liesl Schwabe has an MFA in creative nonfiction from Bennington College. Her work has been published in Agni Online, the *Seneca Review, Post Road,* and in the anthologies *Bare Your Soul* and *Breeder.* She teaches writing at the Fashion Institute of Technology and Yeshiva University and lives with her son in Brooklyn, New York. She would like very much to have a lake to swim in and a porch to sit on one day. In the meantime, she has the free community pool on the other side of the expressway and a fire escape.

Andrea Walker lives in Norwalk, Connecticut, where she enjoys hiking with her two very large dogs (a Weimaraner and Great Dane). She is a member of the editorial staff of the *New Yorker,* where she writes regularly for the "Briefly Noted" section and has contributed to "The Talk of the Town." This is her first published essay.

Lilith Wood is a writer living in New York City. Since her career in an Alaskan cannery, she has been a shoe saleswoman, an editorial assistant, and a radio reporter. She doesn't get back to southeast Alaska very often but likes to explore the Catskills and the rest of New York State when she gets the chance.

About the Editor

Bonnie Tsui is a regular contributor to the *New York Times,* a correspondent for the *Boston Globe,* and a former editor at *Travel + Leisure* magazine. She has also written for *Outside, National Geographic Adventure, O the Oprah Magazine,* and the *Wall Street Journal,* and she is the author of *She Went to the Field,* a history of women soldiers in the American Civil War. A native New Yorker, she currently lives in San Francisco and is working on a book about American Chinatowns. She takes frequent writing breaks to snowboard and swim outside.